Critical Acclaim for Linda McCallister's
*"I Wish I'd Said That!" How to Talk Your Way
Out of Trouble and Into Success*

"I Wish I'd Said That!" is . . . a rule book to help you play the game of business and of life in that most satisfying of modes: the winning mode."

Business First

". . . [T]he content is certainly substantial—and valuable to anyone in business or dealing with difficult relationships. Her precepts, based on 10 years of observation and thousands of interviews (not to mention secondary sources), are straightforwardly presented; each of the six communicator styles—noble, Socratic, reflective, magistrate, candidate, senator—is described well, with easy-to-understand analogies, to Woody Allen, "The Golden Girls," George Bush, and the like, along with explanations of strengths and weaknesses, characteristics, sound, and how-to's of controlling that particular type of communicator. Her discussion of communicating in corporate situations is very specific, including details on negotiating salaries and raises, surviving meetings, and dealing with sensitive issues, among others."

Booklist

"In a work world in which you have to deal with people who may have communication styles as diverse as Lee Iacocca or Woody Allen, *"I Wish I'd Said That!"* demonstrates that how you communicate has everything to do with *who* you are trying to communicate with. After ten years of research and more than 10,000 interviews with workers, professionals and business students, author Linda McCallister has developed a unique *Communication Style Profile,* which measures the six major styles of communication: the Noble, Socratic, Reflective, Candidate, Magistrate, and Senator. This book is a primer on applying this knowledge to control the outcome of important interactions, and to persuade people in a positive manner."

Canadian Manager

"It's not so much what you say, but how you say it. We've all heard this homily again and again, but do we know what it means and how to use it? Linda McCallister does and explains it in a way that is direct, to the point and useful—especially to the business reader. I recommend the book highly. It's not just what she says, it's how she says it."

—Dr. Albert J. Bernstein
Author, *Dinosaur Brains* and
Neanderthals at Work

"If you want to avoid 'pododontia' (foot-in-mouth disease), be sure to read this book and follow Linda McCallister's excellent advice."

—Roger E. Axtell
Author, *Do's and Taboos Around the World*

" '*I Wish I'd Said That!*' has as its hallmark a rich variety of entertaining examples that serve to please as well as instruct."

—Dr. Curtis McCray
President
California State University, Long Beach

"Must reading for anyone concerned with people and results. The six styles cut across cultures and open a window to success in our fast paced global business environment."

—David Sun
President, Sun Microcomputers, Inc.

" '*I Wish I'd Said That!*' will enable you to create success working with others regardless of how their personalities and styles differ from your own."

—Christopher Hagerty
Author, *How to Manage Your Boss*

"Linda McCallister has captured the real pearls of verbal communication by identifying communication styles . . . we each fall into one of her categories. She helps the reader to understand how to use a most vital business skill and parlay it into success."

—Susan Bixler
President, The Professional Image
Author, *Professional Presence* and *The Professional Image*

"I wish I'd said that!"

How to Talk Your Way Out of Trouble and Into Success

LINDA MCCALLISTER, PH.D.

JOHN WILEY & SONS, INC.

New York • Chichester • Brisbane • Toronto • Singapore

Copyright © 1992, 1994 by Linda McCallister.

Published by John Wiley & Sons, Inc.

First Wiley mass market edition published 1997.

Library of Congress Cataloging in Publication Data:

McCallister, Linda.
    I wish I'd said that: how to talk your way out of trouble and into success/by Linda McCallister.
       p.   cm.
    Includes index.
    ISBN 0-471-55551-7(cloth) ISBN 0-471-00857-5(paper)
    ISBN 0-471-17687-7(mass market)
    1. Interpersonal communication. 2. Persuasion (Rhetoric)
3. Persuasion (Psychology) 4. Success--Psychological aspects.
I. Title.
BF637.C45M2 1992
153.6--dc20   92-7586

Printed in the United States of America
10 9 8 7 6 5 4 3 2 1

To
Frankie and Jason,
I Am Because You Are

Why, it's a Looking-Glass book, of course!
And, if I hold it up to a glass,
the words will all go the right way again.

Lewis Carroll, *Through the Looking Glass*

PREFACE

There are six major styles of communication that exist in the world today, and *"I wish I'd said that!"* shows you how to identify and use these styles to influence others, solve problems, and get the results you want at work. You have *total control* over only one thing in your fast-paced, high-stress, global business environment—communication style. If you can control style, you can control the outcome of important interactions. This book shows you how to develop this control.

In his autobiography, Lee Iacocca said, "Motivation is everything . . . and the only way to motivate people is to communicate with them. . . . It's important to talk to people in their own language. If you do it well, they'll say, 'God, he said exactly what I was thinking.' And when they begin to respect you, they'll follow you to the death." Communication style is the language that exists within all languages, and *"I wish I'd said that!"* shows you how to use style to get others to "follow you to the death."

This book will show you how to deal with people who share Mr. Iacocca's communication style—in my classification scheme, he is a Nobel communicator—and how to talk successfully with people who sound like Woody Allen, George Bush, Gloria Steinem, Ronald Reagan, Oprah Winfrey, Geraldo Rivera, Margaret Thatcher, Jesse Jackson, or Jimmy Carter. Each of these people represents a type of communicator; each speaks a unique language within our English language. This book explains how to talk that language and get the results you want at work—or anywhere else.

If you have ever said, "I wish I'd said what I was really thinking," or "I probably shouldn't have said that," or "I said too much; he stopped listening halfway through my pitch," then this book is for you. It is for anyone who would like—once and for all—to feel comfortable and in command when talking with others.

"I wish I'd said that!" shows you how to use style to get ahead and survive in modern, complex organizations. After reading this book, you should be able to forecast what is likely to happen in a particular situation, and ultimately you should be able to control the results of important interactions.

Over ten years, I interviewed more than 10,000 workers, professionals, and business students in an effort to develop my unique and original Communication Style Profile, which measures the six major styles of communication; I call them the Noble, Socratic, Reflective, Candidate, Magistrate, and Senator. These styles form the Communication Kaleidoscope, which turns the very complex process of communication into a simple and easy-to-understand skill that can be used to guide your professional destiny.

The Communication Style Profile Test (contained in the Appendix) is a series of sixty questions that measure how you communicate. This is important because people do not react to *what* you say; instead, they react to *how* you say what you say. Communication success is directly linked to the other person's expectations; the other person expects you to sound just like he or she sounds. You can learn to identify other people's expectations, how to satisfy those expectations, and how to control the outcome of any conversation. If you are attempting to get ahead—or even just survive—in the modern organization, it is crucial that you be able to control what happens in the one-on-one or group conversation. I've provided you with an easy method for gaining this control.

This is not a passive book! Take an active role in the creation and analysis of scenarios that demonstrate what it sounds like when you talk your way into or out of trouble. Through the scenarios, you will see how easy it is to create the sounds of success with many different types of people. I present you with a scenario and ask you to respond. Then I show you how your response will cause or eliminate trouble. The scenarios reveal why one style will not work with all people, and they demonstrate how the Communication Kaleidoscope can be used to create styles that will work with different types of people. I think you will find these scenarios interesting, stimulating, and fun too.

The book is divided into three parts. In Part One, you learn about style, how it works, and how it can be used to control the outcome of interactions. Throughout the book, I use real stories from real people to illustrate how style can be manipulated to create moments of success.

Knowing about style, however, isn't enough. In Part Two, the six styles of the Communication Kaleidoscope are explored, and you learn how to deal with each type of communicator. Once acquainted with the six styles, you will find yourself saying, "Oh my gosh, I do that" or "My boss does that, and it drives me crazy!"

In Part Three, you learn how Communication Style works within the context of a large or small organization, and you learn how to use the Communication Kaleidoscope to get others to willingly do what you want them to do.

The talking scenarios I use throughout the book center on some of the most difficult and often humorous situations we face in our daily lives. They illustrate how communication style can be used as a strategy for dealing with the difficult people who create stress and problems in professional relationships. They reveal how you can use style to keep from destroying your career, and they show you why some people love, and others hate, the way you talk. The scenarios reveal how you can control your own destiny and get the things you want in life without generating resentment or anger.

Communication style is a skill. It is not something you are born with, and it is not something you must accept as fate. You can't do anything about your astrological sign, but you can do something about how you communicate. *"I wish I'd said that!"* shows you what to do and how you can do it better.

Recently I was conducting a seminar based on this book. A middle-aged executive sitting in the first row kept shaking his head and rubbing his brow as I delivered what I thought was a humorous description of the six types of communicators. Throughout the day, he participated in the exercises, but he remained pensive and somewhat distant. At the end of the day, he approached me, looked me in the eye, and in his quiet Noble style simply said, "Thank you. I think you've saved my marriage." He turned and walked out of the room.

He didn't need to say anything more; I knew what he meant. Organizational communication is my area of expertise, but my communication style research applies to personal as well as professional relationships. As you read this book, you will discover that your dominant style of communication is shaped by the work you do, and how you talk at work tends to be how you talk at home. Thus, the same things that irritate or impress your colleagues may irritate or impress your mate. So whether you are looking to improve your marriage or your career, you will find *"I wish I'd said that!"* helpful.

We each view the world through a unique set of glasses. Language helps us define, but communication style helps us interpret the world we see. The Communication Kaleidoscope provides a common framework for interpreting many different worlds.

LINDA MCCALLISTER

Palm Springs, California

ACKNOWLEDGMENTS

It is not possible for me to recognize here everyone who contributed to this project. Over a twelve-year period, thousands of students, workers, managers, professionals, and executives have taken the various versions of my Communication Style Profile test while attending my classes and seminars. Their comments, stories, and suggestions provide the foundation for this book. I am eternally grateful to my students, especially Sharon Eshett, Michael Deforeest, Jeff Kawakubo, and Cathy Crowell, for teaching me how to hear communication style.

I am happy to recognize my friend and mentor, Professor Emeritus W. Charles Redding. As my doctoral adviser, Charles helped me begin my journey into the nebulous world of communication style. He kept the nay-sayers at a distance and allowed me to blaze a trail through uncharted territory. He is the *ne plus ultra* Socratic, but I love him anyway. I owe special thanks to Ann Redding for her kindness, for keeping Charles on time, and for making him answer my telephone calls during those horrible final days of the dissertation process.

To Teri Thompson and Lou Cusella, I offer my undying love. They stood by me and supported me through the darkest and most painful moments of my life. They continue to be my role models.

This book would not exist without Susan Grode, Nancy Stauffer, and John Mahaney. Susan, my attorney, believed in me when no one else did and introduced me to Nancy Stauffer, the world's best agent. Nancy is critical, she is persistent, she is demanding, she is dedicated, she is loyal, she is Noble, and I love her for all this and more. John is my editor, and the person who showed me how to make my styles come alive. His Reflective touch gave a soft ambience to my Noble tones, and his Noble comments inspired me to work harder than I intended.

I am fortunate to have many dear friends. Their encouraging words helped me rise above my own self-doubts, and their supportive actions helped me endure the lonely life of a writer. I am especially thankful to and proud to know Marcy L. Krugel, Gwen Zinchook Ahearn, Kay Alexander, Bobby and Elle Patton, Helena Hacker, Jimmy and Juddi Trent, Bob and Teri Putz, Michael Kuras, LaVern Lindsey, John Beljan, Janet Roncelli, Vala Stults, Ann Marie Peacock, Linda and Bill Gronski, and my dearest comrade, Barbara Crutchfield George.

I am even more fortunate to have family members who serve as my cheerleaders. Nina and Carl Barron, Rita Randall, Paula Skerchock, Jim McCallister, Cindy and Joe Golden, Margaret and Jim Sisson, Pat and Harry Balk, and, my mom, Louise Ford McCallister, have always been there to help me when I have stumbled along the way.

Finally, I am blessed to have two wonderful sons who serve as the lights of my life. Thank you, Frankie and Jason, for your unconditional love and devotion.

L. M.

CONTENTS

Contents

Contents

PART THREE: HOW TO USE STYLE TO TALK YOUR WAY OUT OF TROUBLE AND INTO SUCCESS

Contents

"I wish I'd said that!"

PART ONE

What Is Style and How Does It Work?

Chapter 1

I Wish I Hadn't Said That!

Robert stared in bewilderment as he contemplated his letter of termination. Kay, his friend and colleague, listened with a sympathetic ear.

"How can he say I was abrasive? I wasn't abrasive. I'm not rude. I'm just direct. I say what needs to be said. If you ask me, he's the one who's rude. You can never get a straight answer out of him. He never tells you what he really thinks . . . and what about Carol? You ask her for a simple yes or no answer, and she recites the encyclopedia. They're the ones with communication problems. At least I'm truthful. I say what's on my mind. What's wrong with that? I can't believe I'm being fired because I'm honest. I don't sugarcoat everything I say or bury my thoughts in a sea of words."

Communication. It can make or break a career, build or destroy a marriage, even begin or end a war. It is perhaps the most important thing we do. If we have a problem at work, we say it is a communication problem. If we have a problem in a relationship, we say it is a communication problem.

3

But we typically don't know how to fix these problems, and we often don't know what caused the problem.

This book teaches you how to identify and use the six major styles of communication that exist in the world today to deal with difficult (and not-so-difficult) problems and people at work. It shows you how to influence others and get the results you want, even when the other person is your boss. After reading it, you will know precisely how you can use your own personal style of communication to talk your way out of—instead of into—trouble. You'll know how to develop communication strategies for dealing with the difficult people who create stress and problems in your personal and professional relationships and how to use style to keep from hurting the people you love. You're going to find out why some people love, and others hate, the way you talk. More important, you're going to learn how to get what you want out of life without generating resentment and anger. Let's start, however, by taking a look at what happens when you don't use style to control your own destiny. Consider the true saga of Cindy and the IRS auditor.

In 1987, Cindy received notice that her 1985 income tax return was being audited. Confident that all of her deductions were legitimate, she made the dreaded trip to the ominous IRS building. When she met with the auditor, he explained that she hadn't done anything wrong; this was just a random audit. He asked her to return with her travel log and receipts for her business deductions and assured her that the case could be closed if she could produce these items. Relieved, she returned in three days with all of the requested items.

Two years later, Cindy received notice that she was being assessed additional taxes for 1985. When she called the IRS office, the receptionist asked if she was inquiring about the 1985 or 1986 audit. Cindy stated that she wasn't being audited for 1986, but the young woman replied that both audits were in the file. As ordered, Cindy returned for another visit to the IRS, only to find out that she had a new auditor who was "unable to locate" the original documents she had submitted in 1987. He instructed her to reproduce her records and requested that she sign a release form granting him an extension of time for the 1985 audit since the three-year limitation was due to expire that week. She refused, stating that she should not be held responsible for his incompetency. The conflict began to escalate, and he stated there could be a problem with 1986 if she didn't sign. She asked if she was being audited for 1986, and he replied that he could not reveal that information. This simply added insult to injury, and Cindy let him know what she thought of these tactics—and in no uncertain terms.

Cindy returned the following week with copies of her 1985 documents. A year later, she received a response from the auditor. She was being assessed additional taxes for 1985 and 1986. She sank to the floor, resigned to the fact that she would probably be audited for the rest of her life. But after coming to her senses, she did some research and contacted Pam, who was considered to be the best tax attorney in town. Pam reviewed all of the documents and determined that the deductions were legitimate and completely within the limits allowed by law. She paused, looked at Cindy, and said, "Did you say something to make this auditor angry?" Cindy confessed that, among other things, she called the auditor an incompetent moron. Pam raised her eyebrow, looked at Cindy, and softly replied, "That'll do it every time."

Pam explained that she had seen many unfair assessments and that each case was the result of a communication conflict between the auditor and the taxpayer. She agreed to take the case and assured Cindy that she would win. She also explained that her fees would be almost as much as the tax assessment. Pam took the case to court. She won. Cindy paid the fees, which were only slightly less than the original tax assessment.

The moral of this story is that Cindy talked herself smack dab into trouble. What she said was right; *how* she said it was wrong. Her style of communicating the information caused her more trouble than she ever dreamed possible. It is true that bureaucratic bungling caused the situation to begin with, but it was Cindy's verbal lambasting that caused the auditor to issue the assessment. Cindy won her battle in court, but she lost the war;

she paid a huge amount of money to have the court rule that the auditor was wrong. Cindy tells this story often and laughs as she states, "I have no one to blame but myself. I paid the price for opening my big mouth!"

Communication style—it can guide your destiny in many different directions. Consider the story of Sarah, Bruce, and Roger.

Sarah is a dynamite young professor at a major university. She is an excellent teacher who is popular with the students, and she has already gained a national reputation as an outstanding researcher. She also happens to be attractive and the only woman faculty member in her department. Sarah knows that some of the old guard are resentful of her accomplishments, but she also knows that these fellows are the ones who will vote on whether she gets promoted and tenured.

Bruce, a fellow faculty member, stopped by Sarah's office one afternoon and invited her to lunch. Sarah likes Bruce but finds him annoying because she feels he never comes right out and says what he is thinking. He's pleasant, but she thinks he tells her what she wants to hear rather than what he actually believes. Bruce, however, is an influential senior faculty member, and Sarah is very aware of the importance of organizational politics, so she cheerfully accepts his invitation.

As they reach the parking lot, Bruce points to his brand-new car and asks Sarah how she likes it. Sarah responds,

> "It's great. I love it, but I don't care for the color very much. Couldn't you get it in another color?"

Roger, the chair of the department, stops by Sarah's office several days later and tells Sarah that Bruce came to him and complained about Sarah's rude and arrogant manner. Shocked, Sarah asks Roger for clarification. Roger relates the car incident to her, and Sarah replies,

> "I wasn't rude. He just asked me how I liked his car, and I told him the truth. I wasn't nasty. What should I have said?"

With a bit of a chuckle, Roger answers,

"You should have lied. You should have told him you liked the color."

What do you think? Should Sarah have lied? Your response to these questions is almost entirely dependent on your own personal style of communication because language allows you to define the world you see, and style allows you to interpret and color the world. In the next chapter, I define the world of success by introducing six different styles of communication and explaining how each type of communicator colors his or her world differently. Right now, I am going to introduce you to the Noble, Socratic, and Reflective styles of communication ever so briefly and show you how differently the three types of communicators will respond to the exact same situation. As you read the responses, keep in mind that a Noble is a direct, straightforward communicator who feels obligated to state the truth—like Cindy in the IRS story. A Socratic is a verbose, analytical communicator who is concerned with details, and a Reflective is a warm, supportive communicator who is concerned with interpersonal relations and the need to avoid conflict.

In response to the question, should Sarah have lied? A Reflective might respond,

"Yes, she should have told him she liked the color. It's not actually a lie. It's just more polite. Why hurt his feelings?"

Bruce and Roger are Reflective communicators. That is why Roger offered his particular piece of advice to Sarah. Roger colors his world the same as Bruce does.

In response to the same question, a Socratic communicator, might respond,

"Well, I don't know. That depends. With some people you can be direct, and with others you can't. I don't think she should have lied, but she didn't have to be quite so blunt. Bruce was probably trying to be friendly even though he felt threatened by her. I think there are several ways she could have approached the situation without actually lying. For example, she could have . . ."

A Noble response to this question might be,

"No, she shouldn't lie. If he didn't want to hear the truth, he shouldn't have asked."

Sarah is a Noble. It never occurred to her that her comment would be offensive to Bruce. Nobles believe that everyone should state the truth when communicating with others, and no one should be offended by the truth. If you are a Noble and you accept this premise, then you might also think that this story illustrates a political problem, not a communication problem. Let's explore this thought.

This story actually illustrates how differing communication styles can turn a political issue into a problem. Bruce's insecurities about Sarah's age, productivity, attractiveness, and gender are political issues. His feelings exist in all of us and in all organizations. His attitudes, feelings, and beliefs deal with what he thinks "should be." Office politics are a sum total of what differing people think should be. Communication style focuses on "what is," and the wise use of style can help Sarah change Bruce's feelings about what he thinks should be. Sarah, however, chose an unwise communication strategy and created a political problem for herself. She didn't use her style to help guide her own destiny. Instead, she allowed her style to offend someone who will cast a vote that may alter her destiny.

Before ending this discussion, I'd like to make a brief comment about why I named the styles as I have. I wanted the labels to be descriptive yet as neutral as possible so as not to attach an evaluative connotation to any of the styles. Of equal importance was my desire to have the terms grounded in the rhetorical tradition. The dominant styles were easy. I began with the Nobel, which is very Aristotelian. The Socratic is obviously akin to Socrates, and the Reflective is reminiscent of Plato. The Candidate, Magistrate, and Senator mirror the political aspects of the communication process since most communication is political or persuasive in nature.

HOW TO TALK YOUR WAY OUT OF TROUBLE

Style, the true essence of communication, is a skill. It is not something you are born with, and it is not something you must accept as fate. You can't do anything about your astrological signs, but you can do something about how you communicate. You can read this book and learn how easy it is to feel comfortable and in command when talking with others.

Communication style is concerned with *how* you say *what* you say. This is an important distinction to make because people do not respond to what is said (the actual words). Rather, they respond to how something is said—the style or manner in which the words are used. For example, "close the door," "*close* the door," "close the *door*," and "*CLOSE THE DOOR*" all convey different meanings. The words are the same (the what), but how the words are used differs (the communication style).

If you can control communication style, then you can control the outcome of most interactions. But in order to do this, you must keep one essential thought in mind:

Each person *expects* the other person to communicate exactly as he or she communicates.

We expect the other person to sound as we sound, and when these expectations are not met or when people communicate in a style that is inconsistent with past expectations, communication conflict exists. It is the management of this conflict that leads to control and, subsequently, personal and professional success. Go back and think about Bruce and Sarah. Despite what Bruce thinks about how the world should be, he is what I call a Reflective communicator. He expects communication to be polite, warm, and supportive. He does what he needs to do to maintain this interpersonal decorum, even if that means telling the other person what she wants to hear rather than what he really feels. He withholds his opinions in order to avoid conflict, and he avoids direct confrontation whenever possible (which is why he went to Roger instead of speaking directly with Sarah). When Bruce asked Sarah how she liked his car, he expected a polite, warm, supportive response. What he got was a direct, straightforward opinion that reinforced his belief that the world would be better off without young, arrogant, overachievers who think they know everything.

If Sarah understood Bruce's personal style of speaking, she would understand his communication needs, and she could have used this information to control the outcome of their interaction. This brings us to the central rule that guides all conversations:

If you can control communication style, you can control the outcome of *most* interactions.

As a Reflective, Bruce needs supportive, nonassertive communication that reveals a concern for human feelings. As a Noble, Sarah needs direct, straightforward communication where the honest exchange of information or opinions can occur without concern for personal feelings. Since Sarah is the one whose destiny is at stake, she is the one who needs to control communication style. She must meet Bruce's needs and control her own needs, which he may find offensive, if she wants to control his future behaviors. Ultimately she wants this man to vote for her promotion and tenure. So what could she do to lead him in this direction?

1. She could be truthful (her need) without expressing any negatives (his need). She could say, "I'm so jealous. I wish I could afford a new car."
2. She could avoid the issue and focus on developing a supportive interpersonal relationship. She could say, "A new car, how exciting. I'm

happy for you, and I'll bet you're pleased. Let's take your car to lunch so we can drive in a new car."

3. She could add a quick qualifier if her true feelings slip out. She could say, "I really don't care for the color . . . Well no, I shouldn't say that. Color is personal. Yes, as I think about it, this is a good color. It suits you."

4. She could lie and say she likes the color even when she doesn't.

I am a Noble, so this last suggestion is not my first choice, and for those of you who are having trouble accepting any of these examples, keep one important thought in mind: How Sarah feels about the color of Bruce's car is *not* important. Rather, what is important is her relationship with him and her ultimate promotion. If she doesn't care about their relationship, then she doesn't have to be concerned with his needs and can say whatever she thinks. If she does care, she needs to be able to control her own personal style of communication.

If you are having trouble with my examples because you think Bruce is a hopeless jerk or because you think I'm suggesting that people of lower status should be hypocritical when dealing with people like Bruce, then you are probably a Noble. I say that because Nobles tend to be intolerant of thin-skinned, indirect people like Bruce, and Nobles tend to view face-saving as hypocritical.

If this book is to be helpful, you must set some of those beliefs aside and begin analyzing each of my scenarios from a communication style perspective. Don't criticize or place blame on the people in the scenarios, and don't assume that your style is right and the other styles are wrong. Just consider how communication style can be used to control the outcome of the interaction, and begin developing a tolerance for communication style differences.

I chose this scenario to begin the book because it is so simple, and we need to get the simple problems under control before tackling the difficult ones. Sarah can easily control the outcome of this interaction with communication style. She can't do anything about Bruce's personality or his status in the organization, but she can do something about his style: she can make it work for her instead of against her.

You probably know very little about your own personal style of communication, but by the time you finish the next few chapters, you will understand why you do what you do, and you will be able to identify not only your own dominant style of communication but also that of everyone close to you. By the time you finish reading this book, you will understand specifically how you can use style to create successful moments and control your own destiny. We cannot eliminate organizational politics, but we can use communication style to control or soften the negative impact these politics might have on us. We can also cause ourselves a lot of trouble when we fail to use our style to gain this control.

HOW TO TALK YOUR WAY INTO SUCCESS

For most of us, success and the ability to control our own fate are linked to our ability to lead. Leadership, in fact, is something that concerns everyone. Leaders do not necessarily occupy formal leadership positions, and people with leadership titles are not necessarily leaders. Parents, spouses, teammates, colleagues, and friends can all be leaders if they so desire. In fact, most of us spend a great deal of time trying to get other people to do willingly what we want them to do, and that—in the purest sense of the term—is what leadership is all about. We can force people to do things for a short period of time, but that is not leadership, and those being forced will often sabotage our efforts or get back at us in the end.

Leaders persuade and influence others to accept ideas, to follow, and to take action. Thus, communication becomes the essence of leadership. Without communication, leadership does not exist. Think about it for a minute. How would you get someone to do something without verbal or nonverbal communication?

Communication is the nucleus of almost everything we do. In fact, it is the most important, complex thing we do, and the most competent communicator will emerge as the leader in most interactions. This communication competence is achieved when you are able to control communication style.

Communication is a process—an ongoing, ever-present, constantly changing and building process.* When you decide to communicate something to someone, you begin with an *idea.* You have a visual image in your brain of this thing you would like to communicate to the other person. Your brain begins to select and sort through all of the words and symbols that it knows. Your brain attaches meanings to these words and symbols, and these meanings come from all of your past experiences. Once these meanings are attached to the words, you engage in what is called an *encoding process:* you string these words and symbols together to create or encode a message.

Communication style refers to your encoding processes. It deals with how you say what you say. This is important because the other person tends to react to the way the message is delivered, not the message itself.

The message then travels through some channel to reach the eyes and ears of a receiver, who goes through a reverse process to interpret the message. The receiver *decodes* the message by engaging in his or her own selecting and sorting process. When all of this is done, the best that we can hope for is that the receiver now has a similar idea reconstructed. The receiver then provides *feedback,* which gives you information about how your message was interpreted.

During the feedback stage of the process, the roles are reversed: the receiver becomes the sender and begins to engage in the encoding process. Thus, the circular, ongoing, ever-changing, and constantly building process of communication takes place.

This reconstruction process is complicated by the fact that meanings are derived from each person's past experiences and individual percep-

---

*This description is based on the Raymond S. Ross model of communication that appears in *Speech Communication: Fundamentals and Practice,* 3d ed. (Englewood cliffs, N.J.: Prentice-Hall, 1976).

tions of the world. It is complicated further by the noise that exists in the environment—for example:

The situation.   The context wherein the communication is taking place.

The momentary set.   What's going on at that particular point in time.

The psychological climate.   How each person "feels" at that particular time.

Active participation.   The degree to which each person is actually attempting to communicate effectively.

At best, communication is a difficult, complex process. To see just how complex it is, clear your mind for a second. I'm going to present you with a word, and I want you to try to capture your immediate reaction to it—that is, what thought or meaning pops into your mind when you see or hear the word. Remember, I am going to give you a word, and you are going to capture your immediate reaction to this word. Okay, if you're ready and your mind is clear, the word is *dog*.

What was your first thought? What meaning did you give to the word? If you responded to the word *dog* by thinking the word *dog*, then you are unusual. Chances are that you thought of the word *cat*. If you didn't think *cat*, then the name of your dog, a word that describes some experience you have had with a dog *(bark, bite)*, a word that describes your feelings about dogs *(love, warm, cuddly, hate)*, or a word that describes some aspect of this thing we call "dog" *(animal, tail, furry, big, little)* may have popped into your mind.

You can try this little trick at a party, but it has more impact if you ask others to write down their reaction to your word. You say "dog," and half the people in the room will write down *cat* or one of the other words I just listed. I've been doing this for years, and almost no one writes down *dog*. Some people have very unusual responses. For example, I was using this exercise in a management development seminar I conducted in South Carolina, and as I was going through the room asking each person to state what he or she had written, I came across a woman who had written the word *do*. "Do?" I questioned with some bewilderment. She responded in her soft, southern accent, "You know, dawg doo!"

Dog: a simple three-letter word. Everyone in almost every culture knows the word, but it's the individual experience that gives meaning to it. If this much confusion can exist with a simple little word like *dog*, imagine what happens when you sit down with your friend or lover to explain that you are not happy with something he or she has done. Imagine what happens when you go into your boss and suggest that a company policy should be changed or that you believe you should be given a raise. The idea that you attempt to transmit is seldom—and maybe never—identical to the idea reconstructed by the person who receives your message.

Communication is, indeed, a very complex process. Style of communication is but one aspect of the process, but it is the *one element that we have the most control over, and it is the means by which we get others to do willingly what we want them to do.* A personal story will illustrate this point.

LaVerne Lindsey and I both joined the administrative team at Florida Atlantic University at the same time—LaVerne as the dean of continuing education and I as the director of the Center for Management in the College of Business and Public Administration. There was a long history of feuding between the previous deans and directors over who could offer which courses and how the profits from the center were to be distributed. Unlike the rest of the university, the Division of Continuing Education was not state supported; it was a self-supporting, profit-generating unit. The Center for Management paid a processing fee to the division, but the center was fully controlled and subsidized by the College of Business.

LaVerne was in a higher position, but I had more power because I reported directly to and operated with the full blessing of the dean of the college—and he was the most powerful dean on campus. The faculty in the college earned additional income by teaching in the courses offered through the center. When they earned money, they were happy, and when they were happy, the dean was happy. Prior to my arrival, the center had operated in the red, and there was a lot of wailing and gnashing of teeth by faculty who weren't earning any additional income. Within six months, I had the center solidly in the black, and most of the wailing had ceased. This made me the dean's favorite person, and my financial success gave me a tremendous amount of power on campus because the additional income was used to support underfunded academic programs. The bottom line here is that I was under no obligation to cooperate with the dean of continuing education. I didn't have to do anything she asked, and she had no administrative support to force me to do anything.

One day LaVerne called and asked if I would stop by her home for coffee after work. I knew what she wanted. I ran two very profitable courses through the center that technically belonged to Continuing Education. The courses existed before I took over the center and were in large part responsible for keeping the center afloat when the management courses were not making money. From a financial standpoint, I no longer needed these courses, but I had no intention of giving them to LaVerne.

To make a long story short, we signed an agreement at that meeting that ended the twelve-year feud between the center and Continuing Education. Among other things, I gave her one very profitable course, and she reduced my processing fees to a level that thrilled my dean.

I take no credit for this transaction. LaVerne was the one who successfully used communication style to get me to do willingly what she wanted done. LaVerne communicates as a Magistrate (you'll find out what this means shortly), and there are a lot of things about this style that I find irritating. In fact, many of our past interactions ended in conflict. At this meeting, however, LaVerne controlled those Magistrate characteristics that she knew I found offensive, and she talked to me in my voice—she talked like a Noble. She controlled the outcome of the interaction by controlling communication style. That is what leadership is all about.

I'm often asked which of the six styles of communication is best and if there is a style that is common to the people at the top of organizations. The answer is no: No one style is better than another, and there is no one style that all leaders share. The communication styles are different from each other, but they are not better or worse than each other. As you shall see shortly, we all have the ability to use all of the styles, but most of us choose to use only one style most of the time. Communication style is a matter of choice. It is not something with which we are born and die. It is something that we learn and develop over time, and effective leaders develop the ability to use more than one style.

For some people, leadership means being able to climb the corporate ladder, but not everyone wants to climb this ladder. Certainly there are many other ways of measuring success in life. Nevertheless, for those concerned with ascending the stairway to the top of the organization, a few words need to be said about how communication style can help you do this.

Approximately one-third of the people in this nation work for the government. Another significant portion of the labor force works for nonprofit and/or service departments or organizations where determining a bottom-line dollar profit is difficult at best. Thus, it would be naive to suggest that productivity is the primary basis for promotion. Look around you. More times than not, promotion is based on your ability to get along with others—your communication skills. Yes, there are the whiz kids who get promoted solely on the basis of productivity, and there are those who get promoted for political reasons. For the vast majority of people, however, effective communication skills become the determining factor in promotion decisions.

Here is another true story of a very productive person who was denied promotion because he chose an unwise communication strategy. (This is another university example. I like to use university examples because we do so many things so badly, and I think we tend to learn more from our mistakes. I'll be using examples from all types of organizations throughout the rest of the book, and I even have a couple of examples of university administrators who did something right. For now, humor me by reading this example and keep in mind that university professors train the people you hire.)

Sam is a bright, ambitious, and very productive young professor. Since he had an outstanding publication record, he was given tenure and promoted from assistant professor to associate professor right on schedule and with virtually no opposition. Sam is a bit hotheaded, and he is a Magistrate communicator. As a Magistrate, he has an intense desire to win any argument and a tendency to tell others exactly what he thinks—in great detail.

This combination of traits is irritating, but most of the faculty excuse his offensive behaviors because he is so productive. In fact, several of the senior faculty suggest that Sam place himself up for early promotion to full professor based on his continued record of research. Sam decides that he will apply for early promotion and begins putting together his promotion package, which must be submitted to the various promotion committees. Because this is an early promotion decision, Sam must gain the approval of the senior faculty before he can submit his package to the promotion committees. The approval requires a simple majority vote cast by secret ballot. Sam is confident that he will gain this approval.

True to form, Sam begins this task at the last minute. Three days before the materials are due, he storms into the department office and aggressively begins to chastise Susan, the departmental secretary. In a loud, stern voice, he reprimands her because there are errors in one of the documents. Susan, in her soft-spoken, nonassertive manner, points out that the document is clearly labeled a draft and that he should simply mark the changes he wants. She calmly reminds Sam that turning material in at the last minute creates panic and increases the likelihood of errors. Enraged that she would challenge his remarks, Sam begins a verbal attack against Susan. As his tirade subsides, he turns to Harry, the department chair who has been standing next to Susan through the entire encounter, and demands that Susan be fired for incompetency. Then Sam storms out of the office.

Susan turns to Harry in tears and questions why he had not defended her. Harry replies that he was in shock but assures her that he will speak with Sam and have him apologize. Harry's comments fall on deaf ears. In fact, Sam is so sure that he is right and so committed to winning this argument that he places all of his complaints against Susan in a written memo to Harry demanding that she be fired. Sam sends copies of the memo to all faculty members.

The day after the memo is distributed, the senior faculty vote not to allow Sam to submit his package for early promotion. Nothing is said. Everyone knows why the vote was negative—everyone, perhaps, except Sam.

The Magistrate style of communication is not a bad style, but it is intense and powerful. Like all of the other styles, the Magistrate has positive and negative verbal characteristics. Sam didn't control his communication style. Rather, he allowed the negative aspects of his style to control his behavior. This allowed others to alter the course of destiny that he had plotted for himself.

HOW TO MAKE THINGS HAPPEN IN YOUR LIFE

I would like to end this chapter by sharing a very personal moment with you. When I was in high school, I was very much a Reflective (though I didn't know what that meant at the time). I blushed constantly, and people were always saying, "Oh look at how red your face is getting." To make matters worse, my eyes would fill with tears if anyone raised a voice to me. You see, I had a domineering father who expected my sisters, my brother, and me to listen and not speak, so I learned to be Reflective. I learned to be Noble, however, from a far more compelling life experience.

When I was twenty-one, my first-born son, Frankie, suffered brain damage from a virus. He lapsed into a coma and overnight went from being a healthy, normal child to being hopelessly disabled. He could no longer walk. He could no longer talk. He could no longer feed himself. He could no longer be the source of joy that he had been since birth. The diagnosis was that he had ataxic cerebral palsy and was severely mentally retarded. The doctors stated that the damage was irreversible—he would never be able to walk or talk again—and that he needed to be placed into an institution.

I went to the institution where the admission papers were awaiting my signature, but I left the institution with my young son held tightly in my arms. I did not know what I was going to do with him or how I was going to care for him, but I knew I would never condemn him to a life in that institution.

I rapidly learned that if Frankie was ever to have anything, I had to stand up and speak on his behalf. I was convinced that with proper education, he could gain back at least part of what he had lost. At that particular point in our American history, however, children with multiple handicaps were not allowed to attend public school because they were considered "hazards." Thus, I found myself going to meeting after meeting to fight for his right to an education.

Before each meeting, I would determine my specific goal and I would think about what I was going to say and how I was going to say it. I would anticipate the arguments that would be presented to deny my request and have counterarguments prepared. The last thing I would say to myself before I walked into one of those meetings was, "You are not going to cry!"

I made it through those meetings. I did not budge until I got at least part of what I went in to get, and I did not cry! I didn't cry in the meetings, but it was such a traumatic experience to shift from being totally Reflective to totally Noble almost overnight that I would go into the restroom immediately following the meeting and cry my eyes out. Sometimes I even got sick.

After a while, I stopped getting sick, and I stopped crying. I learned that bureaucratic behavior is very predictable, and I learned that I could control the outcome of those meetings by anticipating what the other person was going to say and by controlling how I said what I said. I learned that I could use communication to survive and create a better life for my son.

The very happy ending to this story is that Frankie is happily married, gainfully employed, and living with his lovely wife, Paula, in Pompano

Beach, Florida. They may not be the two smartest people in the world, but they certainly are two of the happiest and nicest people who walk this earth. Communication style made this possible.

You too can learn how to use communication style to make things happen in your life. You can teach yourself to use communication style to control your own destiny. In the end, the choice is yours. You can ignore style and talk your way into trouble—or you can control style and talk your way out of trouble and into success.

Chapter 2

The Six Styles
of Communication

When you look into a kaleidoscope, you see a well-defined pattern created by the placement of uniquely shaped, brightly colored, pieces of matter. As you turn the lens of the kaleidoscope, you can create an infinite stream of novel and arresting patterns from these finite pieces of matter. Controlling your destiny with communication style is akin to turning the lens of a kaleidoscope. With the communication style kaleidoscope, the well-defined patterns are created by your unique placement of words. Unlike the visual kaleidoscope, however, you have control over the images you wish to produce, and you can recreate the sounds of success whenever you desire. All of the pieces of your communication matter are present within you, and you can turn or focus your verbal lens to create any image you need or want.

Human communication patterns are very identifiable because the average person is redundant; the average person chooses to use the same patterns repeatedly. All of us have three basic patterns of communication that we have developed over time:

- Noble
- Socratic
- Reflective

The six styles of communication are determined by the degree to which an individual uses or combines each of the patterns.*

Everyone has some of the Noble, some of the Socratic, and some of the Reflective pattern, but it is the combination of these patterns that creates your unique communication profile—your personal style of communication. There are six major styles in the Communication Kaleidoscope, and each represents a different sound and a different type of communicator.

---

*The term *Noble Self* was originally used by Darnell and Brockriede in their book, *Person's Communicating* (Englewood Cliffs, N.J.: Prentice-Hall, 1976). Their description of the Noble is considerably different from the profile I present here. Their theoretical descriptions of the Noble Self and the Rhetorical Reflector were incorporated into a test called the Rhetorical Sensitivity Scale (RHETSEN).

I began working with the RHETSEN scale while working on my doctoral dissertation at Purdue University. My research revealed that the RHETSEN scale (developed by Rod Hart, Bob Carlson, and Bill Eadie) lacked theoretical validity: it did not measure what it was supposed to be measuring. In addition, I found that the descriptions provided by Darnell and Brockriede had a kernel of truth in them, but for the most part they were not accurate or helpful descriptions of communicators.

After completing my doctoral studies, I began the long, arduous but very rewarding task of developing the Communication Style Profile test. Thus, the concepts presented in this book are based on more than a decade of research. I have worked with and tested thousands of students, workers, managers, and executives in an effort to develop a scale that will help the average person understand how communication can be used to improve one's life condition.

I will always be grateful to Dr. Roderick Hart for allowing me to serve as his research assistant and for encouraging me to develop my ideas about communication style. I am eternally grateful to Dr. W. Charles Redding for guiding my dissertation to completion, for his continuing support, but most of all for his enduring friendship.

You can learn to use all of the styles and a combination of styles to talk your way out of trouble and to create many different sounds of success.

In this chapter, I provide a brief overview of the six different types of communicators. In the next six chapters, we examine each type of communicator in detail. After reading these chapters, you will be able to listen to anyone for only a few minutes and identify that person's dominant style of communication. More important, you will know specifically which sounds you need to create to get each type of communicator to do willingly what you want him or her to do—without generating resentment or anger.

If you haven't already done so, you may want to turn to the Appendix and take the test to see which style you tend to use most of the time. If you don't like to take tests, then just continue reading, and you will soon recognize yourself in one of the descriptions.

THE DOMINANT STYLES

Everyone has the potential to use all three patterns of communication, but people tend to use one pattern predominantly. If you use one pattern most of the time, then you are a dominant-style communicator. There are three different types of dominant-style communicators:

- The Noble
- The Socratic
- The Reflective

As I briefly describe these communicators, keep in mind:

- We all have the potential to use all of the styles, but we tend to rely on one style more than the others.
- Style is learned. It is *not* a personality trait that will never change.

- One style is not better than another. Each style is simply different from the others.
- Each style has good and bad characteristics.

Before we begin, let me make some comments about this last point. When you are in a stressful situation, you will gravitate toward the style of communication with which you feel most comfortable — your dominant style. There are positive aspects of all six styles — and negative aspects too. And it is the negative aspects or bad characteristics of each style that become worse or more pronounced in stressful situations. Consider for a moment just the three dominant-style communicators. The Noble tends to be a direct and certain communicator, the Socratic tends to be a verbose communicator, and the Reflective tends to be nonassertive. In a stressful situation, these characteristics become exaggerated and more intense. The Noble sounds even more rigid, abrupt, and intimidating. He or she will say with absolute certainty, "This will *never* work!" To the contrary, the Socratic will talk incessantly, and the Reflective will clam up, saying absolutely nothing.

To create some visual images of the six types of communicators, I use examples of celebrities and political leaders who are prototypes of the six styles. Even with the brief descriptions in this chapter, you will begin recognizing the dominant style of people who are close to you. (You may even begin recognizing the style of some you wish weren't so close.)

The Noble: Clint, Rambo, Joan, and Arnold

The Noble is the speak-before-you-think type of communicator. A thought pops into the Noble's mind and rolls right out his or her mouth. Nobles don't filter their thoughts; they simply say what they think.

Mike is the artistic director in a small advertising company. Jim has just spent most of the night completing another rush job. Mike examines the twelve graphic illustrations. He is pleased with eleven of the designs but hands the twelfth back to Jim and says, "This one stinks. You need to do it over again." Mike doesn't tell Jim he likes the other eleven because he figures Jim already knows that, and it doesn't occur to Mike that Jim will take offense to his expression of a simple, honest opinion. Mike is a Noble.

The Noble is a direct, straightforward type of communicator who wants to go from A to Z in a straight line and doesn't want to be bothered with the details in between. Of all the communicators, Nobles use the least number of words to say what they have to say. In fact, if you can't say what you have to say in ten words or less, they don't want to hear it. If you can't write it in one page or less, they don't want to read it.

Clint Eastwood, or at least the characters he plays, is an archetypical Noble communicator. "Make my day," is a Noble statement, and when Rambo says, "Yo!" he, too, is exhibiting Noble communication in the extreme.

Nobles aren't literally noble. They do, however, believe that what they do is right or noble. The Noble is a true believer who truly feels that the primary purpose of communication is the honest exchange of information and opinions. The Noble is the tell-it-like-it-is type of communicator who doesn't think personal feelings should come into play when talking with another person. Nobles don't mean to insult you—they think they should tell the truth (as they see it), and they believe your feelings shouldn't be hurt if the truth is stated.

When Joan Rivers says, "Can we talk," you know she isn't asking you a question, and you know she isn't going to choose her words gingerly. She is going to give you her honest opinion of the person or issue at hand. Joan's audiences love her because she says what other people only think. Some people, of course, hate her because she says what she thinks. If her audience gasps because they think she has gone too far, she simply defends her remarks with, "It's true! Why should he care if I say it!"

You can say almost anything to a Noble, and the Noble will not be offended if he or she thinks you are making an honest statement. Arnold Schwarzenegger was a guest on the "Arsenio Hall Show" one evening, and Arsenio read a comment made by one of the children who appeared in *Kindergarten Cop*. The child was quoted as saying that Arnold Schwarzenegger picks his nose. Arsenio looked at Arnold and giggled as he questioned the accuracy of the remark. The audience roared, but Arnold calmly replied, "Of course. And you don't?" Arnold Schwarzenegger gave a Noble response to a question that he apparently did not find offensive because it was based on "truth." Arsenio Hall, to the contrary, was flustered when Arnold questioned him about similar behaviors. Thunderous laughter arose from the audience as Arsenio stuttered and stammered while trying to evade the question. Arsenio, you see, is not a Noble; he is a Reflective.

Nobles are bottom-line communicators. They will say, "Don't give me all of the details on how you are going to do this. Just tell me what we will end up with. What's the bottom line? When will it be done, and will we make a profit?" Sound like someone you know?

The word *or* is prevalent in Noble speech because Nobles don't tend to see gray areas. Rather, they see things quite clearly as being either black or white, yes or no, go or no go. They will say to you, "Are you going or not? I don't need your reasons. Just say yes or no."

The Noble has considerable difficulty dealing with the Socratic. When the Noble is presented with a problem and states, "I see two possible solutions to this problem. We can either do this or this," the Socratic responds, "Hold on just a minute. I think there are several possible solutions to this problem, and we ought to discuss each possibility!" The Noble cringes with irritation upon hearing these words, and mutters, "Here we go again."

The Socratic: Reagan and Cosby

The Socratic doesn't mean to offend or irritate the Noble, but the Socratic truly believes that each and every point should be discussed before a final solution is selected. This is because the Socratic is the individual who is most concerned with rhetoric and the analysis of details. The Socratic enjoys discussion, negotiation, arbitration, argumentation, and debate.

He or she believes that communication, in and of itself, is a valuable activity and that time spent in conversation is time well spent.

Bill Cosby is the epitome of the Socratic communicator. When he goes into one of his long diatribes to explain a minor point, he is displaying the Socratic style of communication. Much of the humor in the "Cosby Show" stems from the other characters' reactions to his Socratic style of communication.

The Socratic is verbose, has a tendency to use a lot of anecdotal stories, and loves to engage in philosophical discussions of the abstract. Former president Ronald Reagan is a Socratic communicator. When he speaks, he uses anecdotal stories to illustrate his point, and, more times than not, the story is about someone from Iowa or the entertainment industry. You may be thinking that his speeches are written by someone else. That is true, but professional speechwriters don't write in their voice; they write in the voice of the speaker.

The Socratic is easily identifiable because he or she has a penchant for details, and Socratics tend to talk in footnotes. They .tend to give additional information that isn't terribly relevant or necessary for you to understand the topic at hand. If you are not a Socratic, you know you are talking to one when you find yourself saying, "You lost me. Are we still on the same topic?"

Sometimes those of us who are not Socratic get so overwhelmed by Socratic talk that we tune out, and the Socratic has to ask, "Are you still listening to me?" There is a scene in the movie *Amadeus* that I love because it illustrates this point so well. After performing his first opera, Mozart seeks the king's reaction and approval. The king indicates that he enjoyed the opera but that it perhaps had too many notes. Highly offended, Mozart challenges, "I don't understand. There are just as many notes, Majesty, as I required. Neither more, nor less." The king responds, "My dear fellow. There are, in fact, only so many notes the ear can hear in the course of an evening."

For many of us, the Socratic uses more words than our ears can hear.

The Reflective: Woody, Mia, Jimmy, and Arsenio

The Socratic drives the Noble right up the wall, the Socratic thinks the Noble is obnoxious, and while the Noble and Socratic are driving each other crazy, the Reflective is sitting back, patiently listening. This is because the Reflective is the person who believes that the primary purpose of communication is the maintenance or advancement of the interpersonal relationship. The Reflective is the person who is most concerned with the human aspects of the communication interaction, and Reflectives are the best listeners. Woody Allen is an example of a lovable, Reflective communicator, and while former President Carter may not be lovable to some, he is a Reflective communicator.

Reflectives are easily identifiable because they tend to be pleasant to talk with, and they tend to use a lot of qualifiers when they talk. That is, they try to say something positive before delivering the bad news message, and they don't make absolute statements. They don't say, "This will never work." They do say, "Well, I don't know . . . I'm not sure . . . This may not work . . . But then again, it might."

Woody Allen is the master of the qualifier. He creates characters who never quite say what they really feel. In one scene in *Hannah and Her Sisters,* Woody Allen and Mia Farrow ask Woody's writing partner if he will be a donor for their artificial insemination plan. Neither the partner nor the wife says yes or no. Instead, the partner responds, "Gee . . . Well . . . my first reaction after the initial shock is that I'm flattered that you asked me." The wife responds, "Gosh . . . listen . . . I've got to tell you the truth here . . . I'm a little uneasy about this . . . I feel for you . . . I really do . . . I'm going to cry . . . You want my husband to have a child with you?"

For the Reflective, the accurate transmission of information, expression of opinions, and tangible results all play a secondary role in the communication encounter. The Reflective is the individual who will say nothing rather than say something that will alienate the other person. He or she will tell you what you want to hear in order to avoid open conflict.

The Reflective, however, does not feel bound by the little white lie because Reflectives believe that less-than-truthful statements are justified when *you* violate the decorum of the communication interaction. For Reflectives, the communication decorum should be polite, warm, and supportive, and they do whatever they need to do to maintain that decorum.

Reflectives are concerned with human feelings and are typically soft-spoken, nonassertive individuals who often walk away from an interaction frustrated and saying, "I wish I had said what I really thought!"

The Noble *never* walks away and says, "I wish I had said what I really thought." Typically the Noble thinks, "I probably shouldn't have said that." Then he or she reflects about it for a few seconds and decides, "Oh well, he'll get over it!" On the other hand, the Socratic is typically still talking after everyone else thinks the conversation is over.

Yes, three very different styles of communication—not better or worse—just different. The following story—also true—illustrates how these three different communicators respond differently to the exact same situation.

I was supervising two graduate students who were working on a research project. Gloria and Randy hoped to write up their results and have an article published. Gloria came to me one day to explain that they were not making progress because Randy kept avoiding working on the article. After discussing the matter with both of them, we agreed that Gloria would write the article, Randy would have all of the graphs and tables prepared professionally, Gloria would be listed as first author, and Randy would be listed as second author. This agreement seemed to make everyone happy, and Randy admitted that he really didn't have the time required to write the article.

Gloria wrote the article, Randy prepared all of the graphs and tables, and the article was accepted for publication in a well-respected journal. We were all thrilled.

The day the journal arrived, Gloria was in the office with me. She eagerly opened the journal to see the fruits of her labor. Lo and behold,

Randy was listed as first author, and Gloria was listed as second author. (Name order is a big deal in the academic world.) Noble that I am, I immediately called the editor, who explained that Randy had called and stated that the secretary had made an error when she typed the manuscript. He told the editor that he was to be listed as the first author.

During the course of everything that transpired, Randy called Gloria, and during their conversation he said, "I'll bet you hate me." My immediate Noble response to that statement was, "You're damned right I do!"—and I meant it. Toni, our secretary who is a Reflective, said, "No, I don't hate Randy. What he did may not have been right, but he does have a lot of problems. I kind of feel sorry for him." Gloria, who is a Socratic, said (and this is a direct quotation),

> "No, I don't hate Randy. Hate would imply bodily harm. I don't wish Randy any bodily harm. I can, however, say, at this particular point in time, that I don't like Randy very much."

Three very different responses to the exact same situation, and the difference stems from communication style.

Dominant-style communicators are the easiest to identify. They are classic archetypes; they so clearly are what they are. Now let's take a look at how these dominant styles can be combined to create totally different sounds and very different communicators.

THE BLENDED STYLES

Blended-style communicators are a bit more difficult to identify at first because they take two patterns, blend them together, and use them simultaneously. There are only two types of blended-style communicators: the Magistrate, who blends the Noble and Socratic patterns to create a unique sound, and the Candidate, who creates an equally unique sound by combining the Reflective and Socratic patterns. The blended-style communicator does not switch back and forth between the two patterns.

Rather, he or she creates a distinctive style profile by merging the dominant traits of two different patterns.

The Noble, for example, is direct but not verbose; the Socratic is verbose and often directive but not direct or straightforward. The Magistrate blends these two styles; he or she is direct, straightforward, blunt, and verbose—all at the same time. Similarly, the Reflective is a warm, supportive, nonassertive, soft-spoken communicator who is not verbose, but the Socratic is quite verbose. The Candidate—a Reflective-Socratic blend—is warm, supportive, soft-spoken, nondirect, and extremely verbose. In fact, the Candidate talks more than a dominant-style Socratic.

The Magistrate and the Candidate share the base Socratic pattern, but both differ from the Reflective and Noble with respect to one additional and very important aspect: both have an intense desire to win the argument. Each, however, goes about winning the argument in a different manner.

The Magistrate: Geraldo, Dixie, and Muhammad Ali

People tend to have intense reactions to the Magistrate. There doesn't appear to be any middle ground for this Noble-Socratic blended communicator. If the Noble or the Socratic can make an impression on you as a communicator, then the Magistrate can be twice as impressive. If the Noble or the Socratic can anger you with his or her style of communication, then the Magistrate can make you twice as angry. The Magistrate is a very strong communicator—in both positive and negative terms. The other person either really loves or really hates this style.

Geraldo Rivera, Larry King, and Muhammad Ali display the Magistrate style of communication. Think about these fellows. They are not "take 'em or leave 'em" type of people. These Magistrates evoke intense reactions from others. They are not Noble, and they are not Socratic. They are Noble and Socratic at the same time. This creates a style that is very different from the dominant-style communicators.

Magistrates speak with an air of superiority. They feel they are right, there is usually little room for opposing views, and they definitely feel the need to expose the other person's shortcomings. Listen for the air of superiority and to Victor's direct, blunt, detailed, and verbose Magistrate sound as he tells Fred he made an error:

> "That wasn't the smartest move you've ever made Fred. You know we aren't running a charity here. You have to understand that when you agree to change an order, there are a lot of ramifications. I know you don't want to alienate the customer, but the customer isn't always right. They don't always know what's best for them. I personally believe you could have convinced him to keep the order the way it was. I know I could have. I've had a lot of experience, you know. Maybe you can watch the way I handle things the next time. You know, it's not really all that difficult. You have to be a bit of an actor, a bit of a teacher, and a bit of a comedian. You start by letting them think you agree, but then you begin to give them pieces of information and statistics that show your way would be more beneficial. You add a couple of humorous anecdotes when you see them softening, and if that doesn't work, you get a little tough. Let me tell you about how I handled the Barron account last month. Barron is a tough cookie, but I managed to swing him over. I started by . . . etc., etc., etc."

The Magistrate blends together verbal characteristics that at first glance appear incompatible. For example, the Magistrate is both verbose and straightforward. Magistrates tell you exactly what they think—*and* in great detail. Dixie Carter, who plays Julia Sugarbaker on "Designing Women," generates a lot of laughter with this technique. Julia has intense feelings on all topics, and she delivers her diatribes as if she were on a podium surrounded by multitudes of followers. Her oration is typically followed by dead silence or a thunderous ovation from the audience.

Magistrates tend to sound self-righteous, but their harangues can be humorous. They tend to speak as if they were writing one long paragraph, and they jump from one idea to the next without a pause or creating a new paragraph. They tend to use a colorful and somewhat exaggerated description of events, and they speak with enthusiasm, animation, total control, and a bit of braggadocio.

Magistrates don't come up for air once they start a thought, and they don't give you a chance to interject your thoughts. They are totally comfortable with dominating the conversation and in an argument speak louder, talk over the other person and do not hesitate to insult the opponent verbally.

The Magistrate is the most powerful of all communicators. Not better or worse—just powerful. This is because the Magistrate draws upon and actively uses a much larger set of characteristics than does a dominant-style communicator. As you will see in the following chapters, Nobles and Socratics each have thirty or so identifiable communication characteristics they tend to rely upon, but the Magistrate has more than sixty from which to choose. This is both a blessing and a curse for the Magistrate because this profile has double the strengths *and* double the problems. Thus, when Magistrates are communicating well, they are doing it very well, and when they are communicating badly, they are doing it very badly.

If you have ever said, "That is the most dynamic speaker I have ever heard," you were probably listening to a Magistrate. Similarly, if you heard yourself saying, "That is the most obnoxious person I have ever spoken with", you were probably speaking with a Magistrate. They are intense communicators who tell you exactly how they feel, and they tell you in great detail. They are totally committed to winning arguments and tend not to give up. They can be eloquent, and they can be overbearing. They are the best and the worst of two worlds.

The Candidate: Betty White and Jimmy Stewart

The Candidate is a lovable, chitty-chatty type of communicator. Candidates fool you at first because they sound like Reflectives. They are warm, supportive, and very pleasant to talk with, but they talk incessantly, and that's how you know you are talking with a Candidate and not a Reflective. The most talkative of all communicators, this very pleasant, very patient person believes that any problem can be solved if you talk about it long enough. The Candidate, however, is easier to tolerate than the Socratic or Magistrate because he or she does not speak with arrogance; the Candidate maintains the communication decorum of a Reflective.

Betty White, who plays Rose on "The Golden Girls," is a perfect example of a Candidate. She always tries to smooth things over by telling a story about someone she knew who had a similar experience that turned out all right. It's difficult to get angry with Rose, because as long and tedious as her stories may be, she always sounds warm and sincere.

The Candidate blends the dominant characteristics of the Reflective and the Socratic to create a style that is warm, supportive, analytical, and quite verbose. This soft-spoken verbosity is often used to reduce hostility and encourage open communication. When dealing with a hostile individual, he or she will combine the warm, calm, Reflective style with the Socratic question-and-answer technique to encourage conversation until the tension is reduced or eliminated.

Like the Magistrate, the Candidate draws upon and uses a much larger set of characteristics than does a dominant-style communicator. Unlike Magistrates, Candidates are not perceived as domineering communicators. They are, however, perceived as dominating communicators. This is because they lack the Reflective's listening skills and as a result dominate the conversation with incessant talk. Candidates, however, do not have the pushy or forceful tendencies of Socratics or Magistrates and as a result are not considered domineering—just talkative. Albeit, Candidates, like Magistrates, are committed to winning the argument. They sound nicer, but they continue to come back at you until they win.

Like Reflectives, Candidates can be intimidated. Listen as Mary Ann gives an account of a very serious, unsuccessful communication encounter. As you listen, imagine a soft-spoken, warm, and open individual. Notice the one-paragraph structure. Candidates don't stop to breathe or punctuate, and they touch several different topics in the same breath. Keep in mind that the outcome of the story isn't as important as the way she tells the story because, right now, we're just listening for sounds. Later in the book,

I'll show you how to use these sounds to control the outcome of an interaction. In the true style of a Candidate, Mary Ann offers the following story:

For some reason, a bad communication encounter was much easier to come up with, maybe because those are the ones we regret and therefore never forget. Mine's pretty bad. I was a teller at Bank of America, and I totally loved it, the people I worked with were super nice, I was making decent money, and I had friends at another branch I could complain to after an especially busy Friday, or I could fax. One day our new manager, who had been in our branch for only a week, called me into the conference room. I had absolutely no idea what was about to happen, probably because I didn't know her, I didn't know her communication style or even her personality. My old manager was definitely a Noble. Anyway, it turned out I had cashed a check, after accepting a deposit from a customer impersonator. Of course, this little conversation was my chance to defend myself and tell my manager exactly what I did and why. I was so off guard, though, that I practically just sat there like a fool, instead of insisting that the guy signed the check in front of me, had enough to cover the check in this account, and had given me a large deposit, and that most importantly, I had checked his signature card and both signatures matched, and he knew the customer's social security number and mother's maiden name. What else could I have done? Of course that is what I say strongly now, not what I was afraid to say in that little encounter, and that cost me my job. I was very foolish to not see the situation from the beginning, to recount to her the details of what happened, and to save my job. I was so overwhelmed that someone would be so evil, and that I was a victim . . . I have never regretted not saying something more than I regretted not saying something in this instance.

Mary Ann tells her story like a Candidate, but she didn't utilize the strengths of her style to control the outcome of the interaction. She was frightened and intimidated, and she froze. She didn't say anything. She didn't use her style of communication to her advantage, and she lost her job.

Under normal conditions, the Candidate's persuasive effort tends to be quite different from the other communicators. When attempting to persuade, Candidates use personal self-disclosure statements to disarm the other person. The purpose of this disarmament technique is to encourage liking. Once liking has been established, the other person is more inclined to accept the Candidate's position or is more willing to break a rule for the Candidate. Let me illustrate this last point.

Sheila and David belong to a small theater group and have season tickets to the Los Angeles Theatre Center productions. Sheila was complaining to David that she was going to miss the next performance because of a scheduling conflict. As it turned out, David also had a conflict and was unable to go with the regular group. He suggested that the two of them go together on another day and volunteered to take care of exchanging the tickets. When they arrived at the theater and David went to the window to exchange the tickets, he was told that exchanges could be done only twenty-four hours in advance of a performance. He calmly and quietly said, "Oh no, how awful," and then very innocently said,

"I did call in advance and the lady I talked with—I think her name was Jane . . . No, Joan . . . yes, her name was Joan—said that there were seats available and that there would be no problem. I'm sure Joan wouldn't have lied to me . . . she would have no reason. May I just ask you, was she correct? Are there seats available?"

The young woman reluctantly informed David that there were seats available but restated the policy and explained that they were trying to do something about the tremendous number of people exchanging tickets at the last minute. Armed with the ammunition that there were indeed seats available, David set out to disarm this young woman and get her to break the rule and exchange the tickets. He never raised his voice, he accepted total responsibility for his "ignorance" with respect to the exchange policy, and he relayed every word of his telephone conversation with Joan. Each time that she attempted to explain the policy, he would say, "I really don't understand that because . . ." and give a detailed explanation of how he had seen similar situations handled by others. His conversation was animated, and he was able to get the young woman to laugh. He chatted with her about her goals and acting ambitions and shared some anecdotal stories about his own theater experiences. David continued to talk until he had convinced her that she—and she alone—had the power to cause disappointment or joy for a very pleasant, nonthreatening man and his friend who were loyal season ticket holders, and who drove all the way down to see this play for which there were seats available, and who would be more than willing to follow the twenty-four-hour rule should they need to exchange tickets in the future. She exchanged the tickets.

Sheila laughed and gave David credit for hanging in there and talking the young woman into exchanging their tickets. She said she would have just gone to the manager and saved herself fifteen minutes of conversation (very Noble, wouldn't you say?). David laughed and stated that he found the interaction fun. He said,

> "You just keep throwing information at the other person to disarm them and get them to like you. Once they like you, it is easier for them to break a rule to help you out."

This, in a nutshell, is a key factor that distinguishes the Candidate from the dominant-style Reflective or the dominant-style Socratic. The Reflective focuses on the other person—on making the other person feel good or comfortable. The Socratic focuses on the argument—the issue—the rhetoric of the moment. The Candidate uses rhetoric to focus liking on the self. Information combined with liking is then used to disarm the other person and get him or her to agree to the Candidate's position.

Think of the days when some political candidates used to have integrity. Think of Jimmy Stewart in *Mr. Smith Goes to Washington*. Think of the person who doesn't raise his or her voice, who talks and continues to talk until the other person gives in or the problem goes away. That's the Candidate style.

THE DUAL STYLE

If you are not a dominant-style communicator and you are not a blended-style communicator, then you are probably a dual-style communicator. Dual-style communicators develop the Noble style and the Reflective style, *but* they don't blend the styles. Rather, they alternate between two styles, and because they have this ability, they are considered the most strategic of all communicators.

President George Bush displays this dual style of communication. In fact, when *Time* chose Mr. Bush as the 1990 Man of the Year, the cover photo portrayed him with two different sides of the same face. When I saw this photograph, I thought it was an excellent visual illustration of the Senator style of communication.

The Senator: George Bush and Blanche Devereaux

The Noble and Reflective styles are almost complete opposites, yet the Senator has developed *both* styles. The Senator is a strategic communicator who uses these two distinctly different styles of communication to adapt to differing environments. The Senator switches back and forth between being a Noble and a Reflective. The Senator does not blend these two opposing styles together. Rather, he or she allows the situation to determine which style is appropriate. In one situation the Senator may be totally Noble, and in another the Senator may be totally Reflective.

The Senator is a bit of a chameleon and therefore is the one communicator who *cannot* be identified in the first few minutes of a conversation. You must view the Senator in different settings over time before you can identify his or her style. The Senator sounds like a soft-spoken Noble in some situations and exactly like a Reflective in other situations. The Senator uses both styles with ease. To the contrary, it's very difficult for a dominant-style Noble to be Reflective, and some dominant-style Reflectives would rather die than be Noble.

The Senator, unlike either the Noble or the Reflective, is the master of the Hooded-Eye Technique. The Hooded-Eye involves not letting the other person know how you feel on a particular topic. We'll talk more about this later, but for now it is important to note that the Senator uses the Hooded-Eye to gain an information advantage over the other person. In so doing, the Senator becomes a powerful and strategic communicator. Senators plan their communication strategies. They decide when to be Noble and when to be Reflective. During the Persian Gulf conflict, President Bush gave us a rare glimpse at a Senator using both styles in the same situation. He began many of his speeches with a direct statement or warning to Saddam Hussein. In this part of the speech, he was direct, cold, and blunt and often had a stern look or frown on his face. Like a Noble, he frequently pointed his finger to emphasize his point. After he was done redressing Hussein, his voice would soften, and his facial gestures would convey a feeling of concern as he spoke of the men and women stationed in the gulf.

This is an interesting style that provides some valuable insight into how communication style develops. In the early days of conducting this research, we found that people who have high Noble and high Reflective scores tend to be clergy, counselors, minorities, and women who have returned to the paid labor force after being housewives (the nonpaid labor force) for a number of years.

We thought this was a bit unusual, so we began interviewing these people to see what they had in common and if these commonalities contributed to the development of communication style. In our conversations with these dual-style communicators, we found that this unique group of people must interact in two distinctly different types of environments. In an effort to adapt, they develop and use two different styles of communication. Like a Senator who must be sensitive to his or her constituents, they use one style in one environment and the other style in the other environment, as the following story shows.

I was talking with a fifty-year-old woman who had returned to the paid labor force after twenty years as a homemaker. Her scoring pattern indicated that she was a Senator (a dual-style communicator), so I questioned if she found herself using the Reflective style in her home and the Noble style in her work environment. "Oh, no," she responded, "quite the contrary. When I am at home, I am the boss, and what I say goes! When I am at work, I am very calm, and I just enjoy listening and talking with people I like."

It isn't important to know which style she was using in which particular situation. What is important is the fact that she had developed—and was using—two distinctly different styles of communication, and she could alternate between those styles to meet her perceived environmental needs.

This is an important piece of information because it suggests that style is something that is learned. It is not something that we are born with and must accept as our fate in life. Style is environmentally influenced, and if the environment can bring about change, then you can bring about change if you so desire. Communication style is a skill that can be taught and developed.

If you have watched "The Golden Girls," you have witnessed how humor is generated from the use of differing communication styles. Dorothy (Bea Arthur) and Sophia (Estelle Getty) are Noble communicators; Rose (Betty White) is a Candidate; and Blanche (Rue McClanahan) is a Senator. In fact, much of the humor in that show is generated by exaggerating the communication style differences of the four characters. For example, Rose takes the "I know someone who . . ." tendency of the Candidate to the extreme every time she goes into one of her St. Olaf stories. Humor is then generated from Dorothy's Noble reactions to these stories. She may grimace with intolerance, bite her hand to keep herself from screaming, or scream, "Rose. Enough!" While there is humor in the idiocy of Rose's stories, the big laugh comes from the reactions to her stories.

Fast-paced and sharp-witted humor is generated when the two resident Nobles exchange remarks. Dorothy and her mother, Sophia—the ultimate Noble—take the tell-it-like-it-is tendency of the Noble to the outer limits. In one episode, octogenarian Sophia decides that she is going to become a nun. After a nun from the convent arrives, the following conversation occurs,

DOROTHY: Ma. You're joining a convent! Why didn't I know about it?

SOPHIA: Because you're divorced. Technically, in the eyes of the church you don't even exist. . . . I spit on you. [She thinks this may not be viewed as polite by the sister, so she adds] Unless, of course, the sister would like to spit on you first.

A few minutes later Blanche enters the room and displays both sides of her Senator style of communication. She bursts into the room unaware of the nun's presence and exclaims,

BLANCHE: Can you imagine Rose is trying to blame the whole thing on me. That woman has one hell of a lot of nerve. [She notices the sister, smiles, and then shifts into a soft southern, reflective voice and says] Hello. I'm a Baptist.

Imagine the humor that could be generated from an episode of "The Golden Girls" with Woody Allen and Geraldo Rivera as guest stars.

DOROTHY: So tell me, Geraldo. Why *did* you write the book?

BLANCHE: Why, Dorothy, the answer to that question is obvious. He wanted the world to know what a charming . . . open . . . sensitive . . . [breathing heavily] sensual man he . . .

SOPHIA: Balderdash. He wanted to brag about all the girls he bonged.

ROSE: Bonged? I don't remember reading that . . . but you know, I once knew a man named Sven Strudelbonger. Everyone called him Bong for short. Partly because of his name, but mostly because he had a bell in front of his shop, and every time a pretty woman walked by, Sven would bong the bell. Everyone made comments about his large bonger, but I don't know why. I thought the bell was rather small. It was only this big, but then you know . . .

DOROTHY: Rose!

SOPHIA: So Woody. Tell me. How many girls have you bonged?

WOODY: Oh, well . . . you see . . . I haven't really . . . I mean it's not really something I would want to write . . . I mean it's fine that you did, but, you know, personally, I think maybe . . .

GERALDO: Hey, come on Woody. Tell the truth. There's nothing to be ashamed of. We're powerful men. We have a lot of women at our disposal. It's part of our life. You know I wasn't trying to brag. I ask the people who come on my show to expose their innermost thoughts, and I felt I would be less than honest if I didn't expose mine.

SOPHIA: Expose what? Your thoughts or your . . .

DOROTHY: Ma!

You get the idea. Now you write the rest from here, and while you're creating, imagine a world where we could each find humor instead of conflict from our communication style differences. This really isn't a difficult task to accomplish.

If you listen, it is easy to identify someone's dominant style of communication. Even with the brief descriptions that I have provided, you are probably beginning to identify the communication styles of people you know—your father, mother, son, daughter, friend, boss, spouse or mate. You may even be laughing and saying, "Now I know why she drives me crazy." In fact, this information may even keep some of you out of divorce court. With this thought in mind, let's take a look at how you can use this information to talk anyone into doing almost anything without generating resentment or anger.

HOW TO TALK ALMOST ANYONE INTO DOING ALMOST ANYTHING

If you can control the communication style in an interaction, you can control the eventual outcome of a given situation. In attempting to accomplish this goal, remember that each person has a set of expectations about how the other person should communicate. When these expectations are not met, conflict arises. It is the management of this conflict that leads to control and, subsequently, the ability to lead others. It is the management of this conflict that will allow you to persuade others to do what you would like them to do. Let's see how conflict begins.

When you enter into a conversation, you and the other person usually have expectations of similarity: you expect the other person to communicate exactly as you do, and the other person expects you to communicate just as he or she does. Nobles expect Noble talk, Socratics expect Socratic talk, and Reflectives expect other Reflectives. When these expectations are not met, you are both thrown off balance, and communication conflict exists.

In some situations, it is possible to have asymmetric communication expectations. That is, one person may expect the other person not to communicate in a similar style. For example, a Noble or Socratic boss may expect his or her secretary to communicate as a Reflective. When this doesn't happen, communication conflict exists. (In the final section of this book, you'll learn how to deal with these expectations and still get what you want out of an interaction.)

Complementary communication expectations often emerge once two people begin to develop an interpersonal relationship. Once you begin to know and like another individual, you accept or become tolerant of his or her communication style and the inherent strengths and weaknesses. In addition, you may look to the other person to balance or modify the inadequacies that exist in your own style. Let me play the Socratic for a moment and provide you with another story to illustrate this point.

Kelli, a Noble, has worked on numerous advertising projects with Sherry, a Socratic. Over the years, their working relationship has developed into a friendship. Not only have they become tolerant and accepting of their style differences, they have learned to make the best use of the complementary nature of their styles to produce a better product. Sherry encourages Kelli to include details that are essential for understanding, and Kelli encourages Sherry to focus on the main idea and eliminate unnecessary detail.

The understanding of the complementary nature of their communication styles carries over into their friendship. For example, Sherry was offended by a statement made by their boss and asked Kelli for her opinion as to why their boss would have made the comment. Knowing that their boss is an inordinately strong Noble, Kelli matter-of-factly suggested, "She probably finds you interpersonally irritating."

Sherry paused for a moment, looked away to contemplate, looked back at Kelli, and Socraticly replied, "I know you didn't mean to insult me with that statement. You certainly do, however, have a way of getting at the heart of the matter. I suppose if I am really honest with myself, I will have to admit that your assessment of the situation is probably correct."

Adapting to and interacting with differing styles of communication is an important part of leadership. When you fail to adapt or are intolerant of differing styles, you will increase the level of conflict. Managing communication conflict is not difficult if you remember the following four step process:

Steps to Managing Communication Style

1. Understand your own dominant style of communication and the inherent characteristics and weaknesses of it.
2. Identify the other person's dominant style of communication and the corresponding communication expectations.
3. Use all six styles of communication to deal with those expectations and accomplish your goals.
4. Develop new expectations through adaptive and tolerant communication interactions so that accomplishing your goals becomes easier in each future interaction.

Communication style is something that is learned; it is something that is environmentally influenced. Since you spend 50 percent of your waking hours at work, the work environment can have a significant impact on the development of your dominant style of communication. In fact, you are more likely to take your work style home with you than vice versa. We might all like to think that we use different styles in different situations. Socratics especially like to think this, but the truth of the matter is that we don't. We'll talk a little more about this later.

We are all capable of using all six styles of the Communication Kaleidoscope. If you wish to control the outcome of an interaction, to get others to do willingly what you would like them to do, to tell loved ones how you really feel, to control your own destiny, and get the things you want in life without generating resentment or anger, you simply have to adjust your kaleidoscope and create a style that works.

Keep in mind that although Communication Style is not about personality, your personality does interact with your style of communication. It is possible to be a charming or rude Noble, a dynamic or boring Socratic, or a pleasant or devious Reflective. Charming, rude, dynamic, boring, pleasant, and devious are personality traits—not communication style characteristics. Thus, an understanding of communication style may help you control your own style, but your personality can prevent you from using this knowledge in some or all situations.

Additionally, you will notice that in many of the scenarios I present, the storyteller makes reference to the communication style of the other person. Granted, the average person doesn't walk around naming the communication style of the other person, but these aren't average people. These storytellers have attended my training sessions and are attempting to apply their newly acquired knowledge. I share these stories with you because they are real, and they illustrate the types of problems and people we all encounter. Remember, the key to creating the sounds of success is to be able to analyze and plan communication events. The first step in the process is to identify the other person's style of communication. The next step is for you to adjust your style to meet the other person's needs. You can't control or change the other person's style of communication, but you can control yours. In doing so, you can learn to control the outcome of the interaction.

PART TWO

∞

How to Create Your Own Communication Kaleidoscope

Chapter 3

The Noble: Truth in Action

THE NOBLE SOUND

The Noble is actually quite easy to identify, and as we begin our exploration of this unique, sometimes irritating, but often charismatic communicator, keep in mind that everyone has some of the Noble style. This means that you can call upon this style if you need to, even if it isn't your dominant style. Also keep in mind that while some people think of the Noble as crude, others see the Noble as a true leader and admire his or her ability to say what needs to be said—the key characteristic that separates the Noble from the rest of the pack.

Tell It Like It Is!

Susan is an account executive for a Chicago-based advertising firm. Bobby, Susan's colleague and good friend, is also an account executive. They often try their ideas out on each other before presenting to a client. Susan enthusiastically reveals her new sales campaign to Bobby and inquires, "Well, what do you think? Do you think he'll like it?" Bobby, the Noble, replies, "He'll hate it."

The Noble is a tell-it-like-it-is, shoot-them-between-the-eyes type of communicator who typically says what other people only think. The Noble is a direct, straightforward communicator who truly believes that each person should say exactly what he or she feels and that to do less is dishonest, inappropriate, or dishonorable. The Noble may withhold an opinion on an issue that is deemed unimportant, but he or she cannot rationalize a response that is not representative of "true feelings." The Noble is the person who says, "I would rather tell you I won't answer that question than tell you a lie."

The Noble has great difficulty dealing with those who do not accept this same communication premise. In fact, the Noble may become frustrated, irritated, or downright angry with the person who will not say what he or she really feels, and the Noble may view this person as devious or cowardly. As a Noble, you might say, "Good god, Mary! Why didn't you speak up to him? We can't meet those goals. Where is your backbone?" If you say this and Mary is your boss, then you have probably taken one step down—not up—the corporate ladder.

The Noble tends not to be concerned with the personal feelings of others; however, the Noble doesn't expect others to place hurt feelings over and above honest expressions either. In fact, it is almost impossible to insult or offend a Noble if he or she thinks you have expressed yourself honestly. This doesn't mean that the Noble will accept or agree with what is said. It simply means that the Noble believes each person has a right and, for that matter, an obligation to state his or her true feelings, probably because Nobles tend to be bottom-line, results-oriented people.

Joe is a manager with a federal credit union that takes pride in the excellent interpersonal climate that exists throughout the organization. Joe's department is responsible for the collection of delinquent accounts, and he is very aware of the tremendous stress associated with this function. He believes that his staff are working at maximum productivity. At the quarterly goal-setting meeting, Joe responds to senior management's request for a productivity increase. He calmly, without emotion, but with certainty states,

> "Look, a slap on the back and the words, 'job well done' only go so far now. It's time we initiate an incentive program."

The initial shock of this statement quickly diminishes as Joe outlines a program he feels will work. After some revisions, Joe announces the program to his staff, who, in his words, "accept it with open arms."

Joe combined his need to tell it like it is with his concern for results and the bottom line. He said what he had to say and produced a plan to back up his remarks. He used the Noble style to create a moment of success for himself and his staff.

Often a Noble will walk away from an interaction and say, "I probably shouldn't have said that," and after thinking about it for a minute, will add, "Oh well, she'll get over it." The Noble truly believes that the other person should "get over it" because the Noble would "get over it" if the remark in question were made to him or her. Thus, the Noble is not a self-centered communicator. Rather, the Noble is a true believer who expects personal feelings to play a secondary role in the communication interaction; the primary purpose of communication is the exchange of information and honest opinions. The Noble believes that the best way to deal with a problem is to be direct. Sometimes this works—and sometimes it doesn't.

CeCe is a data processing operations manager for a large and profitable savings and loan institution. Kim, a data base specialist, requests time off to interview for a position in the loan quality department. The position offers a promotion and an increase in pay. Internal promotions are encouraged and are part of the corporate philosophy on motivation. As a matter of courtesy, the manager doing the interviewing usually notifies the prospective candidate's current manager. Judy, the loan quality manager, did not notify CeCe.

CeCe is upset by this situation, and while she doesn't know Judy well, she feels she needs to confront her and solve the problem so it doesn't happen again. CeCe walks into Judy's office and asks, "Did Kim inquire about your open position or did you approach her?" Judy indicated that Kim approached her. CeCe responded, "The next time you interview one of my employees, please have the courtesy to let me know in advance."

Judy is not a Noble and is offended by CeCe's blunt comments. She recognizes that she should have called CeCe first, but she also thinks CeCe could have at least said, "Hello, how are you?" before barging into the office. Relations between CeCe and Judy are now strained.

I Know, Therefore You Should Know

The Noble is not a directive and controlling type of individual, as you might initially think. Rather, the Noble is a direct communicator who believes that he or she is in control of the self and a communicator who expects the other person also to be in control. Additionally, the Noble expects the other person to keep the personal self out of the interaction and to communicate in a similar direct, frank, and spontaneous manner.

The Noble openly expresses opinions but is unlikely to share feelings about personal matters. Consequently the Noble does not tend to engage in personal self-disclosure and may be viewed as a distant or very private type of communicator.

Morris is Noble, and his wife, Rita, is Socratic. Rita knows that Morris is angry about something. She tries to question him and get him to open up. Finally, exasperated, she demands, "What's wrong? What are you angry about?" Morris looks at her and responds, "Nothing."

Why did Morris say, "Nothing"? Because Morris *expects Rita to know what's wrong. He* knows what's wrong; therefore, she should know what's wrong. If she doesn't know what's wrong, then it's not worth his effort to tell her.

At the end of this chapter, I'll tell you how to get Morris to tell you what's wrong. Right now, let's take this same characteristic and transfer it to the work situation.

Imagine a Noble manager who observes an employee doing something incorrectly. Does the Noble approach the employee and demonstrate the correct procedures? No. The Noble tends to believe that the employee will figure it out. But somewhere down the line, the employee doesn't figure it out, a major error occurs, and the Noble is left to deal with a crisis that could have been prevented.

Unnecessary crises will not help you get ahead in your organization. Be aware that Nobles occasionally draw upon their Socratic nature and provide direction; however, when this does happen, they are more likely simply to say, "You are doing that wrong. Do it over," and then walk away. They don't explain how the other person should correct the problem—just that it should be corrected.

This need for the other person to be in control of the self is an important issue for the Noble. Nobles truly believe they shouldn't have to tell the other person what to do or how to do it. They think the other person should take control and just do it. If you know a Noble for any length of time, you will hear the words, "Just do it." It's part of their repetitive vocabulary.

Can you see where this one little characteristic might cause the Noble some difficulty?

Eliminate the Chitchat

Nobles talk to produce an outcome, but they often forget that establishing an interpersonal relationship at the beginning of a conversation will have an impact on the outcome. A Noble will walk into your office, sit down, and say, "Okay, let's get to work." There's no pleasant chitchat—no hellos, no comments about the weather, and no questions about your family. You may have blood dripping from your nose, but the Noble sits down and says, "Okay, let's get to work." He or she may pause and say, "Did you know your nose was bleeding?" but then it's back to business as usual.

Nobles don't look at conversation as an interpersonal activity. They look at conversation as having a purpose. They talk to accomplish that purpose, and they don't like to talk if there isn't a purpose. If you ask a Noble, "Do you want to talk about it?" the Noble responds, "No." You question, "But why not?" The Noble responds, "What's the purpose?" You state, "Because it will make you feel better." The Noble responds, "What good will that do? It won't solve the problem."

Nobles tend to think of conversation as something you do while doing something else. The Noble is the one who cleans the desk, files, puts new paper in the printer, or empties the wastebasket while talking with you, and the Noble is the one you can hear clicking away at the computer keys while you are talking with him or her on the telephone.

These characteristics are neither good nor bad. They just *are*. They are the pieces of communication matter that combine to create the Noble communicator. Sometimes these actions are acceptable, and other times they're not. These communication actions have nothing to do with whether the Noble likes or dislikes you. They have everything to do with the fact that the person is Noble. If you know this, you don't have to be offended when the Noble begins straightening her bookshelf while you are attempting to share your innermost feelings.

Be Concise and Say It Quickly!

The Noble is the least verbose of the six communicators. Nobles don't use a lot of words to express their ideas, and they don't expect you to either. If you can't say it in ten words or less, they don't want to hear it, and if you can't write it in one page or less, they don't want to read it. Nobles are bottom-line, task- and results-oriented communicators who want to go from A to Z in a straight line and don't want to be bothered with the details in between. The Noble will say, "I don't want to hear all of this . . . just tell me what we will end up with—what's the bottom line?"

The Noble does not like to be involved in lengthy discussions that focus on all of the details of a situation. Nobles particularly dread communication interactions with Socratics, who are the most concerned with discussion and analysis of details. When the Socratic says, "There are a couple of other points that we need to talk about before we leave," the Noble closes her eyes, shakes her head, and thinks, "We're going to miss lunch again."

Actually Nobles don't need detail in order to grasp the main idea. For example, the Noble is the person who, when reading a novel, will skip the descriptive prose. Nobles don't care about the color of the sky or the scent of the flower. They read the words that are in quotation marks—the dialogue—because that is where the action is, and that is where they can find out what's happening. They also tend to read the introduction and summary sections of textbooks because that is where they can find the main ideas. They don't read the pages in between because those pages elaborate on the details of the main idea, and Nobles think elaboration is synonymous with redundancy.

Focus, Focus, Focus

The Noble is a main idea type of communicator who isn't interested in giving or listening to supporting evidence. Nobles don't want to hear an explanation of why something happened; they just want to know what happened and what's going to be done about it. Furthermore, they seldom provide any supporting evidence or the reasoning behind an opinion or conclusion they have reached. This is not because they haven't done their research but because they know they are telling you the truth—as they see it. Therefore, there is no reason to provide additional or supporting information, and they become irritated or angry if you ask for supporting evidence.

The discourse of the Noble is characterized by order, direction, and control. Nobles are concise, organized communicators; in fact, it is typically easy to outline Nobles as they speak. A Noble will say something like this: "I have three points I'd like to make here. Point one is . . . point two is . . ."

Nobles need and expect this same type of orderly, concise communication from others. If you don't give them the order they need, they will provide it for you. They might finish your statement for you or take your thirty-minute dialogue and provide a three-sentence summary. This need for concise and orderly communication can help you deal with Nobles.

Debbie is a data base specialist responsible for establishing computer user accounts in a large manufacturing firm. She frequently complains that managers don't give her the information she needs to open an account and ends up playing memo tag with some of the managers, which wastes her time and makes them angry. A couple of the managers complained about her "communication games."

Karl, Debbie's supervisor, suggests that Debbie create a fill-in-the-blanks form to make it easier for her to get the information she needs. Debbie restates that she tells the managers precisely what she needs. Karl reminds her that this approach is obviously not working and suggests that she try the form approach.

Debbie created the form. The managers now provide the information she needs, and conflict is reduced.

You might need to know a little more about this story to see the point. Debbie is a Socratic, but her managers are not, and what she defines as precise her managers define as verbose and overly detailed. The managers she was having problems with were Noble engineers. Her Socratic telephone requests and memos drove them crazy; providing a form that met their communication needs by allowing them to provide one word or short responses solved the problem.

The need for order and the ability to focus on the main idea are Noble strengths. The Noble is the person who can go into a chaotic situation and in a short period of time turn disorganization, malperformance, and confusion into organization and productivity. They are quick decision makers and are action oriented. They make good troubleshooters. The

Noble is often the person who is chosen to go in and "clean up a problem." Unfortunately, the Noble tends to leave a few bodies lying in the hallway as he or she goes about creating order out of chaos.

Hit-and-Run Missions

Nobles are frank, spontaneous, direct, and often abrupt communicators, but they are not argumentative. In fact, they tend to avoid argumentation and debate and instead engage in what I call hit-and-run communications. The Noble will walk into the room, tell you what he or she thinks, and then turn around and walk out before you have a chance to respond. The Noble isn't interested in arguing with you but simply wants you to know that he or she has a different opinion. The Noble accepts that you are entitled to your opinion—as wrong as it may be.

The Noble reserves argumentation for the really important issues. Negotiation and compromise are verbal strategies that the Noble may engage in if the issue at hand is important. More times than not, however, the Noble will simply accept that a difference of opinion exists and discontinue any further discussion on the topic. The Noble will say, "Look, I feel this way, and you feel another way, and neither of us is going to change our minds, so there is no reason to continue this discussion." If you're a Noble, you don't have a problem with this statement. If you're not a Noble, this type of statement creates some real conflict.

Often a Noble won't even provide this justification. He or she will simply say, "Yeah, sure, whatever." This doesn't mean the Noble agrees with you. It just means he or she isn't willing to argue the issue.

No Gray Areas

The use of the word "or" is prevalent in the speech of a Noble. Nobles tend to make a lot of categorical statements. They view things as black or white but never gray. They look for an immediate response or reaction to a situation, and they can clearly see that there are only two possible solutions to most problems. They make either-or statements and attempt to force you into a yes-no response. They will say, "Don't go through all that. Just say yes or no. Are you going or not? Yes or no?"

This one little characteristic can actually help you control the Noble. If you want the Noble to do something, simply offer a choice between what you want done and something you know the Noble doesn't want to do. Nobles offered a choice between two alternatives tend to make a decision. You have to be quick and stay alert, because the Noble may come back with a third alternative. If that happens, rapidly respond, "That's not an option," and provide two other alternatives. Have your list of either-ors prepared in advance, and you should be able to control the Noble's behavior.

You Should, You Must, You Will

Another thing to listen for in the speech of a Noble is the use of "should," "must," and "will" statements. The Socratic also makes should, must, and will statements, but they have different meanings. For the Noble, a should, must, or will statement is a simple opinion statement. For the Socratic, a should, must, or will statement is a directive. For example, if a Noble says, "You should get your hair cut," he or she is really saying, "You should get your hair cut because I would get mine cut if it were that long; however, you do what you want because it's your hair." The Noble will not tell you how to do something or suggest that you have to do it; the final decision is yours because you should be in control of yourself. But when the Socratic says, "You should get your hair cut," he or she is giving you a directive—you *should* go and get your hair cut. As you will see in the next chapter, this is because the Socratic is a very directive, persuasion-oriented communicator.

Actions Speak Louder Than Words

The Noble tends to be a rapidly speaking, animated communicator who uses wide, sweeping hand and body gestures—probably because Nobles use the fewest words of the three types of communicators, and the nonverbals help to supplement their sparse usage of words. The following Noble–Socratic story illustrates these characteristics.

Laura is a Noble communicator, and her very dear friend, Marcy, is a Socratic. Over the years, they have learned to adjust to their style differences. Marcy talks on and on, and Laura doesn't listen. Laura is abrupt; Marcy ignores these statements or tries not to be offended.

One evening over dinner, Marcy began going on and on about the poor service. Finally, Laura said, "Marcy, stop complaining. We won't leave a tip, and we'll go somewhere else for dessert." Laura didn't want to argue with the waitress, but she did want to express her opinion about the service by not leaving a tip. Marcy continued to complain throughout the meal, and Laura continued not to listen to her.

As they got up to leave, Marcy put her part of the money on top of the check and said, "Put your money here, and let's leave." As Laura began to walk out, the waitress, who also must have been a Noble, approached Laura and said, "Excuse me. I'd like to point out that the tip was not included on the check." Laura, being equally Noble, responded, "And I'd like to point out that you were a rotten waitress, which is why we didn't leave a tip!" Just then Laura noticed Marcy walking as quickly as she could out of the restaurant.

When she reached the parking lot, she saw Marcy standing by the car roaring with laughter. "What's wrong?" she inquired. Marcy responded, "You should have seen yourself. You and that waitress were nose to nose, and when you started to talk, your finger went up in the air, and you shook it right in her face."

Ah yes, the wide-sweeping, nonverbal gestures of the Noble. We don't want to argue with you, but if we are forced to, we will stand there with our hands on our hips and our eyes squinted. If we are going to make a point, you can bet that our fingers are going to be tapping on the desk or table. Nonverbal communication and the sparse usage of words are important characteristics of the Noble style of communication. Watching the

Noble, instead of listening to him or her, will provide you with some great insight into what's going on in the mind of this distinctive communicator.

Be Like Me

As you can well imagine, or as you may have personally experienced, the Noble has some major communication problems. Foremost is the fact that the Noble is terribly intolerant of people who do not have a similar style of communication. They tend to reveal their intolerance through their facial expressions, by doing other things while the Socratic is talking, by talking over the Reflective, by telling the Socratic to get to the point, by totally ignoring all non-Nobles, by finishing the other person's sentence, by summarizing the other person's comments, and by attempting to force the other person into a yes-no response.

Them's Fightin' Words

Nobles also create a defensive communication climate through the use of absolute and final statements. Nobles say, "This will never work!" As soon as an absolute statement like this is uttered, at least three people in the room will begin to think, "Oh yeah! You just watch me make it work!" Absolute and final statements create a defensive or even combative communication climate. As a result, Nobles find themselves in verbal battles that they would rather avoid.

The Noble can sound abrupt, and the straightforward style of communication tends to intimidate some people. These characteristics create a closed communication climate. The other person will say, "For goodness sake, don't ask him. He's likely to tell you what he thinks in front of everyone." If you are trying to gain respect and recognition, you don't want to create a closed communication climate. To the contrary, an open communication climate, in which people are encouraged to express their thoughts and ideas, is important to friendship, love, life, and leadership.

Nevertheless, under the right conditions, these combative and intimidating sounds can actually produce the results you want.

I worked for a man named Gary Luing when I was in Florida. He was the dean of the college, and I was the assistant dean. He is a Reflective, but we made our style differences work for us. He used to laugh and refer to us as the dynamic duo, and he got a great deal of pleasure out of referring to the Noble as the Obnoxious. He used to tell me my fuse was too short, and I used to tell him that his was too long. We worked together as a team because we found humor in our differences, and we were aware of and respected each other's strengths.

*One day Gary came to me about a crucial issue being considered in the academic senate. He said it was extremely important that the proposition be passed because our college would lose a lot of resources if it failed. He knew full well that the professors from the other colleges would vote against the proposition if they thought the College of Business would benefit from it. He asked me to go to the senate meeting and use my strongest Obnoxious style of communication to speak **against** passage of the resolution. I reminded him that the style was called Noble and agreed to do what he asked.*

We both understood his strategy. He knew they were likely to vote against anything we appeared to want. To be absolutely sure they voted this way, he wanted me to present our ostensible position in an absolute, certain, and intimidating manner. You see, academicians automatically take the opposite position when an issue is supported in this manner. As predicted, the senate passed the resolution even though it was in our best interest and not theirs. Our little communication strategy worked, but I have to admit that it didn't do much for my image.

Information Underload

Information underload is another communication problem generated from the Noble style of communication. Because Nobles have a total disdain for details, they do not provide enough detail when giving direction, and as a result, the other person doesn't understand what is expected. Furthermore, Nobles tend to be impatient or reactionary communicators, which results in poor listening habits.

HOW TO GET THE NOBLE TO DO WHAT YOU WANT

This profile of the Noble style of communication is neither good nor bad; it is simply different from the Socratic and Reflective styles. Sometimes the style works, and sometimes it doesn't. The other person is actually the determining factor in whether the style will work.

Liz is the director of human resources, and her company has recently enacted a dress code. Allen is a vibrant young supervisor who is fond of wearing blue jeans although the dress code states they are not acceptable attire. Liz talks with Allen, she counsels him, she jokes with him, and she even pleads with him. Finally, Liz has enough. She once again calls Allen into her office and says,

> "Look, I'm tired of being dumped on by my boss, and I'm tired of dumping on you. Get rid of the blue jeans, and do it now!"

Allen got rid of the blue jeans because Liz finally spoke to him as a Noble. In her previous attempts, she had relied on her warm, supportive, Reflective style, which always left Allen with the impression that she didn't like the jeans but it was no big deal if he continued to wear them. When she finally spoke in absolute Noble terms, he heard what she was saying.

Allen's blue jeans may not seem to be an important problem, but they were a major source of stress for Liz. Every time he showed up in jeans, Liz was reprimanded by her boss, and it was beginning to look as if she wasn't capable of managing others. Her Reflective style wasn't working, so she had to go to the style that Allen expected to hear: she had to speak as a Noble.

The point to this story—and all of the other stories I have been providing—is that *you* have to be the one to control style if you want to control the outcome of the interaction. The other person doesn't have to do anything. If you want to create a successful moment, you have to control your style to meet the other person's communication needs. You do not lose control or give up anything when you do this. To the contrary, you gain control because you gain the ability to get the other person to do willingly what you want him or her to do.

"Truth in action" perhaps best describes the Noble style of communication. Additionally, the Noble has a communication premise that guides his or her behaviors. In attempting to explain, predict, and control the Noble, or to be able to control your own style-associated behaviors if you are a Noble, it is important to understand this premise:

The Noble Communication Premise

The Noble is a true believer who expects the personal feelings of the self to play a secondary role in the communication interaction. The Noble believes that the primary purpose of communication is the exchange of information and honest opinions.

This premise brings about a set of easily identifiable verbal and nonverbal characteristics and behaviors. An awareness of these characteristics can help you identify Noble communicators. If you listen and watch carefully, you can identify an individual's dominant style of communication during the first five minutes of conversation. You can then work with the dominant style characteristics and manipulate them to guide and control the outcome of an interaction. The repetitive verbal and nonverbal characteristics of the Noble are summarized in the list on the following page.

Noble Communication Characteristics

The Noble:

Is direct, straightforward, frank, and spontaneous
Assumes control of the self
Expects the other person to control his or her self
Openly expresses opinions on issues
Rarely engages in personal self-disclosure
Feels obligated to state his or her "true" feelings
Expects the other person to express "true" feelings
Focuses communication on the main idea
Uses words sparingly
Avoids lengthy discussions involving details
Tends not to supply supporting evidence for conclusions or opinions
Avoids argumentation and debate
Engages in hit-and-run communication interactions
Has an orderly, concise sense of communication decorum
Expects orderly, concise communication from the other person
Makes directional-opinion (should, must, will) statements
Makes categorical, either-or statements
Expects yes-no responses
Tends to be a rapid-speaking, animated communicator
Tends to use wide, sweeping hand and body gestures
Tends to make absolute and final statements
Provides the bare facts when giving directions or sharing information
Tends to be an impatient and reactionary communicator
Tends to have poor listening habits
Sounds abrupt and certain when speaking
Has the ability to intimidate
Tends to be intolerant of other styles of communication
Tends to be a task, results-oriented communicator
Tends to be most concerned with the bottom line
Tends to say the things other people think but don't say

To begin controlling your own destiny through communication style, you need to gain an appreciation for and an understanding of the strengths and weaknesses of each style. It is equally important to begin seeing the humor in style. If we can laugh or even smile when we hear the sounds of difference, then we can begin developing a tolerance for difference. This is, ultimately, what peaceful coexistence is all about.

Noble Strengths

Assertiveness. The Noble has the ability to accomplish his or her goals in an interaction while taking the needs of the other into consideration.

Organization. The Noble has the ability to organize and summarize thoughts and ideas in oral and written communication interactions.

Focus. The Noble has the ability to "cut through the garbage" and identify the central issue.

Credibility. The Noble speaks with confidence and authority. Thus, his or her remarks are usually given serious attention and consideration.

Animation. The Noble has the potential to be an energetic and entertaining speaker because of the rapid and concise use of words, the use of wide, sweeping hand and body gestures, and the ability to vary vocal tone and facial gestures.

Leadership. All of the other strengths combined with the Noble's action-oriented style and desire to make quick decisions helps him or her project an image of a powerful leader.

Attention to these strengths can help guide the outcome of an interaction, but equal attention must be given to the problem areas.

Noble Weaknesses

The problem areas of any style prevent the other person from listening to or being persuaded by the message. Sometimes the problem area actually causes the other person to do the opposite of what you are advocating. For

Nobles, their trouble-talk can be described as curt, crisp, terse, and pithy, sounds that create the following communication problems:

Aggressiveness. The Noble has a tendency to go from being assertive to being aggressive. This creates feelings of hostility. Nobles know they can win by intimidation, and although this may be the appropriate strategy in some situations, the long-term negative effects of aggression are undesirable. Aggressive communication behaviors create a closed and defensive communication climate. Thus, interpersonal conflict increases and productivity decreases.

Inattentiveness. The Noble doesn't pay attention to details or to another person who is speaking. This lack of attention increases conflict because it generates errors and causes the other person to feel alienated and angry.

Absoluteness. Nobles have a tendency to be extremists; everything is black or white, right or wrong. They have difficulty seeing the gray areas and tenuous nature of some issues. The certainty with which they speak causes the other person to become defensive and often angry.

Intolerance. Nobles have difficulty playing organizational games because of their intolerance for differing styles of communication. They expect everyone to be direct, straightforward, and totally honest, and this just isn't the way the world works.

You now have a complete overview of the Noble style of communication. You have a checklist of easily identifiable characteristics, and you can listen for and observe these in your own speech and the speech of others. Now let's see how you can use this information to control your destiny.

Controlling the Noble

Dealing with a Noble is very easy because Nobles are predictable, uncomplicated communicators who don't get their feelings hurt easily. In talking with the Noble, you might find these guidelines helpful:

1. Be direct and simply say what you have to say.
2. Be concise and orderly.

3. Start your conversation by stating your purpose or conclusion first.

4. Identify your main points and ask if the Noble would like additional information.

5. Don't be offended or intimidated by Nobles. Learn to ignore some of their statements. They don't mean to offend you; they just don't filter their thoughts before they speak.

6. Tell the Noble if he or she has done or said something that bothers you.

7. If you want the Noble to do something, give two alternatives from which to choose.

I told you earlier that I would give you some hints on how to get "Morris" to open up and tell you what's wrong. Let's look at those first two guidelines, and see if we can get Morris to talk. Remember, you want to be direct, straightforward, concise, and orderly. You might say,

"Morris, I know you are Noble and don't like to talk about these things, but I am not Noble. I don't have the ability to guess what's in your mind, and it is unfair and unkind of you to expect me to do that. Now tell me what's wrong."

Or you might say,

"Morris, I know you are Noble and don't like to talk about these things, but if you were to say something, what might you say?"

Or you might say,

"Morris, I know you are Noble and don't like to talk about these things, so I am going to ask you some questions, and all you have to do is say yes or no. (After you ask three or four questions that require only a yes or no response, the Noble will say, "Okay, okay, I'll tell you!")

Or you might say,

"Morris, I know you are Noble and don't like to talk about these things, so here is a three-by-five card. I'll leave the room. You write down what's wrong, and then put the card on the table."

This last suggestion isn't as farfetched as you might think. Morris will either laugh and just tell you what's wrong or will use the card!

Now let's see if we can create a behavior out of guidelines 3 and 4. Suppose you have a report to do for a Noble, and you are a Socratic. You can meet both of your communication needs by attaching a one-page summary memo to your detailed report. The Noble will read the memo, and, if more information is needed, he or she will look at your report. The truth of the matter is that the Noble probably will not look at your report. This, of course, gives you a lot of power because you can guide the Noble's behavior by controlling the flow of information. Use this power wisely.

It is particularly important to pay attention to guidelines 5 and 6 when your subordinate is a Noble and you are not. When communicating with a Noble, it is essential that you understand that the Noble really doesn't mean to be offensive, but when a thought pops into the Noble's head, it will proceed to fall out of his or her mouth. If you become offended by the remark, you have unnecessary conflict that could be damaging to your career. But if you simply call attention to the problem, the Noble will attempt to correct the behavior. The Noble may get angry with you at first, but he or she will get over it and attempt to address the problem. For example, let's say you manage a Noble supervisor who walks past his employees each morning without saying "good morning." You try to explain to him that his staff think he is angry when he comes in and doesn't at least greet them. He responds, "You're too sensitive." What do you say? You will control the Noble's behavior if you say something like this:

> "Yes, that may be true, but I think it would help morale if you would say hello when you come in instead of just walking past everyone without speaking. If morale is improved, productivity will improve."

The Noble can relate to this statement because you have shown how interpersonal behaviors affect the bottom line. The Noble may appear irritated when you first give this response, but I assure you that he or she will think it over, and in most instances there will be a change in behavior.

Now let's take a look at the seventh guideline. Nobles are either-or, reactionary communicators. If you know this and you want to get the Noble to do something, then simply provide a choice between two alternatives—either two alternatives that are equally acceptable to you or one alternative that you know will be totally offensive to the Noble and the other alternative the thing you want him or her to do. (There are, of course, other combinations that you can use.) The point is that the Noble thinks in either-or terms, and if you want to persuade the Noble, then you must meet this communication need.

Suppose your boyfriend or husband is a Noble. You want to go to the movies, but you know he is going to say he wants to stay in and watch television. To increase your chances of success in getting him to go to the movies willingly, ask him to select between (1) two different movies, (2) a movie or the ballet (which he hates), or (3) a movie or painting the living room. You select the pairing you think will work best. If he says, "Neither. I want to stay home and watch television," you say, "That's not one of your options."

If you are a male reading this book and you think that was a sexist example, I'll change the scenario. Suppose your wife is a Noble, and you want her to (1) go camping, (2) agree on the purchase of the car of your choice, or (3) agree to the purchase of season football tickets. Select a scenario, and write out what you would say using the either-or strategy. (You ought to be getting pretty good at this by now, so I will not provide a suggested response.)

Two Nobles have little trouble communicating with each other; it's the people who are listening who have the trouble. To an outsider, a non-Noble, Nobles may sound as if they are angry, rude, or unfriendly. To the Nobles, they are just "telling each other like it is."

Listening to two Nobles can be quite humorous. If nothing else, it is fast paced. Two Nobles making decisions on how best to approach a complicated project will exchange a series of either-or alternatives. This either-or Noble characteristic is actually a key to getting Nobles to do what you want them to do.

HOW NOBLES CAN GET OTHERS
TO DO WHAT THEY WANT

If you can imagine, for just a minute, Margaret Thatcher talking with Alice in Wonderland, then you can imagine how non-Nobles respond to your style. Communication conflict between Margaret and Alice is indeed inevitable. This conflict, nevertheless, is controllable or manageable. Conflict becomes manageable if you do the following:

- Determine your goal or purpose. Ask yourself why you are engaged in the interaction and what you would like to accomplish. For example, if your goal is to intimidate the other person, you don't have to read any of the following steps; you can be as Noble as you like, and you'll accomplish that goal. If you don't wish to intimidate, then you need to be concerned with the remaining guidelines.

- Listen and identify the other person's dominant style, and then address his or her communication needs by drawing upon and using your other two, less dominant, styles of communication.

- Use your communication strengths to guide the conversation.

- Attempt to control your communication problem areas.

Controlling the Socratic

You know that a Socratic has a need to talk and a need to be concerned with the analysis of details. If you want to get the Socratic to do something, the following list of dos and don'ts should help.

Do allow the Socratic to talk without showing your intolerance.
Don't complete his or her sentences or abruptly ask, "Is there a point you're trying to make?"
Do force yourself to listen and be attentive.
Don't clean your desk, file papers, or empty the wastebasket while the Socratic is speaking.

Do force yourself to provide additional information and detail in your responses.

Don't say "just because" or "because I said so" when the Socratic asks for justification.

Do ask the Socratic if he or she needs any additional information.

Don't say, "I already explained that," when the Socratic asks for clarification.

Do plan for the interaction to take longer than you think it should.

Don't use absolute statements because the minute you make one, you will be in for a detailed discussion or debate.

Obviously you cannot just ignore your own communication needs in these interactions, but you can make an effort to address your needs while still meeting the needs of the other person. Suppose you are working with a community volunteer whom you value and want to motivate, or a powerful member of your board of directors, or an influential government official. This person gives you elaborate directions every time he or she asks you to do something. You find this irritating so you decide you would like to gain some control of the interactions without instigating unnecessary conflict. Depending on the type of relationship you have with this person, the importance of the task at hand, and the timing, you might decide to address your own need for concise and orderly communication by keeping a yellow pad in front of you and writing down the main points this person is attempting to communicate. You may want to keep this list, and the next time this person attempts to reiterate the list of directions, you pull out the list and say,

> "You gave me such excellent directions last time that I decided to save them for future use. I understand every single detail, but you can be assured that if I have any questions, I won't hesitate to come in and ask for your assistance."

Let's make this a little more difficult. Suppose this person irritates you and makes you feel less than competent when he or she gives elaborate directions. Because you have read this book, you know that the Socratic doesn't think you are dumb. You know Socratics give directions because that is what they need and would want from you, but you can't control your irritation any longer. Write what you would do on a sheet of paper. Don't read ahead until you complete this exercise.

If you said you would be assertive and attempt to accomplish your goals, consider the needs of this person, and still reduce hostility, then you are responding as a leader who is using communication to control outcomes. An assertive, Reflective-Noble-Socratic response might sound something like this:

> "I admire your ability to attend to details, and I take pride in the products we produce. But I am having one heck of a time with the directions you provide. I'm the type of person who gets very frustrated with a lot of directions. It makes me feel as if you lack confidence in my abilities, and I know you don't intend to make me feel this way. So, I'd like to propose that I do the project and give you a draft to review. You can then indicate if any additions or deletions are necessary."

You might be wondering why I'm talking about taking direction from someone else in a book for leaders. Regardless of our positions, all of us take direction from others, and those giving direction may be less competent than those of us receiving the direction. As leaders, we must be able to interact successfully with all types of people, and leadership does involve the giving and receiving of direction. When all is said and done, leadership emerges as a consultative or collaborative process—not a dictatorship.

Let's change this scenario a bit and see how you can handle a Socratic employee. Suppose you have an excellent employee who is very productive and loyal but who drives you crazy because she is so Socratic. You have asked for a brief summary of the problem situation in the Detroit office. Halfway through her lengthy and detailed response, you realize you've stopped listening and have lost track of the main points. What do you say?

If you said, "You rambled on so much that I lost the point of what you were saying," then you responded as a Noble but not as an effective leader. Instead of becoming irritated with the lengthy or rambling response of a Socratic, the Noble leader needs to work on developing less direct, less defensive ways of saying, "You ramble." A less direct way of making this point might sound something like this:

> "I'm not sure I totally understand your line of reasoning. I'm going to summarize the points I think you were making, and we can see if I have interpreted you correctly."

Controlling the Reflective

When talking with a Reflective, Nobles have to remember to give attention to the interpersonal aspects of the interaction. Nobles seldom have trouble getting a Reflective to do something, but if they want a Reflective to *want* to do something or want a Reflective to give an honest opinion, then the following guidelines will be helpful:

- Take time to engage in some pleasant, courteous dialogue before getting to the business at hand. Establish a positive interpersonal climate before discussing issues.
- Be patient, and don't put words in the other's mouth.
- Avoid the use of absolute or final statements.
- Ask open-ended questions that encourage a thoughtful response like, "How do you feel about this issue?"
- Force yourself to listen and be attentive.
- Control your nonverbal facial gestures so they don't intimidate the Reflective into saying what you want to hear instead of what the Reflective really feels.
- Plan for the interaction to take more time than you think it should.

In many ways, the Reflective admires the Noble style of communication, so when speaking with the Reflective, draw upon your communication strengths. Once you have established a warm, supportive communication climate, feel free to focus on the main idea and be as animated as you wish. The Reflective sees you as a credible, interesting, and dynamic communicator when you aren't being overly Noble. When you are being overly Noble, the Reflective thinks you are rude and obnoxious. When this happens, the Reflective will try to avoid conflict and tell you what you want to hear rather than what he or she really feels. In the end, this strategy will increase conflict.

There is one final thought that you as a Noble should keep in mind when communicating with a Reflective: you don't always have to say exactly what you think! Consider the importance of the issue and how the other person will feel when you say what you have to say. Also consider whether your remarks will bring about a change in behavior. Sometimes it isn't worth the effort or the resulting pain to say what you have to say. Sometimes it is better to say nothing—and that advice comes to you from a true Noble.

You have not read much of this book yet, but I'll bet my first royalty check that you already have a firm idea of what needs to be done to get the results you want. The ability to persuade others to do what you want them to do is almost totally dependent on your ability to control your communication style. There are but two simple rules to keep in mind as you continue reading this book and begin to control your own destiny by creating moments of success with communication style:

1. Leaders develop tolerance for differing styles of communication.
2. Leaders do not force their style on others.

If you keep these two rules in mind and if you begin thinking about how you can go about meeting the communication needs of the other person, you are well on your way to becoming an effective leader.

I share one more Noble example with you before ending this chapter.

Oprah Winfrey was talking with a man in the audience recently, and I chuckled as I observed that the man's face was directly level with her breasts.

No sooner had that thought popped into my mind than it fell out of Oprah's mouth. She matter-of-factly asked the man to stand up so his head wouldn't be in her breasts.*

The audience laughed, I laughed, and now all of you know—Oprah's a Noble.

Phil Donahue is also a Noble, and his talk show style is that of a Noble. (People who have watched him for a long time say he has changed over the years. Since I didn't see him during his early years, I can't comment on that observation.) He's a good listener, but he completes the person's thought or uses the blunt, tell-it-like-it-is statement to create humorous moments. Recently he was talking with an attractive woman on a show devoted to the topic of divorce and dating. As she was tactfully trying to explain why she had no sex life, he candidly completed her thoughts by suggesting she wouldn't go to bed with a bimbo.* She laughed and, like a Reflective, stumbled over her words while indicating agreement with his remarks. (A bit of trivia clarification here: *bimbo* is a male, and *bimbette* is a female.)

Whether I am writing or speaking about communication style, I always start off with the description of the Noble because the Noble won't wade through a discussion of the Socratic or Reflective before hearing about himself or herself. Now that all of you Nobles know about your own style and that one of your problems is lack of attention to detail, I hope that you will continue with the rest of the book describing all of the other styles. But just in case this strategy hasn't been totally effective, I end this chapter with a private message to the Nobles:

"Listen up, Nobles! You have to develop a tolerance for all styles if you want to be an effective leader. You develop this tolerance by understanding all the styles. You'll develop this understanding by reading all of the chapters. Don't skip to the final section of this book because the information won't do you any good if you don't understand all of the styles."

---

*I have paraphrased this incident based on my viewing of the show.

Chapter 4

The Socratic:
Thoughts That Breathe,
Words That Burn

THE SOCRATIC SOUND

The Socratic and Noble worlds are very different—yet also very similar. The Noble and Socratic do not get along communicatively, but when they are paired together on a project and they make their style differences work for them, they will produce a product that is surpassed by none. Their styles are almost perfectly complementary; what one lacks, the other has. A weakness in one is a strength in the other. The problem is getting these two strong-willed, confident, and sometimes bull-headed communicators to agree to let their style differences work for them.

Let's begin with a successful Socratic interaction (so Nobles can see that the Socratic style can be used to create moments of success), a conversation between Kevin, a Socratic stockbroker, and Mr. Feldman, an investor. Mr. Feldman is a fifty-five-year-old, wealthy, conservative American who is a Reflective. As you read this encounter, listen for the Socratic sound.

Mr. Feldman has a portfolio of approximately $1 million in various certificate of deposit (CD) accounts that are coming up for renewal. He is reluctant to have any capital at risk and is not likely to consider switching to mutual funds given the lack of guaranteed return. Kevin, however, would like to convince Mr. Feldman to convert his CD accounts into mutual fund investments.

KEVIN: Mr. Feldman, you currently have invested $1 million in CDs at about 8 percent, and indications are that CD rates will be going down.

MR. FELDMAN: Yes, but I am assured that the money will be there when I retire.

KEVIN: Not really. You have an investment that is yielding 8 percent. Of this amount, 4 percent is going directly to inflation; additionally you are faced with federal taxes of 31 percent and state taxes of about 9 percent, which takes another 3 percent of your money. This means that you are actually making only 1 percent on your money. (Kevin illustrates this fact by taking a one-dollar bill and tearing pieces off as he indicates the different factors. He then hands Mr. Feldman a very thin strip of the one-dollar bill.) Now if inflation goes up or CD rates go down, you will actually be losing money.

MR. FELDMAN: Yes, but I will at least have the capital.

KEVIN: But as these factors occur, the capital will be worth less and less, and you will have to dip into the principal, which will reduce your return further. Mutual funds are not a guaranteed investment. However, from its inception, the stock market has had a return rate of over 12 percent by investing in just the Standard and Poors 500. Research statistically shows that by investing in the market for a period of fifteen years, the chances of making a 15 percent return on your money go up to 70 percent and the chances of losing your capital go down to zero. (Kevin shows Mr. Feldman an article to support this statement.) A mutual fund gives you the power of a highly trained management team that is investing in over 150 companies. My suggested portfolio includes both global and domestic funds so you are insulated against fluctuations in the value of the dollar. The return on the five mutual funds I am recommending has averaged over 18 percent for the last ten years. Though many have done well for a longer period of time, performance past that period is not relevant as it applies to another business cycle.

MR. FELDMAN: What is the charge of investing?

KEVIN: Mutual funds vary in investment charges from load fees of 8.5 percent down. There are break points at which the fees are lower, so your average cost per fund will be 4 percent. However, it is of no importance what the fund charges are, because returns are calculated after the maximum load fee is taken out.

MR. FELDMAN: What do I pay you?

KEVIN: The major portion of the load fee is reallocated to me as a dealer allowance of commission. I have no other charges. The company will continue to charge you a fee of about 3 percent a year for administration, but it is, again, taken into account in the return statistics.

MR. FELDMAN: What do you suggest I do?

KEVIN: Start out with $100,000 and see how comfortable you feel with the investment. As you feel more comfortable, you can invest more.

Within one month, Mr. Feldman had invested the entire $1 million and has since referred several clients to Kevin. Kevin, the Socratic, smiles as he says, "It only cost me one hour of time and a dollar bill."

This is a successful communication encounter because it worked. It is a Socratic communication encounter because it is detailed, analytical, and verbose. Notice how Kevin provides a minihistorical review of the stock market and how he supports his assertions with research statistics — all Socratic characteristics.

Talk, Talk, and More Talk

Ah, yes. The Socratic style of communication—it is very different from the Noble style. Like the Noble, however, the Socratic style of communication is distinctive and easy to recognize. The Socratic is the individual who is most concerned with rhetoric and the analysis of details, and he or she believes that communication, in and of itself, is the primary purpose of verbal interactions. Socratics like to talk, they enjoy talking, and they do talk—a lot. It is this tendency toward verbosity that causes the Noble or Reflective to describe the Socratic as boring.

Socratics believe that time spent communicating is time well spent, and they view argumentation as a desirable and constructive exercise during which each person explores and expresses his or her thoughts on the issue at hand. In fact, of the three types of dominant-style communicators, the Socratic tends to be the most argumentative. But to the Socratic, this is not a negative. Socratics see argumentation as positive and view a good debate as exhilarating.

Socratics openly engage in and enjoy discussion, debate, negotiation, and arbitration exercises. In fact, when you need someone to represent you in a negotiation or arbitration situation, the Socratic is the best person to send. A Noble will issue ultimatums and alienate the other side, and a Reflective is likely to give everything away to the other side. But the Socratic will continue to talk and negotiate until the other side makes concessions. The Socratic will stay all night talking if necessary, and sometimes the other side will give in just to avoid listening to the Socratic. This is particularly true if the person or people on the other side are Nobles.

Never Leave a Detail Unexplored

Socratics are deliberate in what they say, to whom they will say it, and under what conditions they will say it. As a result, they can sound much like Nobles. Their penchant for details and discussion, however, clearly separates them from the Noble.

This attention to detail is both a strength and a problem for Socratics. As a strength, Socratics attempt to look at the total picture, and they have the ability and desire to sort through the gray areas as a way of reducing hostility. That is, if they sense that the other person is angry or not in agreement with what is being said, they will continue to discuss every possible aspect of the topic in an effort to achieve agreement and reduce hostility. This attention to detail also allows Socratics to produce polished final products. On the downside, attention to detail often turns into attention to irrelevant details. Socratics can become too picky, and non-Socratics find it tedious to listen to them. As a result, non-Socratics tune out, and Socratics find themselves saying, "Are you still listening to me?"

The Ruling Hand of Socrates

The Socratic style of communication is similar to the method of teaching Socrates used in which a series of questions leads the answerer to a logical conclusion. The Noble will tell you his or her conclusion or bottom line right up front. The Socratic doesn't do that. Socratics predetermine the logic of the situation and attempt to lead the other person in the interaction to reach the same conclusion through a series of questions and answers. Socratics, of course, believe that this conclusion is the appropriate and logical one and typically will not give up until you too reach this very same conclusion. As such, the Socratic tends to be the most directive and controlling of the three dominant-style communicators.

This Socratic question-and-answer technique can be troublesome because it appears that the Socratic is lecturing the other person, and this creates a defensive and combative communication climate. However, if the other person understands that the Socratic is just being Socratic and not lecturing or talking down to him or her, then conflict may be reduced.

Socratics are persuasive communicators and do well in advertising and public relations. They understand the process of persuasion and use the process effectively. Nobles, in contrast, usually don't attempt to persuade; they just tell you what the end result should be and expect that you will do what you believe is appropriate. They won't think you're very bright if you don't do what they would do, but then, they believe you have the right to be wrong. Reflectives listen and ask questions and, depending on the situation, may offer an opinion. As a rule, they do not exert a tremendous effort to convince or persuade. The Socratic, however, vigorously attempts to persuade and lead the other person in the interaction to accept the final conclusion as appropriate, logical, and desirable. And the Socratic will continue to engage in the discussion until this goal is achieved.

Socratics tend to be very persuasive communicators, but they are the *least persuadable* of the three dominant-style communicators. It is almost impossible to get Socratics to change their minds once they are made up — perhaps because they feel they have so thoroughly researched the topic that it is not possible for them to be incorrect.

You Should, You Must, You Definitely Will!

Socratics do not necessarily say the rhetorically appropriate thing to say. They do, however, mediate and contemplate what they are going to say, and there is a certain amount of order and calmness in their words. Socratics are straightforward, but unlike Nobles, they do not tend to use absolute statements. In fact, Socratics seldom speak of anything in absolute terms, and they aren't likely to make either-or statements or expect yes-no responses. When the Noble provides a bottom-line statement, the Socratic responds,

"Well you know, there are a lot of ways to measure the bottom line. After all, what *is* a 'real' bottom line? There are a lot of things that we have to consider other than just the cost of the materials and amount of sales. There are the human costs, the environmental costs, and the . . ."

Sound familiar?

Socratics have the ability to look at the total picture and sort through the gray areas in a situation. This can be a valuable asset in the workplace, particularly when attempting to engage in problem-solving activities or when to facilitate conflict resolution between two warring parties. This ability, however, is often overshadowed by the Socratic tendency to be directive.

Like Nobles, Socratics make should-must-or-will statements. Unlike the Noble, the Socratic statement is a directive to do something. For example, the Noble might utter the words, "You should put that report in a nicer binder," but the Noble is actually saying, "If that were my report, I'd put it in a nicer binder, but it's your report so do what you want with it." The Noble may think you are silly if you don't change the binder, but he or she really doesn't care if you don't. The Socratic cares. When the Socratic utters the words, "You should put that report in a nicer binder," he or she is giving you a directive: you *should* put it in a different binder. Thus, the Noble and Socratic may occasionally sound alike, but their words have very different meanings.

Presenting the Prima Facie Case

When attempting to persuade or discuss an issue with another person, Socratics construct a prima facie case complete with supporting evidence and a plan of action. They then expect the other person to present a rebuttal exploring the issues raised in the original argument. In constructing a case, Socratics draw upon their analytical abilities and their penchant for details.

Lisa is a claims representative for a large, reputable life and casualty corporation. She is given a case that is over three years old, which the former defense representative has been unable to settle. The case involves a woman whose car had been struck by a Salvation Army truck insured by Lisa's *firm. Lisa explains her strategy in attempting to get a settlement for under $10,000:*

"I began by thoroughly reading the file and listing all events in chronological order. I found that the woman had a prior history of claims for back injuries dating back twenty years. The same attorney represented her in four prior cases. There was no damage to either vehicle in this case, but the woman was claiming a back injury. I had all this information in front of me, along with the three offers I was prepared to make, when I called the plaintiff's attorney. The attorney asked for $20,000. I asked him to justify the amount. When he finished with his evasive speech, I reviewed her prior history with him, and I cited physicians' statements from her medical records. I offered him $2,500 as a nuisance settlement. He counter offered with $3,500. I settled."

Lisa called her corporate defense attorney, who had advised her earlier that she would be lucky to settle for $10,000. The attorney wasn't in, so she left message of the settlement. A few days later, Lisa received a letter congratulating her on the low settlement. The attorney also said he would like to meet her the next time he was in town.

Lisa's Socratic style of communication helped her to gain recognition in her corporation.

Talking in Footnotes

Perhaps the most distinguishing characteristic of Socratics is that they talk in footnotes. The Socratic begins telling you something, then takes a slight detour and drops down to the footnote to provide some tangential information about the topic, then goes back to the topic, then drops back down to another footnote, and so on. Those who don't talk or think in footnotes get lost in the maze. Then they look at the Socratic and say, "You've lost me. What are we talking about? Are we still on the same topic?"

Stories, Reviews, and Parenthetical Asides

Another identifiable characteristic of Socratic speech is the excessive use of clauses, phrases, and parenthetical asides. The footnote, the parenthesis, the dash, the comma, and the semicolon are heard in the speech of the Socratic as readily as they are viewed in the written communications produced by this rhetorical communicator.

Suppose your boss is a Socratic. She needs you to take a report down to Dave and pick up some papers that he has for her. She hands you the report and says,

> "I need you to take this down to Dave in engineering. You know Dave. He's a tall, husky fellow with curly blond hair and a ruddy complexion. He graduated from Whittier College a few years back, and, actually, it is kind of cute that he blushes a lot when he talks even though he tries to project a tough image. He is a very liberated young man, and I like that. He's very easy to work with and fun to be around."

At this point, you have totally forgotten that your boss wants you to take the report down to this fellow, about whom you know more than you ever wanted to know. The parenthetical aside is additional information that isn't particularly relevant to the topic at hand, and it is very characteristic of the Socratic style of communication.

Nobles tend not to provide supporting evidence. Socratics provide more evidence than a Noble or Reflective wants or needs. They tend to rely on the use of anecdotal stories, but they also tend to use the same anecdotal stories—over, and over, and over again. Other people become very familiar with the Socratics' repertoire of stories, and when they see you leaving an interaction with a Socratic, they will laughingly ask, "Did he tell you the story about . . . ?"

Socratics engage in lengthy, elaborate historical reviews. If you ask a Socratic why a policy or problem exists, he or she will take you back to day one and give you a historical review of the problem—complete with names, dates, places, and times.

The other person in the interaction is often in awe of the Socratics' ability to recall minutia—unless the other person happens to be a Noble. Nobles may be impressed with Socratic recall ability but prefer not to be subjected to this elaborate transmission of information. In fact, Nobles may disparagingly remark that Socratics can remember your zip code.

When transmitting information, Socratics assume familiarity on the part of the receiver. That is, they speak as if the other person shares the same field of experience and is familiar with the people and events being described. For example, a Socratic does not say, "I was reviewing the purchase order forms with two of my employees." A Socratic does say, "I was reviewing the SG3-2 materials with Joanne and Jason in my office yesterday around noon."

Delivering the Monologue

Socratics enjoy playing the role of philosopher. They do not want to be bound by the concrete, tangible elements in a situation. Rather, they become immersed in the discussion of the abstract, and at times it may appear as if they are having a discussion with the self. In fact, you may find yourself looking around the room to see if anyone else is there because you're not sure who is involved in the discussion. If you are the Socratic, then you are not looking around. At the end of your monologue, however, you may find yourself asking, "Did that make sense to you? Do you understand the point I'm trying to make?" In an effort to keep you from reexplaining your position, the other person will respond, "Oh yes. I understand."

Listen as Amanda explains how her tendency to engage in monologue speaking created an unsuccessful communication encounter with her boyfriend:

My boyfriend had some friends visiting him from Indiana, and it was their first time visiting California. My boyfriend thought it would be a nice idea to take them down to Tijuana one day while they were here. I didn't care for this idea too much because there are so many other things to do and see in southern California that I felt would be more enjoyable for them.

I explained that the last time I was down in Tijuana, it was very dirty, congested, and depressing. I proceeded to rattle off every alternate destination I could think of — Santa Barbara, San Diego, Catalina Island, Palm Springs, and Ensenada were a few of the ones I mentioned. Unfortunately, I didn't stop with this. I had to go on and name every restaurant and attraction we could visit if we chose one of the other destinations. Then I even suggested other modes of transportation, like the train or a boat to Ensenada.

I just wanted to make sure we explored all of the possibilities, and in my own mind, I wanted to make sure we were doing the right thing. Instead I made my boyfriend mad with my information overload, and he just said, "Forget it. We're going to Tijuana."

I think if I had just chosen two alternate destinations and picked out restaurants, attractions, and modes of transportation for each, I could have presented him with two very clear, concise alternatives. If I had done that, there would be a good chance he would have chosen one of the alternatives, and I wouldn't be stuck going down to Tijuana this weekend.

This tendency to engage in monologue speaking is a key to understanding the Socratic style of communication. Socratics have to verbalize their entire thought processes. They have to hear what they are thinking before they can make a decision. Thus, they speak to persuade the self, not necessarily the other. The other person often becomes irritated with the Socratic monologue because it appears as if the Socratic is lecturing at or speaking down to the other person. In reality, the Socratic isn't speaking with anyone but is just trying to hear his or her own thoughts. The Socratic has to do this, and if you know this, then you won't be offended by the monologue.

If, Then, Therefore We Should

Just as the use of the word "or" is prevalent in the speech of the Noble, the use of the "if, then, therefore" statement is prevalent in the speech of the Socratic. Socratics love to engage in theory construction communication interactions. They use hypothetical situations, hypothesis statements and if-then-therefore-we-should statements to illustrate a point and attempt to convince you of the merit of the issue under discussion.

Winston Churchill Revisited

As you might well imagine, Socratics are the most verbose of the three dominant-style communicators (the Candidate is the most verbose of all six types of communicators); they tend to use four to five times more words to say what they have to say than does the Noble. Socratics have an affinity for words and tend to have large vocabularies, which they use to win arguments because the other person in the interaction doesn't want to admit that he or she doesn't understand what was just said.

The Socratic never appears to be at a loss for something to say, and because of his or her love affair with words, the Socratic has the potential for communication eloquence. This doesn't mean that Socratics always achieve this potential. Socratics can be boring and tedious speakers, but the potential for communication eloquence is there—if the Socratic chooses to develop this potential. Remember: it is possible to control, utilize, and manipulate your style of communication to bring about a positive outcome to an interaction, but you have to work at it. You have to want to make your communication style work for you—not against you.

Information Overload

Socratics, like Nobles and Reflectives, have some special communication problems. Foremost is the tendency to engage in information overload. In the zest to be totally accurate, the Socratic often inundates the other person with more information than is wanted or needed. The result is that the other person tunes out the Socratic, and a closed communication climate is created.

Listen as Guadalupe, a Reflective, provides her perceptions of a Socratic engaging in information overload:

The worst experience I've had in a work environment occurred when I began working for an insurance company as a data entry clerk, and the person assigned to teach me the computer operations for that facility was a Socratic. This training experience was made worse by the fact that he had a very slow, monotone voice that tends to lull the listener to sleep.

When I asked, "How do I change the printer for the different type forms that need to be printed out?", he replied,

"You want to line up the forms according to this little blue pen mark near the carriage roll of the printer and make sure the first line to be printed is just below the printer ribbon so the policy numbers can fit into this little box on the form. You have to practice printing policies before you really get the hang of setting up the paper because this printer is very old and the ribbon needs to be changed often. To change the ribbon, you have to lift up this top part and the ribbon comes right off; the extra ribbon is in that drawer. Be careful because the ink gets all over the place, and sometimes the printer keys get stuck in the ribbon, and you have to go into the supply room to get pliers to turn the keys back to their proper position."

This type of conversation went on for the rest of the day for each and every task I was supposed to learn. I was eventually given another instructor on different days. I dreaded even asking my first instructor any questions because I knew he would go on and on and on, and before I knew it, I would be tuning him out and daydreaming.

If you find yourself frequently saying, "You're not listening to me," or "Are you listening to me?" then you are probably a Socratic who is engaging in information overload.

Socratics have a problem with redundancy. They use favorite expressions or stories to the point that they become distractors. The other person stops listening to the Socratic because he or she figures, "I've heard this before." This tendency to be redundant creates a closed communication climate, as does the Socratic tendency to engage in nonstop conversations with the self. The Socratic has a problem with overtalking and—like the Noble—has poor listening habits. The redundancy, the nonstop conversation with the self, and the poor listening habits create a situation where the other person just stops listening. Other people may appear to be listening, but in fact they are wondering if and when the Socratic is ever going to shut up.

The Socratic style of communication is neither good nor bad; it is simply different from the Noble and Reflective styles.

HOW TO GET THE SOCRATIC TO DO WHAT YOU WANT

"Thoughts that breathe, words that burn" captures the essence of the Socratic style of communication. Like the Noble, the Socratic has a communication premise that guides his or her behaviors. In attempting to explain, predict, and control the Socratic or to be able to control your own style-associated behaviors if you are a Socratic, it is important to understand this premise:

The Socratic Communication Premise

The Socratic is the individual who is most concerned with rhetoric and the analysis of details. Socratics believe that communication, it and of itself, is the primary purpose of verbal interaction.

This premise brings about a set of easily identifiable verbal and nonverbal characteristics and behaviors listed on the facing page.

An awareness of these characteristics can help you identify Socratic communicators. If you listen, you can hear these characteristics in the speech of a Socratic. If you listen and watch carefully, you can identify an individual's dominant style of communication during the first five minutes of conversation. You can then work with the dominant-style characteristics and manipulate them to guide and control the outcome of the interaction. In gaining control, it is important to recognize the strengths of the Socratic communicator.

Socratic Strengths

Rhetorical sophistication.   The Socratic has the ability to be an influential public speaker, and he or she uses a well-developed vocabulary to arbitrate or negotiate interpersonal interactions.

Persuasiveness.   Socratics have the ability to reduce hostility and guide behaviors with the use of words.

Analysis.   Socratics have the potential to be successful problem solvers because of their ability to see issues from many perspectives.

Thoroughness.   Socratics have the ability to produce a polished final product because of their attention to detail.

Credibility.   A Socratic speaks with confidence and from a base of knowledge; thus, his or her remarks are usually given serious attention and consideration.

Illustration.   Socratics have the ability to paint visual images with words. They use anecdotal stories and hypothetical examples to help the other person share or experience a similar moment in time.

Socratic Weaknesses

The problem areas of any style prevent the other person from listening to or being persuaded by the message. In some instances, the problem area

Socratic Communication Characteristics

The Socratic:

Enjoys the process of rhetoric and enjoys talking
Tends to be verbose, with an affinity for words
Has a penchant for details
Tends to analyze everything
Views argumentation as desirable and constructive
Presents his or her position as a prima facie case
Expects the other person to present a rebuttal that matches the
   the issues raised in the original argument
Openly engages in discussion, negotiation, debate, and arbitration
Utilizes the Socratic method of teaching
Utilizes persuasive message techniques
Resists persuasive efforts by others
Asks questions for which he or she already knows the answer
Uses discussion of the gray areas to reduce hostility
Tends to use anecdotal stories and hypothetical examples
Indulges in lengthy, elaborate, historical reviews
Assumes familiarity on the part of the listener
Engages in philosophical discussions of the abstract
Makes hypothesis statements and if-then-therefore statements
Makes should-must-will directive statements
Avoids absolute and categorical statements
Tends to verbalize his or her entire thought process
Uses clauses, phrases, and parenthetical asides
Tends to speak with footnotes
Tends to engage in information overload
Tends to have poor listening habits
Tends to be directive and controlling
Tends to be redundant
Tends to lecture at the other person
Tends to engage in nonstop conversation with the self
Tends to make excessive use of descriptive adjectives, modifiers,
   and parenthetical asides
Tends to have a well-developed vocabulary
Has the potential for communication eloquence

actually causes the other person to do the opposite of what you are advocating. Socratics tend to have the following communication problems:

Rhetorical rigidity.   The Socratic has a tendency to take constructive argumentation into destructive argumentation. Socratics are so sure they are right that they become inflexible and refuse to give up until the other person "admits" that the Socratic is right. The argumentative communication behaviors create a closed, defensive, and hostile communication climate.

Verbosity.   Socratics have a tendency to be redundant, engage in nonstop conversations with the self, and engage in information overload. These problems create a closed communication climate; the other person stops listening to the Socratic.

Arrogance.   Socratics have a tendency to lecture the other person or to speak in a patronizing voice. This patronizing communication style creates hostility and increases interpersonal conflict.

Rudeness.   Socratics have a tendency to interrupt or talk over the other person.

Dogmatism.   Socratics have a tendency to try to control and direct the other person. Socratics really believe they have the "right" answer, and they feel it is their duty to get the other person to see the light. The directive and controlling nature of the Socratic increases interpersonal conflict.

Socratics are a bit more difficult to deal with or persuade than are Nobles because they are more complex. Imagine attempting to persuade Tweedledee to accept your position on an issue with which you know he does not agree. Things aren't exactly cut and dried with the Socratic. Nonetheless, Socratics are predictable communicators. In dealing with the Socratic, try to keep the following guidelines in mind:

• Don't expect any interaction with a Socratic to be brief.

• Don't become defensive or offended when the Socratic begins to lecture you. This is part of the Socratic style, and it doesn't necessarily have anything to do with how he or she feels about you or your intelligence. It has more to do with the Socratic need to verbalize an entire data set when making a point.

- Learn to appreciate the Socratic recall ability.
- Look for the humor in the parenthetical asides.
- Don't be offended when the Socratic asks you to do revisions on what you thought was a final product.
- Use the Socratic thoroughness, attention to detail, and anecdotal stories to your own benefit.

These last two guidelines are crucial in dealing with Socratics. If the person you are talking with is a Socratic who has not read this book and is not attempting to control the offensive aspects of his or her style, then it is up to you to do the controlling. It is up to you to be flexible and to make the Socratic style work on your behalf.

Nothing is ever complete enough for the Socratic, and if you expect the Socratic to accept your project or proposal on the first try, you will be frustrated. As a professional, you take pride in your work and never hand a draft of anything into your boss or client. You probably do several rewrites, and then you are probably irritated when your boss or client request changes on your "final" product. You can reduce your own irritation with this type of behavior by changing your approach and using Socratic characteristics to your benefit. Instead of bringing your boss or client a final product, let him or her see the product in various stages. At each stage, ask the Socratic for input. Have the Socratic review the penultimate draft of whatever it is you are working on and then say,

"It looks as if we have all the bugs worked out, and we are ready to go to production with this thing. Take one last look and make sure there isn't anything else that you would like added or changed."

After your boss or client examines the project and indicates that everything is in order, then say,

> "Are you sure there is nothing else? This is the last chance to speak or forever hold your peace."

This won't guarantee that your boss or client won't ask for additional changes on your product, but it does introduce a certain amount of guilt. Thus, the Socratic will at least apologize before asking for the changes, and your hostility will be reduced. The Socratic will say,

> "I know I said I wouldn't make any more changes, but there is just one more little thing that needs to be done, and then I promise I'll leave it alone."

Your own hostility is reduced when the Socratic makes these remarks because the focus is on the Socratic obsession with details, not your inability to perform.

You can make Socratic thoroughness work for you by delegating detail tasks to a Socratic. Leaders, of course, are able to delegate effectively, and it is even possible to delegate to your Socratic boss. Suppose you and your boss are planning a special event. You know your boss is a real stickler about details, so you sit down with him or her and say,

> "You are so much better with the details than I, and we both want this activity to be a success, so why don't you make a complete list of everything you think needs to be done, and I'll see to it that it gets done."

In doing this, you've saved yourself a lot of aggravation and effort. Depending on your relationship with your boss and your own ability to deal with details, you might suggest that the two of you sit down together and generate the list. Whatever approach you take, be sure to turn this list into a formal checklist of activities, and be sure to save the list. If perchance your boss calls attention to the fact that some detail was not taken care of, then you pull out the list and say,

"Yes, I can see how we missed that. It wasn't on our list. I'll add it to our list, and next year when we do this, we won't forget it."

Finally, you can use the anecdotal story to control Socratic behaviors. The Socratic uses the story or hypothetical example to help you visualize his or her experience. If you want to change a Socratic perception or persuade a Socratic to do something, use an anecdotal story or hypothetical example to illustrate your idea. If you can't think of a story or create an original example, then use one of the stories or examples that the Socratic is so fond of using.

If you begin by expecting the Socratic to communicate like a Socratic and then you attempt to make his or her characteristics work on your behalf, you will manage communication conflict and improve your chances of controlling the outcome of the interaction. People are often judged by how well they work with their superiors. The examples and techniques that we have discussed also work when the person you are leading or working with is a Socratic or a Reflective.

There is one thing you can be absolutely sure of when two Socratics get together: they will fight for on-air time. There is going to be a **lot** of conversation; the Socratics will interrupt each other and talk over each other; there will be lengthy philosophical monologues; and the conversation will veer off in so many directions that an observer is sure to get lost in the sea of words. I say "observer" because it is a sure bet that with two Socratics in the room, the Nobles and Reflectives aren't going to be doing much talking.

To feel the impact of two Socratics talking, try to imagine Jesse Jackson and Margaret Mead discussing the most significant sociological changes of this century. Then try to imagine what it would be like to contribute something meaningful to that conversation. Better yet, try to keep track of the main points each attempts to make. Can you feel the impact?

For the most part, Socratics enjoy involved discussions with other Socratics, but perhaps too often these discussions turn into heated and angry arguments. The tendency to be argumentative and inflexible can create some real problems when two Socratics are on opposite sides of an issue. If they are on the same side of an issue, everything is fine; they will just engage in normal Socratic behaviors. If they are on opposite sides of an issue, resolution of the conflict can take a long time. Indeed, resolution may not be possible.

It is not uncommon to hear one Socratic criticize another Socratic for being too verbose. Herein lies the key to the Socratic. Socratics really think they are right, and they believe that what they have to say is important. Thus, for two Socratics to get along, both have to acknowledge that they are Socratics, and both have to acknowledge that there is merit in the other person's idea! As you can well imagine, this is no small feat to accomplish.

If both you and your boss or you and the person you are leading happen to be Socratics, you probably have one additional problem to deal with: you have difficulty getting things done on time. At this point in this book, I don't have to explain why this problem exists.

HOW SOCRATICS CAN GET OTHERS TO DO WHAT THEY WANT

As I did with the Noble, I must end this chapter by talking directly to the Socratics who are reading this book. Go back and read the four-step process for controlling the outcome of an interaction (p. 45), and keep in mind that you are the one who must adapt if you want to create moments of success. You cannot change anyone else; the only one you can change is yourself. If you want to be in control, you have to be the one to meet the other person's communication needs.

Controlling the Noble

You know that the Noble has a disdain for details and becomes uncomfortable with lengthy, slow-moving conversations. If you want to get the Noble to do something, then consider this information about his or her communication needs and do the following:

1. Plan ahead. Prepare and organize your thoughts and requests in advance, and know precisely what you want to say before you walk into the interaction.

2. Provide the Noble with a time schedule for the interaction.

3. Do not just drop in on the Noble to "discuss things."

4. Force yourself to limit the amount of detail you provide when passing along information. When possible, provide a summary of the main points with backup information available in a written document.

5. Don't become offended or arrogant when the Noble makes an abrupt or absolute statement.

6. Don't lecture at the Noble. It will cause hostility.

7. Control your desire to engage in argumentation.

8. Offer a specific set of alternatives for the Noble to consider.

9. Force yourself to listen and be attentive because the Noble is only going to say it once.

10. Don't be offended if the Noble starts to clean the desk or file while you are speaking.

Let's take a look at a couple of these guidelines and see if we can hear the sound of control. The first three guidelines address the time and order communication needs of the Noble. If you walk into an interaction with a Noble and say, "If you have a few minutes, I'd like to discuss something with you," the Noble will immediately become defensive because he or she expects your "few minutes" to turn into a lot of wordy minutes. If you want to control the outcome of the interaction, you say,

"Hi, Mark. I need about seven minutes of your time. I have three questions about the Cuevas account that I need answered before I can move forward. If we can deal with this now, it will help me close the account today."

If the Noble responds that he or she is busy and can't talk with you at the moment, quickly respond,

"I'm available at one and again at three this afternoon. Which is more convenient for you?"

Chances are the Noble will pick one of those two times or might say, "Oh, what the heck. You're here now, so let's take care of it!" But if the Noble says he or she is not available at those two times, then immediately respond,

"I need to take care of this today. When will you have seven minutes to help me with this problem?"

Now let's take a look at guideline 8. We talked about this earlier, so this should just be reinforcement. The Noble is an either-or kind of person, and since you know this, you can make this characteristic work for you to control the outcome of the interaction. For example, if the Noble says, "I think you ought to fire him or transfer him to another department," you respond,

"Yes, those are possibilities. We could also put him on probation or give him some additional training and evaluate him in thirty days. Which do you think will work best?"

In each of these interactions, you have provided the Noble with structure, order, and choice—the communication needs that guide the

Noble to respond positively in an interaction. Now let's look at that final guideline.

If it *really* bothers you when the Noble does other things while talking with you, then say so. The Noble can deal with a candid remark and will attempt to change the behavior if he or she is aware of the fact that it bothers you. Simply say,

> "I have to be really honest with you. I feel like a nerd when you file while I'm trying to talk with you. Could you wait to do that until we are done?"

This response is direct and frank. The Noble can deal with this, and believe me, the Noble will make an attempt to change his or her behaviors if the Noble thinks it is necessary to develop your relationship and if the Noble wants to maintain your friendship.

I was totally unaware of the fact that I used to clean my desk or do other paperwork while people were speaking with me. Then one day I was sitting in my office, and a fellow graduate student came in to talk with me about a project. Ritch Sorenson is a person I like and respect, and I was really taken back when he stopped our conversation and said,

> "Linda, you really hurt my feelings. You're always doing something else when I come in to talk with you, and it makes me feel as if you want me to leave. Don't you like me? I thought we were friends."

I felt awful when I heard those words! I apologized, assured Ritch that I did indeed value his friendship, and I explained that my hyperactivity had nothing to do with him or my feelings for him. His willingness to be open with me helped me to recognize something about my communication style that was offensive to others. Since that day, I have made a concerted effort not to clean my desk while talking with others, unless I want the person to go away, I know the other person is also a Noble, or I ask the other person if it is okay if I clean my desk while we talk.

My friend Bill is the epitome of a Magistrate; he says exactly what he thinks, in great detail. He talks incessantly and has a tremendous sense of self-worth. It would never occur to Bill to be offended if I clean my desk while he talks. Sometimes when he aggravates me, I even turn off the light and usher him out the door while he is talking. Bill is a bright person, and most of the time, I like to hear what he has to say. I know it's going to take him a long time to get through his monologue, and I know I'm Noble, so I say,

> "Bill don't be offended if I clean my desk while we talk. I am really interested in hearing what you have to say. So you just go ahead and talk. I'm listening."

Bill tells me to go ahead and clean because it doesn't bother him at all, and then he begins his monologue.

You cannot ignore your own communication needs when speaking with a Noble, and I am not naive enough to think that all Socratics are going to reduce what they have to say down to ten words or less every time they are confronted with a Noble. There are a couple of things that can be done to meet your own needs while still making the Socratic style palatable to the Noble.

- Issue warnings and acknowledge the Noble communication needs when you know you have a lengthy bit of information to convey. Say, "I know you hate it when I go into great detail on these matters, but it is really crucial that you know the whole story here. Bear with me, and I'll try to get through this as rapidly as I can."

- Number and organize your points when you have a lot of information to give the Noble. Nobles can tolerate the detail if it is well organized.

- Learn to appreciate the Noble need to be honest. You always know where you stand with a Noble—and that's not all bad.

- Look for the humor in the Noble style. As a Socratic, you like to use anecdotal stories. Watching and listening to Nobles can provide you with a ton of anecdotal stories.

Keep in mind that Nobles are action-oriented people who need to be doing something while you are speaking. It actually helps them to listen when they engage in some sort of activity, especially if your communication is going to be lengthy. Their minds wander if they are forced to just sit and listen, but if they have something else to do "while" listening, they relax and don't attempt to rush you or cut the interaction short. If you are a Socratic who can talk and work at the same time, then you can jump right in and help the Noble with the activity. Simply say, "Let me help you with that while we talk." If you can talk and work at the same time, you and the Noble can become excellent work partners, and this is a good thing to keep in mind if you are a Socratic and your boss is a Noble. One final thought on this issue: you can put money on the fact that the Noble **is** doing something else while chatting with you on the phone.

Controlling the Reflective

The main thing that you as a Socratic need to be concerned with when speaking with a Reflective is your tendency to be verbose. Reflectives will not interrupt you; they will just let you go on, and on, and on. They will smile and listen politely as you dominate the conversation, but when you leave, they sigh and say, "What a ghastly person. I do hope I don't offend people by going on like that!"

The Reflective is a patient communicator who enjoys interpersonal conversation, so you don't have to worry about the time factor as you would with a Noble. But there are some things that you need to be concerned with if you want the Reflective to provide you with an honest reaction. The following points may be helpful in getting the Reflective to respond honestly or in getting the Reflective to want to do something you would like him or her to do:

1. Take time to engage in some pleasant, courteous dialogue before you get to the business at hand.
2. Don't speak in a patronizing tone of voice or flash your vast array of

knowledge. The Reflective will react by telling you what you want to hear instead of what he or she really feels.

3. Be patient, force yourself to listen, and be attentive to the Reflective's communication needs.

4. Don't talk over the Reflective.

5. Remember to give the Reflective a chance to talk.

6. Probe for input and reactions to whatever is being discussed.

7. Teach the Reflective some Socratic techniques as a way of getting the Reflective to open up.

Let me explain this last guideline. If the Reflective is reluctant to provide you with an honest opinion, ask him or her to provide a hypothetical example or an anecdotal story. Suppose you want a Reflective to evaluate honestly the way you handled a particular situation; you might say, "If the greatest leader in the world were to have handled this situation, what do you think he or she would have done differently?" This approach will allow the Reflective to be honest because he or she can rationalize that the opinion is actually that of the greatest leader. In that way, the Reflective doesn't have to worry about hurting your feelings. Let's try another example.

Suppose you know there is a problem in your work group, but you're not quite sure of the cause. You are fairly sure the Reflective knows what's going on, but she's reluctant to give you information because she "doesn't want to get anyone in trouble." You might try this Socratic approach:

"Sally, suppose you are a screenwriter, and you are going to write a movie about the problems in our office. Tell me a little bit about your plot, and describe your good guys and your bad guys."

The Reflective, like the Noble, becomes bothered with too much information. Reflectives are patient communicators who like to think or reflect before making a decision. The more information they have, the longer it takes them to make a decision. If they become inundated with information, they will avoid the decision completely. As a result, you must be careful not to overwhelm the Reflective with information and details. If you want to help the Reflective to make a decision, make good use of a highlighting pen and summary sheets just as you would with a Noble. Highlight or summarize the main or important points, and be sure to include a statement about how the people involved will be affected by the action to be taken.

Finally, whether you are talking with a Noble or a Reflective, try to curb your tendency to think out loud. Think about what you have to say, organize what you have to say, and then say it. And remember, some people do not feel uncomfortable with silence.

With this Noble statement in mind, I conclude this chapter by reminding you of the two rules that will help you get the results you want:

1. Develop tolerance for differing styles of communication.
2. Do not attempt to force your style on others.

Chapter 5

The Reflective:
The Sweeter Banquet
of the Mind

THE REFLECTIVE SOUND

Reflectives, like Nobles and Socratics, have a distinct and consistent style of communication. Reflectives believe that a polite, warm, calm, and conflict-free decorum should exist when communicating, and they will do whatever is necessary to maintain that decorum.

Tracy, the manager of a retail store, is trying to get Jessica, a salesperson, to clean the store each night at closing time. Jessica neglects this responsibility despite the fact that it is part of her job description. Tracy observes that the other managers often leave notes for employees informing them of tasks that need to be done, but she feels this type of communication has negative results. She feels that it is important to have face-to-face interactions.

Tracy approaches Jessica and attempts to tell her, without being direct, that the store needs to be cleaned:

"The store has been a little messy lately; I guess it has been busy."

This approach does not work, so Tracy tries again:

"Jessica, I know that cleaning the store is not fun, but it is something that must be done every day, so what I did is I cleaned this section of the store for you so there won't be too much for you to do tonight."

Tracy did not clean anymore after this encounter, but Jessica did continue to clean the store nightly as expected.

The Nobles and Magistrates are probably choking on their coffee as they read this little interaction and saying, "Just tell her to clean like she's supposed to!" But that's not the Reflective style, and in fact, this is a true story; Tracy *did* get Jessica to do willingly what she wanted her to do.

Always Polite, Warm, and Supportive

The Reflective is a nice person to talk with because the Reflective is the person who is most concerned with the interpersonal aspects of the communication interaction. The accurate transmission of information, expression of opinions, and tangible results all play secondary roles in Reflective communication encounters. This is because Reflectives believe that the maintenance or advancement of the personal relationship assumes precedence over all other functions and goals during an interaction. Reflectives are truly concerned about the human feelings in the interaction. At times, they are motivated by their concern for their own feelings and a desire to have others like them. At other times, it is a concern for the other person and a desire not to offend or hurt the other person that serves as a motivational force. At all times, the Reflective is concerned with the avoidance of open confrontation.

The Little White Lie

Like the Noble and the Socratic, the Reflective has clearly established rules and guidelines governing the decorum of the communication interaction.

Violation of these rules by the other person is justification for a statement that is less than truthful. For example, if a person is rude, forceful, or intimidating, the Reflective may say what the other person wants to hear even if that is not what the Reflective really feels. The Reflective feels justified in using the little white lie because it helps to maintain the polite, calm decorum of the interaction. Once the Reflective leaves the interaction, however, he or she *does not feel bound by the response!* This is because the Reflective feels that the offender was wrong to violate the decorum of the interaction in the first place. Thus, the less-than-truthful statement is justified if it reinstates the warm, supportive, polite, and calm decorum of the communication interaction.

It Is Better to Say Nothing

Typically Reflectives will say nothing rather than say something that will hurt or alienate the other person. In addition, they will say nothing if expressing an honest opinion will cause the other person to become angry with or displeased by what is said. Thus, Reflectives withhold opinions, but they don't necessarily provide false opinions, and they will tell you what you want to hear rather than what they really feel in order to avoid conflict.

In general, Reflectives avoid open conflict by withholding negative opinions, but this creates another type of conflict because the nonresponse is often interpreted by the other person as a statement of agreement. In reality, however, the Reflective has not agreed or disagreed; he or she has simply not expressed an opinion. When the other person moves forward and later finds out that the Reflective isn't going to do or support whatever was discussed, conflict is generated that can be directly attributed to communication style differences. The other person states with anger, "Well, this is just great! You said you'd support the proposal, and then you didn't. Thanks a lot!" But the Reflective *did not* actually say he or she would support the proposal. The Reflective didn't say anything in an effort to avoid conflict, but conflict was generated anyway.

Reflect Upon It a While

Reflectives don't necessarily reflect off the other person and say what that person wants to hear. Rather, they tend to reflect off the situation. That is, they like to think before they take any action. They will walk away from an interaction and think about it for a while before giving an opinion. Similarly, Reflectives do express their opinions, but they do it in a very different manner than does the Noble or Socratic. Reflectives walk away from a conflict situation, reflect on what was said, and then return at a more opportune time to express their opinions. If pressed for an opinion, and the opinion is going to be contrary to that expressed by the other party, Reflectives select their words gingerly or will simply say what you want to hear. Then they will proceed to do whatever they want to do without regard for what they have told you.

Let's Share Feelings

Reflectives are reluctant to express strong opinions but do openly engage in personal self-disclosure. They will share their innermost feelings and will allow the other person to do the same. In fact, other people frequently tell their problems to the Reflective. To be even more factual, other people constantly tell their problems to the Reflective. If you are a Reflective, you are probably shaking your head and saying, "Yes, that's right. Everyone tells me their problems, and then I don't get my work done." And do you know why everyone tells you their problems? That's right — because you listen, and because you don't give advice. If you are a Reflective and you want people to stop telling you their problems, then give them some advice on how to solve the problem. The minute you give them the advice, they will find a reason to end the interaction. People who tell you their problems don't actually want advice, they just want someone to listen. Give them a solution to their problems, and they stop talking because they have lost their listener.

Rogerian Response Techniques

Reflectives are good at getting other people to open up, and this is a very positive trait from a leadership or management perspective. Reflectives use what is called Rogerian response techniques to encourage other people to disclose their feelings or provide additional information. Empathic statements show an understanding of what the person is feeling, and mirror statements reflect back (in the form of a question) the same words the person is using—for example:

RYAN: I'm really angry about these changes.

OZZIE: You're really angry about the changes? (mirror)

RYAN: Not angry. Just upset.

OZZIE: I understand. (empathic)

RYAN: It's not that I don't want to do the changes. It's just that I'm uncomfortable when we miss a deadline.

A restatement of the exact words the person is using and paraphrased responses are examples of Rogerian response techniques that encourage the speaker to explore other aspects of the matter and help the speaker evaluate his or her feelings about the problem—for example:

RYAN: With these changes, the report will have to be redone. It's going to take two or three weeks to change it.

OZZIE: Two or three weeks? (restatement)

RYAN: Well, maybe not quite that long. I'll be working with Jason, and he's sharp technically, but he's not the easiest person in the world to work with.

OZZIE: I see. (empathic)

RYAN: Nothing very major, but on a job like this, I'd like to feel that my partner is open to a lot of give and take.

OZZIE: You feel that it would be difficult to exchange ideas with Jason on this project? (paraphrasing)

RYAN: No. Not really. He's just real opinionated, but then again, I guess I am too.

A counselor named Rogers (hence the term Rogerian) popularized these techniques as a way of getting people to open up and as a way of helping people reach their own solutions. They are noncommittal, nonjudgmental responses that encourage the person to say more. When Reflectives respond to a statement by saying such things as, "Uh-huh . . . I see . . . Yes, go on . . . I understand how you might feel . . . You mean you don't think we should do this because . . ." they are utilizing Rogerian response techniques to encourage the other person to continue talking, to share their feelings, and/or to provide additional information.

Now the Nobles, Magistrates, and Socratics may be thinking that these techniques are wimpy. Nevertheless, these communication techniques are extremely helpful when you are dealing with a difficult or hostile individual or when you are trying to get information from someone who isn't eager to provide that information.

Qualify Everything

A second effective people-oriented communication technique utilized by the Reflective is the verbal qualifier. A qualifier is a positive statement that is delivered before the bad-news message, or it is a statement that modifies or qualifies an absolute statement. For example, if a Reflective makes an absolute statement like, "This will never work," he or she will add a qualifier that will reduce the defensive nature of the remark. The Reflective will add, "But who knows? Maybe it will, so let's give it a try." This qualifying statement takes the sting out of the absolute statement and reduces the need for the other person to respond defensively.

Suppose that I am your Noble boss and that you have given me a report that contains several errors. As a Noble, I might walk up to you, place the report in front of you, and say, "This report is full of errors. I want you to correct the errors and have the report back to me in an hour." You take the report, but you certainly don't dare ask any questions about the errors because I have created a closed communication climate with my abrupt directive.

Now suppose that I am your Socratic boss, and you have handed me the same report. As a Socratic, the first thing I am going to do is to pull up a chair and sit down with you because I know our conversation is going to take some time. I pull out the report and proceed to explain every error, why I think it occurred, how I think it occurred, how I think it should be corrected, and how you might avoid making the same error in the future. It's a sure bet that you're not going to ask me any questions because by the time I am finished, you are ready to tear your hair out, and you're thinking, "All right, all right. I understand. Go away. I know what to do!"

Now suppose that I am your Reflective boss. We are dealing with the same report with the same errors. As a Reflective boss, I will make use of the qualifier and say,

> "I am normally very pleased with the reports you do for me. I do, however, have a problem with this one. I have noted several errors that I would like you to correct, and then I'll need the report back within the hour. Please don't hesitate to ask for help if you have any questions on what needs to be done."

This Reflective response makes use of the verbal qualifier to lower you natural tendency to be defensive when confronted with a criticism of you work. With the defensive barrier removed, you are more likely to b motivated to want to make the corrections and to want to avoid errors i the future. In addition, the Reflective response creates an open communi cation climate by encouraging you to ask questions. This is importan because errors often result when an individual doesn't understand how t do something. If the person doesn't feel free to ask questions, future errors are almost inevitable.

I'm Listening

Reflectives make good use of verbal and nonverbal reinforcers. The nod of the head and the verbal responses of "I see . . . uh-huh . . . I understand" reinforce that the Reflective is listening. The fact that the Reflective is listening helps reinforce your importance in the interaction. In fact, if you have to give a speech and you are nervous, just look for the Reflectives in the audience. They are the ones nodding their heads, smiling, and giving you nonverbal encouragement to continue. If you direct your speech to the Reflectives in the audience, your anxiety will subside. These nonverbal behaviors are very supportive. They say to you, "It's okay. You're doing just fine. Go on."

Listening is a Reflective strength. Of the six types of communicators, the Reflective is the best listener. If you want an accurate account of something that was said, ask the Reflective because he or she was probably the only one listening. The Socratic was thinking about his or her next remark, and the Noble was thinking about getting out of the room. The Reflective was listening.

Patience Not Progress

Reflectives are patient communicators. They have no sense of communication immediacy and believe in thoroughly thinking through issues and actions. They reflect, they think things over, but they do not tend to verbalize those thoughts. The Socratic tends to think out loud and verbalize his or her entire thought processes, and the Noble simply verbalizes the end product of the thought process. The Reflective just sort of thinks about things, and maybe he or she will—or maybe he or she won't—tell you about the end product.

Reflectives are the least directive and controlling of the three types of communicators. They listen, offer help, and ask questions, but they rarely provide solutions. Reflectives talk things over and offer suggestions in an effort to help the other person reach his or her own solution to the problem. Reflectives do not typically tell the other person what to do. Furthermore, Reflectives search for improvement rather than elimination of a problem. As a result, they tend to be more tolerant when working with people and more successful when working with people who have personal problems.

The downside of this attribute is that Nobles, Magistrates, and Socratics tend to feel that the door has been left open so they really don't have to do what the Reflective requests. Think back to the story of Liz and Allen. Allen didn't get rid of his blue jeans until Liz issued the Noble ultimatum. The ultimatum is not the chosen Reflective way, but Reflectives need to be able to draw upon this technique on some occasions just as the other communicators need to be able to utilize some of the Reflective techniques.

Speak Softly and Don't Carry a Big Stick

Reflectives are the most flexible and easiest to persuade of the three dominant-style communicators. They listen to the other person. In addition, they don't think in absolute or final terms, so they tend to be open to ideas and can be persuaded to change their opinions when presented with a rational argument. Socratics and Nobles love to go out to lunch with Reflectives because when asked to suggest a possible location, the Reflective responds, "It doesn't matter. Where would you like to go?" Reflectives actually do have an idea of where they would like to go to eat, but they offer to let you make the selection because they feel that is the polite thing to do.

Reflectives are not forceful; they do not argue; they are rarely aggressive; but they can be assertive if the issue is really important. For example, Reflectives tend to be protective and will defend someone who is being verbally abused. They will attempt to defuse the hostility in an interaction by saying something like, "I understand why you are upset, but don't you think you are being too harsh with him?" If the situation is too volatile to defuse, the Reflective will wait until the interaction is over and then do something that is unique to Reflectives: walk out of the interaction, befriend the abused individual, and then apologize on behalf of the abuser! The Reflective will say, "I'm really sorry that he talked to you that way." The Reflective doesn't feel responsible for the abuser's behavior but does believe that the decorum of the communication interaction has been violated, and he or she feels the need to restore harmony.

A Reflective recently explained to me that she actually feels embarrassed for the abuser. She said, "It is difficult to understand how anyone can behave that way and not be embarrassed." You see how our communication premise guides our behaviors and colors the way we see the world. For the Reflective, the maintenance of the communication decorum takes precedence over all else.

Reflectives are typically soft-spoken, unassertive individuals, and their discourse is permeated with words like "perhaps," "maybe," "however," "somewhat," and "might." In addition, the discourse of the Reflective is sprinkled with empathic words like "we," "help," "together," "share," and "concern." "I'm sorry" is a Reflective giveaway. The Reflective can be heard offering apologies for everything negative that happens to the other person—even if the Reflective had nothing at all to do with the negative occurrence.

Reflectives will apologize for negative consequences that they had nothing to do with, but they are reluctant to accept ownership for negative feelings that they really have, and they tend to shift the negative feeling to a third party. Suppose you are a Reflective, and you have to talk to one of your workers about body odor. As a Reflective, you will not say, "I have noticed that you are having a problem with body odor." As a Reflective, you will say, "Some of your workers have noticed that you have a problem with body odor." We'll talk about how this approach will cause trouble in the last chapter of this book.

I Wish I Had Said What I Really Thought

Reflectives are not without communication problems; the most serious of the problems is the personal frustration that they feel about their inability to speak up and be assertive. Reflectives frequently walk away from an interaction with their fists clinched and eyes squinted saying, "Gee, I wish I had said what I really thought!" When Reflectives do say what they really feel, the other person tends to be so shocked that he or she will immediately apologize or obediently follow the Reflective's orders. Listen as Katrina explains how deviating from her Reflective style helped her solve a problem with her boyfriend.

Derrick always seems to get frustrated with me because I am "quiet and timid." I always try to explain that this is just the way I am. He complains that I hold things in, and he's right—I would rather not say anything than cause a fight.

Well finally, I couldn't hold things in any longer, and I told him we had to talk. Well, he's not the "let's sit down and discuss our problems" type, so he didn't want to listen. At this point, I got really frustrated and started to cry. Out of frustration, I yelled at the top of my lungs, "You're really starting to piss me off, and you're being a real ass! Turn around and look at me when I talk to you!"

Well, I think he was shocked that I could yell and actually get mad, but it worked. I finally got to get things off my chest, and we were able to come to a compromise.

The Credibility Gap

Credibility is often a problem for Reflectives because of their reluctance to be directive or assertive. Their ideas and suggestions are often ignored in meetings because they don't speak with confidence. Reflectives become totally depressed when they make a suggestion that is ignored and then five minutes later a Noble or Socratic is hailed as a savior for making the same suggestion. Furthermore, strong-willed individuals with hidden agendas take advantage of the courteous Reflective style by talking over or interrupting the Reflective as he or she speaks. This places the Reflective in a one-down position and erodes his or her credibility. If the Reflective wishes to be viewed as credible or believes that the point he or she is trying to make is important, then the Reflective should say, "Excuse me, but I wasn't finished with what I was saying. I'd like to continue." This, of course, is a Noble response, but it is an effective way of making sure your ideas are heard. You can remain calm and soft-spoken during the interaction, and your Reflective sense of communication decorum will remain intact.

Reflectives are master equivocators, and the use of equivocal statements also casts doubt on the credibility and dependability of the Reflective. The ambiguous and uncertain nature of Reflective position statements creates a feeling of reluctance in the other person. The other person doesn't know where the Reflective stands and is reluctant to involve the Reflective in the decision process.

While Reflectives do engage in supportive communication interactions, their disdain for conflict often results in the creation of a distrustful communication climate. Reflectives are viewed as deceitful when they use the little white lie or remain silent on an issue. In their efforts to keep everyone calm and content, they can be viewed as conniving. For example, Reflectives refrain from gathering a group of people together to work out a solution to a problem because the risk of conflict is too great. Instead Reflectives visit each person in an attempt to orchestrate the solution before the group gathers. Sometimes, depending on the people involved, this can be a good strategy. Often, however, the people involved begin to communicate with each other and start to feel as if they are being manipulated. As a result, a climate of distrust is created.

Finally, the Reflective tendency to engage in noncommittal communication contributes to the climate of distrust and a closed communication climate. That is, the other individual may simply avoid communication with the Reflective and say, "Don't bother asking him; he won't tell you what he really thinks anyway."

The Noble, the Socratic, and the Reflective can all create closed communication climates. They just do it in different ways.

HOW TO GET REFLECTIVES
TO DO WHAT YOU WANT

Like all other communicators, the Reflective has a communication premise that guides his or her behaviors. In attempting to explain, predict, and
control the Reflective or to be able to control your own style-associated
behaviors if you are a Reflective, it is important to understand this premise:

The Reflective Communication Premise

The Reflective believes that the primary purpose of communication is
the maintenance or advancement of the personal relationship. The
accurate transmission of information, expression of opinions, and
tangible results play a secondary role in the communication encounter.

This premise brings about a set of easily identifiable verbal and nonverbal
characteristics and behaviors:

Reflective Communication Characteristics

The Reflective:

Is concerned with the human feelings in an interaction
Believes the communication decorum should be polite and conflict
   free
Attempts to maintain a warm, calm, and supportive communica-
   tion decorum
Will make less-than-truthful statements to maintain the communi-
   cation decorum
Avoids open conflict by withholding negative opinions
Often says what the other person wants to hear rather than what
   he or she really feels

Will apologize for negative consequences for which he or she is not responsible

Will shift ownership of his or her real negative feelings to a third party

Openly engages in personal self-disclosure

Uses Rogerian response techniques to encourage others to talk

Has no sense of immediacy—engages in delayed communication responses

Uses qualifiers to reduce hostility

Uses verbal and nonverbal reinforcers to create a supportive climate

Avoids directive and controlling statements

Tends to be a patient listener

Uses empathic responses, restatements, paraphrases, summaries, and probing questions

Offers help and asks questions but rarely provides solutions

Tends to be flexible and persuadable

Avoids absolute statements

Tends to make equivocal position statements

Attempts to defuse communication hostility

Tends to be soft-spoken and nonassertive

Experiences personal frustration because of an inability to be assertive

Has difficulty establishing credibility

Can be viewed as conniving or deceitful

Will say nothing rather than say something that will offend

Tends to use empathic words like "share," "concern," "we," "help," "together," and "sorry"

Tends to be a pleasant person with whom to talk

Allows others to tell him or her their problems

An awareness of these characteristics can help you identify Reflective communicators. Like the Noble and Socratic, there are strengths and weaknesses of this style.

Reflective Strengths

Accuracy. Reflectives have the ability to engage in active listening techniques, which encourage others to provide honest information and allow for the accurate transmission of information.

Patience. Reflectives tend to think before they act, thus avoiding unnecessary conflict. In addition, the Reflective takes the time to hear the person out and avoids making a premature decision.

Supportiveness. Reflectives have the ability to make the other person feel good about the self, and Reflectives are able to reduce defensive behaviors when delivering the bad-news message.

Openness. Reflectives have the ability to create an open communication environment in which individuals feel free to speak honestly.

Conciliation. Reflectives have the ability to help other people solve their own problems. They are able to serve as the peacekeeper between two warring parties.

Empathy. Reflectives have the ability to tune in to the needs of the other person and respect the confidential nature of the interaction.

Reflective Weaknesses

The problem areas of any style prevent the other person from listening to or being persuaded by the message. In some instances, the problem area actually causes the other person to do the opposite of what is being advocated. Reflectives tend to have the following communication problems:

Passiveness. Reflectives have a tendency to back away from controversial issues. They tend not to say what they really think, and this causes personal frustration for the Reflective and the other person. This passive tendency causes the Reflective to lose out on career opportunities because the other person views the Reflective as weak.

Vulnerability. The Reflective tends to be easy prey for the strong-willed because of his or her tendency to be passive or nonassertive.

Reflectives are verbally attacked because the other person knows the Reflective will back down.

Indecisiveness.   Reflectives tend to be overly concerned with personal feelings and the pleasant communication decorum, and this results in indecisiveness. The ability to be decisive and directive, when necessary, are problem areas that can prevent the Reflective from achieving personal and professional goals.

Noncredibility.   Reflectives are not viewed as credible communicators because of their soft-spoken, unassertive, noncommittal style. In addition, the tendency to say what the other person wants to hear instead of what the Reflective really feels establishes the Reflective as a dishonest or devious person in the eyes of the other.

It is fairly easy to get a Reflective to do what you want. It is not easy, though, to get him or her to do it without resentment or thoughts of sabotage. It is also fairly easy to make yourself look like a heel or a bully when you pressure a Reflective into doing what you want. Furthermore, a stubborn (personality trait) Reflective can infuriate you and make you look pretty silly by "forgetting" to do what you have requested.

If you want to avoid some or all of these negative reactions, then there are a few basics to remember when you are talking with a Reflective:

1. Take time to develop the interpersonal aspect of the conversation.

2. Attempt to include or draw the Reflective into the conversation.

3. Use a self-disclosure or I-message* combined with a qualifier and a what-if statement to gather honest information.

4. Avoid bullying the Reflective into doing what you want. He or she will get you in the end.

---

*I-messages are the opposite of you-messages. They are statements accepting ownership of the problem instead of statements blaming someone else for the problem. "I'm really upset about the things that happened today," is an I-message. "You really made a mess of things today," is a you-message.

5. Avoid the use of absolute or final statements.
6. Make reference to and show a concern for the human needs in any situation.

If you are attempting to motivate a Reflective or you really want an honest opinion from a Reflective, it is important that you not violate the Reflective communication decorum. If you do, Reflectives will placate you or comply with your directive but will not internalize your message. Furthermore, given the opportunity, they will quietly sabotage your directive. Reflectives are reserved and soft-spoken, but that does not mean that they are stupid or without strong opinions, so when you walk into a room to talk with a Reflective, take the time to be courteous and develop the polite, supportive communication decorum before you get down to the business at hand. This will get the conversation off to a good start and increase your chances of getting the Reflective to accept the position you are attempting to advance.

As a leader, it is important to include or attempt to draw the Reflective into the conversation. Many good ideas are lost because the Reflective is ignored. If you want to tap into those good ideas, you can simply say to the Reflective,

"Tony, you've been sort of quiet through this discussion. How do you feel about the plan?"

When you make a concerted effort to draw Reflectives into the conversation, they do respond, and in problem-solving situations, it is important to get ideas from everyone who will be involved with the final solution. When you don't get this informaion, the chances of sabotage are greatly increased.

Finally, non-Reflectives have great difficulty dealing with Reflectives who don't say what they really feel. Nobles and Socratics are distrustful of Reflectives and will complain, "I can never tell what's *really* on her mind." To avoid this destructive conflict-producing interaction and to gather honest, accurate information from the Reflective, you can use two very simple verbal techniques. First, you can combine a self-disclosure statement or I-message with a probing question:

> "I'm feeling very uneasy with this conversation. I sense that you are not telling me how you really feel. I want us to be able to solve this problem. Can you tell me how you would like to see the problem resolved?"

The final sentence might also sound like this:

> "Do you have any ideas you can share with me?"

If you are a Noble or Magistrate, you are probably thinking that you could or would never talk in this style, but believe me, Reflectives *will* respond to an interaction structured in this manner. If you want to control the outcome of the interaction, you have to force yourself to learn how to use this style.

Additionally, you can use the qualifier and what-if statement to generate honest responses from Reflectives. You can say,

> "I know you never say anything that will hurt the feelings of another person, but if you were to criticize this plan, what would you say?"

In presenting this question, you have allowed the Reflective to make a critical statement in a nonthreatening manner, and the Reflective communication decorum has remained intact. In addition, you have used Reflective communication techniques to get the Reflective to engage in open communication. You have addressed the Reflective communication needs and in the process have controlled the outcome of the interaction.

Talking with a Reflective can be a pleasant experience. The difficult part of interacting with Reflectives comes when you attempt to get them to say what they really feel. But this is not an insurmountable problem.

"Polite" and "nice" are two adjectives that come to mind when describing a conversation between two Reflectives. Visualize former president Carter talking with Mother Teresa—a serene picture indeed. The inability to make a decision, however, is a problem that can be observed when two Reflectives engage in a communication interaction. Let's listen to Carl and Nina as they attempt to decide on how they should celebrate her birthday:

CARL: Where would you like to go for your birthday?

NINA: Oh, it really doesn't matter. What would you like to do?

CARL: Dinner at the Cove would be nice, but it's your birthday, so you should be the one to decide. We can go where you like.

NINA: The Cove would be nice.

CARL: Now I don't want you to say that just because I suggested it. Is there some place you'd like better?

NINA: No, not really. I really like Chez Maison, but that's a little too expensive. You like the Cove, and that will be just fine.

CARL: Now let's not worry about the price. I just suggested the Cove because it's on the water. If Chez Maison makes you happy, then I'm happy.

Would you like to place bets on where Carl and Nina will go to celebrate Nina's birthday?

HOW REFLECTIVES CAN GET OTHERS TO DO WHAT THEY WANT

Now it's time to talk frankly with the Reflectives. If you are a Reflective and the other person is a Noble or Socratic, then you might feel a little like Abraham Lincoln meeting the Mad Hatter. You know that communication conflict is inevitable, but you also know it is controllable. Let's review the main points for controlling conflict:

• Determine your goals or purpose.
• Listen and identify the other person's dominant style. Meet the needs associated with the style.

- Use your strengths to guide the conversation.
- Control your communication problem areas.

As a Reflective, the best thing you can do in dealing with both the Noble and the Socratic is to develop your assertive communication skills. It is possible for you to do this and still maintain the polite, warm, and supportive communication decorum that you desire. By making use of some of the assertive techniques, which already are part of your style, you can meet your own needs while giving consideration to the needs of the other person. At the same time, you can attempt to reduce hostility. The following assertive techniques can be very helpful:

Assertive Techniques for Reflectives

- Make use of I-messages.
- Make use of nonverbal support for your assertions.
- Make use of grain-of-truth statements.
- Make use of the verbal qualifier.

Let's start with the I-message. When you use the personal pronoun "I" instead of "you," you are assuming ownership of the problem and taking responsibility for your own actions, feelings, needs, and desires. I-messages help to decrease defensiveness on the part of the other person because they eliminate personal attacks and accusations. The focus is on the person who is attempting to be assertive, not the other person. Let's try a scenario and hear what it sounds like when you talk your way into trouble and what it sounds like when you use communication style to talk your way out of trouble.

Suppose your boss has transferred some projects to your department that really should be handled by Charlie and his staff. Your boss has done this because you and your staff have a reputation for excellence, and

Charlie has a reputation for not getting work done on time. While you find this confidence in your abilities flattering, your staff is already overworked and irritated with doing the work of two departments. You approach your boss and talk your way into trouble by saying:

> "The people in my department are getting fed up with doing the work of two departments. You don't deal with Charlie. You just give us his work to do. My people are really getting angry."

Your boss might respond to this statement by getting angry with you or lecturing you on the need for the competent people to take up the slack of the less competent or by expressing confidence in your ability to convince your staff that they shouldn't be angry. It is not likely that your boss will respond by changing his or her behaviors.

Let's try using communication style (changing how you say what you say) to talk your way out of trouble and control the outcome of this interaction. You can say,

> "I must admit that I am uncomfortable with this assignment. On the one hand, I am pleased that you have this type of confidence in me and my people. On the other hand, I feel angry and frustrated when I am asked to assume projects that should be completed by Charlie and his group. What can we do to help Charlie meet his responsibilities?"

In this statement, you accept ownership for the problem instead of blaming your boss. You also guide the solution by redirecting attention to the need to change Charlie. You are attempting to control the eventual outcome of the interaction by effectively using communication style.

Nonverbal support for your assertions—eye contact, facial expressions, gestures, spatial relationships, vocal cues (rate, pitch, intonation, and vocal quality), silence—is essential. These nonverbal behaviors are used to support or to be consistent with your verbal assertions. For example, assertive statements lose impact if your vocal cues are apologetic or timid. And if the vocal cues are argumentative or accusatory, they have impact but also produce—rather than defuse—hostility and conflict. A calm, firm, conversational tone is the most effective vocal cue to use when attempting assertive communication.

Your posture and gestures must be consistent with your message. If you are hovering in a corner biting your nails as you say, "I think we should reword that advertisement," it is not likely that anyone will give serious consideration to your assertion. Similarly, if you are standing with your arms folded and your lips clinched tightly together, it isn't likely that the other person will believe you when you say, "No, I'm not angry."

Your eye contact and facial expressions can communicate avoidance, shyness, insecurity, uncertainty, severity, hostility, and any number of other feelings. In addition, your spatial relationships can signal confidence, support, warmth, retreat, or attack. The point to remember is that you project your belief in your own self-worth when your nonverbal communication supports your verbal assertions.

The grain-of-truth statement is an interesting technique that provides a defense against manipulative criticism. With this technique, you simply accept whatever is true about a criticism and then move forward to decide what should be done—if anything. For example, let's go back and visit Charlie and your boss. Suppose your boss responds to your I-message by saying,

"I thought you were a good manager, but now you are refusing to help out with this work."

This message is meant to make you feel guilty and to get you to do the work so your boss can avoid dealing with Charlie. If you allow your boss to make you feel guilty and you do the work, your boss is off the hook. But you are angry and feel as if you are being used. You can change the outcome of this interaction by using the grain-of-truth statement. You can say,

"It is true that I am a good manager, and I take pride in the quality of my work. I cannot, however, produce quality work for myself and

Charlie. I think you can help all of us produce quality work by dealing with Charlie."

With some people, this statement may produce the desired result. With others, this is just the beginning of a verbal volleyball match. In the end, the person who is able to control the communication style will control the outcome of the interaction.

Your ability to make use of the qualifier—the positive statement before the bad-news message—and your ability to engage in personal self-disclosure are helpful assertive communication techniques. Suppose you are dealing with a Magistrate, who is monopolizing the conversation. You might say,

> "You make some very interesting points. But I'm feeling a bit uncomfortable about not contributing to this conversation. I'd like to express my opinions on this issue. Would you like to hear some of my ideas?"

This response makes it difficult for the Magistrate to continue ignoring your needs. But for the sake of analysis, let's say the Magistrate responds,

> "Actually I'm not interested in your opinions. I have thoroughly researched this issue, and I am quite sure that I have identified the real problem."

How would you respond?

If the Magistrate were your boss, your answer might be different from a response to a Magistrate who is your friend or colleague. Additionally, your response will differ depending on your purpose or the goal that you hope to achieve through the communication interaction. Suppose this Magistrate is your boss, and this issue is not one that you feel you need to fight for right now, but you do want to begin training your boss to behave differently. You might say,

> "I respect your right to refuse additional information, and I will proceed as you have ordered. If you change your mind and decide

that you would like to consider my information, I will be happy to share it with you."

You smile politely as you deliver the last sentence and then quietly leave the room to continue with your work.

Let's take this one step further. Given the brief description you already have of the Magistrate, how do you think he or she will respond? If you think that the boss might begrudgingly ask for your information or that he or she would come back later and attempt to get your information without appearing to acquiesce to your statement, then you are beginning to understand how you can use communication style to control the outcome of interactions.

Controlling the Noble

Let's combine what you know about assertive communication techniques with what you know about the Communication Kaleidoscope and see how a Reflective can control a Noble. Consider the following:

- Nobles don't mean to be offensive. They just believe they should say what they really feel. As a Reflective, you must force yourself to give an honest opinion and avoid saying what you think the Noble wants to hear.

- Don't be offended if the Noble doesn't take time to engage in friendly chitchat, but remember you can change this behavior by asking the Noble something about himself or herself.

- Provide the Noble with a choice between two alternatives when you want him or her to do something.

- Say what you have to say without being overly concerned with hurting the Noble's feelings.

- Attempt to make your communication concise and orderly, and remember to include a bottom-line statement; explain the end result.

Controlling the Socratic

In dealing with the Socratic, keep the following in mind:

- Use your active listening techniques to keep some order in the conversation and to clarify what has been said or agreed upon.
- Make use of verbal qualifiers to make sure that the Socratic allows you time to speak.
- Do your research, provide supporting evidence for your assertions, and provide detail.
- Be patient and understand the Socratic need to be verbose and overly detailed.

I am frequently asked which style of communication is *the* best style. The answer to that question is that none of the styles is the best one. It isn't the style that brings about personal or professional success. *It is the ability to use style to gain control and guide the outcome of an interaction that creates opportunities for success.* Successful people have the ability to use their dominant style of communication to make things happen and to draw upon their other two less dominant styles to produce desired outcomes. One style is not better than another; each style is just different.

Chapter 6

The Magistrate:
The Good, the Bad, and
the Really Ugly

THE MAGISTRATE SOUND

Frédéric is from France. He is a salesman, and he is a Magistrate. As you read his description of his attempt to persuade a person he identified as a Noble, listen for the Magistrate sound. While Frédéric offered this story as an example of an unsuccessful communication encounter, note that he doesn't accept the blame for what went wrong. The blame falls on the other person, who "was stuck to his position." I have underlined some key phrases that are prevalent in the speech of a Magistrate.

Last year I was at a boat show taking a survey for a French marine product. I met a man who represents a U.S. product that is similar. I did not know the man. I just spoke with him for several minutes. I think he was a real Noble in the way he tried to avoid arguments, make absolute statements, and never recognize that I was right on certain points.

My goal was to show him the product (I had some pictures) and prove to him that it had many more uses and advantages than the product he was representing.

I had some pictures showing the product in different uses, but he never admitted that this product was different from the one he was representing. I did not expect him to reject his own product; I just wanted him to recognize that my product was a new concept.

He was stuck to his position. All he was able to say is that he could see no difference.

Frédéric felt this was an unsuccessful communication encounter because he didn't win; he wasn't able to *prove* that he was right. This is an unsuccessful communication encounter but not because Frédéric didn't win. It is unsuccessful because Frédéric isn't able to accept responsibility for what happened in the encounter. To the contrary, he sees the other person's unwillingness to be persuaded as the problem. Frédéric misanalyzed the interaction because of his Magistrate need never to be wrong.

Herein lies the secret of the Magistrate and the most obvious characteristic that separates this communicator from the Noble and the Socratic: the Magistrate is totally committed to winning the argument; the Magistrate must always be right.

The Magistrate is a committed communicator who believes that the honest exchange of opinions and information and the analysis of details are the primary reasons for communicating. The dominant characteristics of the Noble and the Socratic are blended together to create a communicator who is direct, straightforward, and analytical. At first glance, this combination of communication characteristics appears to be ideal for someone who aspires to lead, and in fact, the Magistrate can be an illuminating leader. The dark side of the Magistrate, however, can lead those who would be led to think of him or her as little more than a would-be dictator. Those are some pretty strong words, but you must keep in mind that the Magistrate is a powerful communicator.

Power Personified

Magistrates are powerful from the perspective that they are intense, often dynamic, and often overbearing communicators who elicit intense reactions from others. This is partially because the Magistrate draws upon and actively uses a much larger set of characteristics than does a dominant-style communicator. Where the Noble or the Socratic each has thirty or so identifiable communication characteristics that they tend to rely on, the Magistrate has more than sixty from which to choose. This is both a blessing and a curse for the Magistrate because this profile has double the strengths and double the problems. When Magistrates are communicating well, they are doing it very well, and when they are communicating badly, they are doing it very badly. There doesn't appear to be any middle ground for this Noble-Socratic blended communicator. If the Noble or the Socratic can make an impression on you as a communicator, then the Magistrate can be twice as impressive. If the Noble or the Socratic can anger you with communication style, then the Magistrate can make you twice as angry. The Magistrate is a very strong communicator—in both positive and negative terms.

Tell It Like It Is and in Great Detail

Usually it is easy to identify a dominant-style communicator during the first five minutes of conversation, but it is a bit more difficult with the blended-style communicator. The Noble tends to be straightforward but not verbose, and the Socratic tends to be verbose but not straightforward, and neither is confusing. Magistrates are simultaneously straightforward and verbose. They will tell you exactly what they think, and they will tell you in great detail, and they will state it over, and over, and over again. This can be very confusing if you are trying to determine the speaker's dominant style so you can control the interaction. You will be asking yourself if the person is Noble or Socratic. The answer, of course, is that the person is both.

Listen to Nick as he explains an unsuccessful communication encounter he had with his friend Gene. This isn't a work-related example, but I've chosen to use it because it demonstrates the classic Magistrate sound. Note Nick's direct, straightforward, and verbose storytelling style. Also note the air of superiority and certainty in his words, and pay particular attention to the fact that he doesn't actually accept responsibility for the failure of this communication encounter even though the assignment called for him to provide a story where his style caused him a problem. This is because Magistrates typically don't admit failure or defeat. In this story, it is because Magistrates don't accept partial victories. Also notice his criticism of Gene's Magistrate style of communication.

Gene is a friend I've know for ten years. Gene and I played football in high school and college together. For nine years, we played next to each other. Gene and I spent the last five years rooming together on the road games. We complemented each other on and off the field. Gene is a naturally gifted athlete. Gene's ability only increased when he came here to play football. He was one of the best linebackers this school has ever had.

Gene is with no doubt a Magistrate. If one asks Gene a question, especially about himself, one must be prepared for a loooooong response. He definitely thinks he is the best with words. Others think he's great. I know all his lines. After all, I am one of his best friends.

My goal with Gene is one that I haven't had much success with. Size, strength, and quickness are three important qualities when one moves into Division 1 level of college football. In order to get bigger and faster, Gene started using about half a dozen chemical substances. I never told Gene what to do while we were playing. After all, I tried the same stuff for a twelve-week period. Therefore, from experience and friendship, I felt I had a right to talk to him. Gene had been using the juice [chemicals or steroids] for over three years.

When our eligibility was gone, Gene kept using the juice. Gene isn't physically addicted to the juice; he has a psychological addiction. He thinks he looks bigger and better when he is using it. It isn't that the juice makes you look better; it just gets you to the point you want to be at but at an accelerated rate.

Gene turned twenty-three last November. On his birthday, Gene was no longer covered on his parents' insurance. Prior to his birthday, he went in for a complete physical examination. He told me the doctor said he had inflammation of the liver. He was still on the juice. I knew it. The doctor knew it, and a select group of guys in the gym knew it.

Being Gene's friend, spending ten years together as friends, and five years together as partners on and off the field, I told him what I thought the only way I knew how. I called him a stupid son of a bitch and told him he was going to kill himself. I asked what his mom and pop would do if he was gone. I asked him what his little brother, Justin, would do if he was gone. Justin idolizes him.

Gene isn't completely off the juice, but at least he is down to only one drug. I don't think there will be success until he is thoroughly chemical free. Every once in a while, he forgets his goal of independence. So every once in a while, I get in his face and remind him what he needs to do. After all, it's a sickness—he is addicted. The day is coming, but we haven't been completely successful yet.

This touching story shows the sensitive, open side of a communicator who is clearly a Magistrate. It also shows the Magistrate's absolute commitment to persuasion. There are many other factors influencing Gene's drug addiction, but Nick assumes that his powers of persuasion will ultimately make the difference. I hope he's right.

The Magistrate isn't quite as intimidating or abrupt as the Noble, although he or she can be overbearing. This is probably because verbosity and analysis are the dominating characteristics of Magistrates. Thus, they will tell you how they feel about an issue, but their opinion tends to be floated in a sea of words.

Magistrates are concerned with their own rhetoric, but they don't feel the need to be totally honest all of the time. If they think you can "take it," they will "tell you like it is." If they don't think you can take it or the issue isn't important, they will soften the way they tell you that you are wrong; they will, however, always let you know you are wrong. A personal story will illustrate this point. As you read the story, keep in mind that the event took place during the Persian Gulf conflict, and because there are three major military bases near my home in Palm Springs, it is not unusual to see war planes flying overhead.

Vala and I are having lunch on my patio as a bomber flies overhead. We both marvel at the structure, and Vala comments that the jet will be landing at the Palm Springs airport, which is approximately two miles away. I indicate that a bomber jet would not land at this airport, and I suggest that the pilots are probably headed for the air force base just over the mountain. Vala tries to convince me that she is right but gives up after a while.

Following lunch Vala states that she is going to take a quick run to the store for soda. I tell her there is a whole case of soda in the pantry. Vala says it's not the kind she wants, and she leaves.

Vala returns nearly an hour later, and when I ask what took her so long, she calmly replies, "I was at the airport climbing up on the bomber that didn't land there. It was quite a thrill."

This is an example of the Magistrate in action. This was not an important issue, but Vala had to prove she was right. Can you see where this Magistrate characteristic could cause some problems in an interpersonal or work relationship? It didn't cause a problem between Vala and me because she is a dear friend and I accept the fact that she is one of the strongest Magistrates I know. In fact, she is such a strong Magistrate that I can be a totally obnoxious Noble when I'm with her, and it doesn't faze her at all. This, however, isn't the way things work in the workplace.

Steve is an extremely bright young supervisor in the aerospace industry. He is at the top of his class in his M.B.A. program, and he loves the process of argumentation. He is stimulated and challenged by a good debate, but he can be overbearing when attempting to make his points.

Steve and several other supervisors are called into a meeting with Ruth to discuss some employee problems. Steve doesn't report to Ruth, but she is one step higher than he, so she technically is his superior. During the meeting, Steve began to debate the course of action Ruth was outlining. He began to play the devil's advocate and suggested retaliatory actions that are employee might take. Their voices began to escalate as they both tried to force their position on the rest of the group.

STEVE: If I'm the employee, and you start putting those sorts of restrictions on me, then I'm going to start losing my loyalty. I'll start slowing down, producing less than I'm capable of producing.

RUTH: Then I'll write you up. I'll reduce your hours. You'll get time off without pay.

STEVE: Then I'll start sabotaging the projects, or I'll start marshaling the troops together to block your efforts.

RUTH: (Shouting) Then I'll fire you.

STEVE: (Shouting back) Then I'll sue you.

The room fell silent.

RUTH: I'm going to write you up for this.

STEVE: For what? I'm just trying to bring up some of the points we need to be concerned with.

RUTH: You're insubordinate.

STEVE: I wasn't being insubordinate. I was just trying to play the role of devil's advocate. I'm trying to show you how the workers think and how they will respond.

Ruth complained to her boss. Her boss went to Steve's boss, Steve was forced to sign an official reprimand, and he was given time off without pay for insubordination and being "argumentative."

After the reprimand meeting where Steve was not allowed to say anything in his own defense, Ruth's boss told Steve, "I wanted to fire you, but your record is too good." Steve's record is more than just good; it's outstanding. But his Magistrate style of communication stopped his rising star. He had to press his point. He had to prove that he was "right, " and it cost him his career. He may have been totally right in his analysis of the problem Ruth was presenting, but the way he stated his position caused him significant harm.

Everyone lost in this situation. If Steve had a valid point to make, it was lost, and the company will suffer the consequences of an environment that discourages open debate and discussion. Steve kept his job but lost his credibility and marred his perfect record. He is now looking for another job, and another American organization has lost a good employee because the people in charge don't understand the importance of communication style. This entire incident could have and should have been handled better.

Like the Socratic, the Magistrate feels a need to help you see the "truth." Unlike the Socratic, the Magistrate does not tend to use the Socratic question-and-answer technique to get others to accept a particular point of view. Rather, the Magistrate will provide a lengthy lecture in an attempt to "teach" you the "correct" answer.

Win at All Cost

Magistrates can be distinguished from dominant-style Socratics by listening to the way they handle debate and discussion. Dominant-style Socratics actively engage in debate and discussion with others. They find the exchange of ideas and verbal competition exciting. For the Socratic, the thrill of winning the argument comes from matching his or her verbal agility against that of the opponent. If the opponent lacks the rhetorical sophistication to engage in the game of words, the Socratic takes no thrill in winning. The Magistrate simply wants to win the debate and isn't interested in your argument. Magistrates sound like Socratics because they present the same lengthy, detailed, prima facie case, but they differ from Socratics in that they don't expect or want a rebuttal. They will interrupt you, talk over you, or engage in Noble hit-and-run tactics by leaving the room. This is another example of the simultaneous use of Noble (hit and run) and Socratic (prima facie case building) characteristics. The bottom line is that the Magistrate will present the argument but doesn't want to hear your argument. The Magistrate is driven by the need to win the argument; nothing else matters. If you listen, you can hear this pattern when Magistrates speak.

Another example of the simultaneous use of differing characteristics is that Magistrates manage to avoid absolute and categorical statements (Socratic) while still being abrupt and certain when speaking (Noble). For example, the Noble will say,

"This will never work!"

The Socratic will say,

"There are a number of issues that will determine the feasibility of this project. First, we should consider the time involved, and the number of people we will need to produce a quality product within the time allotted. If we then consider . . . etc., etc., etc., then it may be reasonable to assume that the chances of success may be somewhat slim. This, of course, does not rule out the possibility of success, but it does raise some serious doubts. My personal opinion on the matter is that it probably won't work. You may have a different opinion that we should discuss."

The Magistrate will say,

"The chances for success are slim. Let me explain why I question the feasibility of the project. First, there is the problem of time combined with our manpower situation. We don't appear to have enough time given the number of people. Even if we were to push our people, the quality of the product becomes questionable. If we then consider . . . etc., etc., etc., then it is reasonable to assume that success is questionable. My personal opinion on the matter is that it won't work."

Read the three statements out loud. Listen for the sound of difference, and listen for the distinctive sound of certainty in the Magistrate's words. Like the Noble, the bottom line or conclusion is presented first, and there is certainty in how the ideas are expressed. Like the Socratic, the entire thought process is presented. Unlike the Socratic, however, there is no request for input from the other person.

Do As I Say, Not As I Do

The Magistrate is the one communicator who doesn't necessarily want the other person to sound as he sounds. That is, Magistrates display one behavior but expect the opposite behavior from the other person. For example, they avoid the use of categorical and either-or statements, but they expect yes-no responses from the other person. In addition, they engage in information overload, but they expect **you** to provide the bare facts when giving directions or sharing information. In short, they talk, but you should listen.

Think back to the example of Ruth and Steve. Ruth is a Magistrate, but she would not accept the same style from Steve. Also think of Nick and Gene. Nick is a Magistrate, but he was critical of that same style displayed by Gene.

The Peacock Strut

Perhaps the greatest Magistrate strength is the ability to be concerned with the bottom line and the details. As a result, Magistrates produce a polished product without the help of others and can be viewed as totally competent individuals. But even this seemingly positive characteristic turns out to be a double-edged sword. The Magistrate's self-contained abilities cause the other person to think of him or her as a know-it-all. Indeed, he or she may know it all, but a blatant display of knowledge tends to serve as a source of irritation—as opposed to admiration—for the other person.

Magistrates tend to think of themselves as experts—on just about everything. They assimilate information quickly and then repeat this information to others as if the knowledge originated with the Magistrate.

Pat is a singer. She's been around forever, she knows just about everyone, she has tons of stories to tell about the old days, and she provides her opinion and advice — in great detail — on any topic. She is the ne plus ultra Magistrate. Jason arrives at the recording studio and introduces his friend Amanda to Pat. He tells Pat that Amanda works for Neil Diamond.

PAT: Neil Diamond? That's great. He's a hell of a nice guy. Great songwriter but not the greatest singer.

Amanda is taken aback and a bit offended by the remark. Pat attempts to justify her statement.

PAT: Hey, I'm not saying anything bad. I know him. He's a great guy, and he's one hell of a songwriter, but he doesn't have the greatest voice in the world. I remember when he first hit town. No one wanted to hire him, but he writes . . . boy can he write, and that's how he got started. They wanted his songs.

Pat continued to go into detail about what transpired during that time. She wasn't making anything up. She knew her facts, but Amanda didn't find any of it impressive. Later Jason took Amanda aside and said, "Hey, look. I know she's overbearing, but if you're ever in trouble or need help with anything, Pat is the one to call. She may be obnoxious, but she's almost never wrong."

Pat will tell you she's <u>never</u> wrong.

Yes, the Magistrate is very much like a peacock. The beauty and grace of this magnificent creature is marred by the cackling sounds emoted when he spreads his colorful tail feathers and begins to strut and prance.

Magistrates tend to have the most difficulty dealing with people at work. When I mention this in my seminars, the Magistrates smile, shake their heads, and say, "Yeah; my boss tells me I rub people the wrong way." Like Steve, Magistrates are often described as argumentative, and they often find themselves in fights, both verbal and physical.

The Great Orator

Magistrates create a dramatic and animated style of communication by combining their Socratic affinity for words and well-developed vocabularies with the wide-sweeping nonverbal gestures that are typically associated with the Noble sparse usage of words. Great orators and actors emerge when the simultaneous use of these differing characteristics is perfected. If you think of Richard Burton and Vanessa Redgrave, you will get a sense of the oratorical style of Magistrate communicators.

Read portions of Earl's speech below and listen for the oratorical sophistication of the Magistrate. Let me first, however, set the stage.

In my graduate seminar in human resources management, I have the students debate controversial social issues that affect business and organizations. The assignment is designed to help develop logical and analytical thinking and speaking skills, and I encourage the students to take the position that is actually contrary to their own beliefs. If a student is in favor of a particular resolution, he or she will speak against the issue.

Earl was the first affirmative speaker the night when the topic was, "Resolved: English should be the official language of the United States of America." Some of the students in the class got a big kick out of Earl, and some of the students found his Magistrate style of communicating irritating. He did tend to be argumentative, but his outlandish remarks were often very humorous. He usually came to class in shorts and a t-shirt, but the night of the debate, he arrived in an expensive three-piece suit and stoically sat in the front of the room eagerly awaiting the beginning of the debate. He stood up and slowly but confidently strolled to the podium. He paused, looked directly at the audience, pulled out a small American flag from behind his back, placed it on the front of the podium, and with all the grace, poise, and style reminiscent of Aristotle himself, he delivered the following words:

"America, God bless her soul, is a great nation. She is a nation with a diverse population whose inhabitants originate from many sources. This has created a great challenge for her—a challenge so great that a lesser nation could not face it. America must be a culture of many cultures. She must allow her children to maintain and freely express their different cultural heritages. At the same time, however, she must cause the vastly different groups to bond into one single functional unit. This has been attempted by the establishment of widespread patriotism and the belief that her free and democratic system is the best known to mankind. But one thing has caused America to fall short of her goal. That one thing is her failure to establish one common and dominant way for her children to communicate. The failure to establish English as the official and dominant language has caused a great harm to America. That harm grows worse."

Earl spoke with great passion, and he was careful to support all of his assertions with evidence. He used quotations, statistics, illustrations, and metaphors to build his prima facie case, and he delivered his message with style and grace. As he came to the end of his speech, he lowered his voice and concluded,

"English has always been a part of becoming American, but more so in the past than in the present. The relevant ease of communication in a single language has provided a kind of national glue—a common thread to the creation and development of our nation. Our nation is spread over a wide area and harbors diverse interests, beliefs, and national origins. A threat to that common bond has emerged in the increasingly strident political campaign for separate foreign-language teaching. Thank goodness, most immigrants do not support such an effort. The bilingual system fails students and society as a whole. It is a system of cultural maintenance—not language acquisition.

> *Estas en los estados unidos—apprendre la lingua!*
> *Vous êtes au les États unis—apprener la langue!*
> You are in the United States—learn the language!

Baseball, hot dogs, Mom's apple pie, and the English language. America—the beautiful—her flag—long may it wave."

He picked up the flag and waved it above his head. The room was silent, and then everyone—including those arguing the opposite view—broke into applause. They didn't applaud his ideas; they applauded the way he expressed those ideas. The Magistrate can indeed be a master orator.

If you want to witness this sound for yourself, rent a copy of the movie video *Patton.* George C. Scott's speech in front of the huge American flag is a prime example of the Magistrate style of communication.

The Double-edged Sword

Perhaps one of the Magistrate's most endearing qualities is that he or she says the most outlandish things. Nobles say what other people only think; but Magistrates go one step further. They personally self-disclose while saying things that other people only think. They openly express their prejudices, and they won't hesitate to comment on their own inadequacies or failure. They make good use of humor when they do this, and from this perspective, they are entertaining communicators. They have the ability to take center stage and are memorable speakers. They are memorable, but that can be good or bad, because they are double-edged sword communicators. Magistrates are intense people, and as a result, others have intense reactions to them; we love them or hate them.

Think of David Letterman. It's hard to take a middle-of-the-road position on Mr. Letterman. You either love him, or his style drives you right up the wall.

It is possible to love and hate this double-edged sword communicator at the same time. I love having Magistrates in my classes because they do make the most outlandish comments, and I can count on them to get a good discussion going. But—and this is a big but—I hate it when they come in to argue about a grade.

HOW TO GET MAGISTRATES TO DO WHAT YOU WANT

Like the three dominant-style communicators, the Magistrate has a communication premise that guides his or her behaviors:

The Magistrate Communication Premise

Magistrates are concerned with rhetoric, the analysis of detail, and the straightforward presentation of opinions and information. They are paradoxical communicators who simultaneously display differing verbal characteristics, but they expect a dissimilar style of communication from others.

In attempting to explain, predict, and control the Magistrate or to be able to control your own style-associated behaviors if you are a Magistrate, it is imperative that you understand the Noble and the Socratic styles of communication. If you skipped those chapters, go back and read them. The Magistrate doesn't use Noble in one situation and Socratic in another. Rather, he or she weaves the two styles together to create a unique blended style characterized by the simultaneous use of differing characteristics. Thus, in order to distinguish the Magistrate from the Noble or the Socratic, it is important that you be able to identify his or her paradoxical communication characteristics found listed on the following page and hear the best and the worst of two worlds.

The Magistrate's Simultaneous Use of Differing Characteristics

The Magistrate:

Is direct and straightforward but also is analytical and verbose

Tends to be tactful but also provides honest opinions

Presents a prima facie case but also engages in hit-and-run communication

Avoids absolute and categorical statements but also is abrupt and certain when speaking

Focuses on the main idea but also presents the entire thought process

Avoids either-or statements but also expects yes-no responses from the other person

Engages in information overload but also expects minimum information from the other person

Is concerned with the bottom line but also is concerned with details

Has an affinity for words but also uses wide, sweeping nonverbal gestures

Can be a very impressive or a very irritating speaker

Is a double-edged sword communicator who elicits intensive reactions from others

Unlike the Noble, the Magistrate:

Avoids the use of absolute statements

Can be overbearing

Is totally committed to winning the argument

Unlike the Socratic, the Magistrate:

Tends to avoid input from the other person

Tends to avoid the Socratic question-and-answer technique of persuasion

Magistrate Strengths

An awareness of these characteristics can help you identify the Magistrate and enable you to distinguish this blended-style communicator from the dominant-style Noble or Socratic communicator. It may take a bit longer to pinpoint this style, but if you listen and watch carefully, you can hear the simultaneous use of differing characteristics. You can work with these blended-style characteristics to guide and control the outcome of the interaction. In gaining control, it is important to recognize the strengths of the Magistrate style of communication.

Rhetorical sophistication and animation. The Magistrate has the ability to be a great orator. He or she combines the Socratic's well-developed vocabulary with the Noble's energetic and entertaining nonverbal gestures to create the potential for oratorical excellence.

Focus and analysis. The Magistrate can identify the central issue and is able to see the issue from many different perspectives.

Thoroughness and credibility. The Magistrate is viewed as a totally competent individual because he or she produces a polished final product and speaks with confidence, authority, and from a base of knowledge.

Illustration and organization. The Magistrate's strength as a negotiator, arbitrator, writer, or speaker stems from his or her ability to paint visual pictures with words and to organize thoughts and ideas.

Magistrate Weaknesses

The problem areas of any style prevent the other person from listening to or being persuaded by the message. In some instances, the problem area actually causes the other person to do the opposite of what you are advocating. Magistrates tend to have the following communication problems:

Verbosity and inattentiveness. The Magistrate has a tendency to talk and not listen but nevertheless expects the other person to listen and not talk. These behaviors create a closed, hostile, and defensive communication climate.

Arrogance. The Magistrate has a tendency to lecture the other person or to speak in a patronizing voice, which increases interpersonal conflict.

Rudeness. The Magistrate has a tendency to interrupt, talk over, and ignore what the other person has said.

Dogmatism. Magistrates have a tendency to be directive and dictatorial. They issue orders or directives and expect others to follow without question or debate.

Intolerance. The Magistrate tends to be intolerant of his or her own style of communication. Magistrates expect the other person to respond as a Noble or Reflective, and expect the other person to be very attentive despite their own inattentiveness.

The Magistrate is the one communicator who doesn't expect the other person to communicate in a similar manner. The Magistrate expects the other person to respond as a Noble or as a Reflective; however, the Magistrate will not be persuaded by a Reflective effort. Thus, the Noble style of communication is the key to controlling the outcome of an interaction with a Magistrate. The Magistrate can be persuaded by a solid Socratic analysis, but you must first get him or her to listen to that analysis, and you do that by being assertive. You may find it necessary to say,

"Hold on a minute, Herb. I have something I need to say on this subject. I listened to you, and now I'd like you to listen to me. I have two points I want to make. I want you to listen to those two points, and then tell me how you feel about them."

If you are a Reflective and think this is too assertive, you might say,

> "Herb, I find your analysis very interesting. I don't happen to agree
> with all of your points, and I would like you to listen to my analysis as
> I have listened to yours. May I proceed?"

One of these statements will get your foot in the normally closed door of the Magistrate. You may have to remind him or her that it was agreed that you could speak without interruption, and then you must be prepared to listen as he or she provides a very certain and yet Socratic response to your assertions. You must continue to assert yourself throughout the interaction and be able to shift from Noble to Socratic, and vice versa, as the encounter progresses.

I was speaking with John, one of my M.B.A. students, who is currently teaching high school English. He was describing the "run-ins" he was having with his principal. In Los Angeles, like everywhere else, there are a lot of problems with the school system. John felt obligated to verbalize these problems and to tell the principal how to improve the situation. John was recounting the arguments that he and the principal had engaged in because he wanted to know if I thought the principal would deny him tenure. I tried to explain that the principal had the power to deny him tenure and that if he didn't control the dictatorial aspects of his Magistrate style, he could lose his job. John kept talking over me, so I finally put my fingers on his mouth and quietly said, "Shhh. Stop talking for a minute and listen to what I am saying."

John stopped talking and listened as I gave him some advice about how to begin to repair the rift between his principal and him. John did listen, but the advice came too late. The next week John came to class and said, "You were right. He fired me."

I was able to put my hand on John's mouth without offending him because Magistrates don't mean to be offensive. To the contrary, they want you to like them, and they want you to think of them as special. That could be why they are so committed to winning or being right. They think if they are right, you will have more respect for them. What I am saying here is that the Magistrate will not punch you in the nose if you tell him or her to be quiet so you can talk. Magistrates want to be loved like everyone else. You have to be willing to hit them between the eyes with your message.

It is possible to persuade a Magistrate, but you can't be mild-mannered in your attempt. The following example is of a Magistrate being persuaded.

David is a claims manager for a major insurance company. Brian is another claims manager who is a lawyer. David identifies Brian as a Magistrate. He describes Brian as "superficially authoritarian who typically wins his arguments by the sheer volume of facts at his command."

David wants to convince Brian of the correctness of his view on a legal matter so that they might proceed with a resolution to a contractual claim. David explains his approach:

"When I gained the opportunity to get a word in edgewise, I quickly stated the issue, brought up some background legal issues (the nature of the claim so defined), and cited a case on the issue that established the precedent in the matter. I left him with the task of verifying my reference, which he did. This made it easy for him to accept this point so we could proceed with the resolution of other issues."

David typically communicates as a Senator, but in this situation, he used Magistrate techniques to persuade a Magistrate, and he was successful. He concisely presented a prima facie case, allowed Brian to accept ownership of the decision, and left him with the task of verifying the reference. In doing this, he met Brian's need to be "right."

In summary, the following three rules (added to the guidelines presented earlier in the book) will help you control the Magistrate:

1. Be assertive and use the Noble style to control the flow of conversation and information.

2. Be prepared to listen to a lengthy but certain Socratic response.

3. Flatter Magistrates. Let them know that you think highly of their opinions before you attempt to persuade. Indicate that acceptance of your position will enhance their credibility. Then give them the opportunity to research or verify the points you raise. Once they do this, they will come back and offer the solution as if it were their own.

When they do come back and present your idea as their own, don't argue. Just accept the fact that you successfully used communication style to get the Magistrate to do what you wanted him or her to do.

It is intriguing to watch and listen to two Magistrates attempting to persuade each other. At minimum, the interaction is tense, even when they agree on an issue. When they are on polar sides of an issue, the word "tense" takes on a whole new meaning. Perhaps the best way to get a feeling for the verbal intensity generated by two Magistrates is to visualize a racquetball match between two A players. Both players attempt to hold center court, and each player attempts to move the other out of center court by hitting the ball hard, fast, and low. Neither player will give the other breathing room for fear that center court will be relinquished, and the spectators cringe as the flailing rackets come within centimeters of drawing blood.

Two Magistrates can be very exciting to watch. Can they persuade each other? I've never seen it happen, but that doesn't mean it can't or hasn't happened. The chances that it will happen are greatly increased if one person attempts to control the communication style component in the interaction. One thing is certain: the Magistrate who has been persuaded will be back for round two and an attempt at being the persuader.

How Magistrates Can Get Others to Do What They Want

You will notice that persuasion is not listed as a communication strength for the Magistrate although it is a strength for the dominant-style Socratic.

This is because Magistrates vacillate between being powerfully persuasive in the public arena and totally inept in interpersonal encounters. As eloquent orators, Magistrates can persuade an audience of thousands to move mountains, but in the one-on-one interaction where dialogue is supposed to be a two-way street, the Magistrate can be a dismal failure.

In the interpersonal encounter, persuasion in an interactive process; both parties must converse, and both must take part in the game of words. Since the Magistrate doesn't play the game of verbal agility, he or she does not succeed as a persuader — not even with the Reflective. Thus, if you are a Magistrate and you would like to control the outcome of the interaction, you must add three guidelines to those already presented in the previous chapters. In fact, let's call these rules, not guidelines:

Rules to Help the Magistrate Be Persuasive

1. You must listen and not just talk.
2. You must allow the other person to present a rebuttal to your prima facie case.
3. You don't always have to win.

Mario followed this advice and found that it helped improve his relationship with his wife.

In the past when my wife and I had discussions, I would almost always dominate the conversation. Last week my wife came home after a very trying day where some things back at the corporate offices had been said about her that really distressed her. We started to discuss the problems as usual, and as usual, I had all the the answers — being a Magistrate. But I began to think back to our HRM [human resources management] class and what I had learned. I realized that she did not want to hear me or any of my solutions. She just wanted to talk. I sat patiently and listened as she unloaded her terrible day. Afterward my wife thanked me for listening and for being there.

This is a prime example of what this book is all about. Magistrates constantly talk their way into trouble because talking without listening is part of their style. If they can control this style weakness, they have a shot at talking their way out of trouble. If they can control this weakness, draw on their communication style strengths, and meet the communication needs of the other person in the interaction by following the guidelines presented in this book, they can control the outcome of the interaction.

Chapter 7

The Candidate:
The Good, the Bad, and
the Hardly Ever Ugly

THE CANDIDATE SOUND

The Candidate is a pleasant, patient, and talkative communicator who believes that any problem can be solved by talking about it long enough. The dominant characteristics of the Reflective and the Socratic are blended to create a communicator who is warm, supportive, analytical—and verbose. Candidates are soft-spoken storytellers, who truly want the other person to like them and who try not to hurt the other person's feelings but will talk incessantly—albeit tenderly—to prove a point. To try to visualize the Candidate sound, think of Betty White as Rose on "The Golden Girls" or Joe Regalbuto as Frank on "Murphy Brown." For those of you who can remember back this far, think of Georganne on the "Mary Tyler Moore Show" or the lovable Gabby Hayes. On the silver screen, Katherine Hepburn's character in the *African Queen* and Chief Dan George's character in *The Outlaw Josey Wales* will give you a good view of the Candidate in action.

Focus on Liking

The Candidate tries to create a feeling of liking. Even with strangers, the Candidate will attempt to establish a personal relationship by making self-disclosure statements and by narrowing in on the personal aspects of the other person. Candidates really want others to like them. This makes them very vulnerable, and as human beings, we tend to be kinder to vulnerable people. This, in a nutshell, is a key factor that distinguishes the Candidate from the dominant-style Reflective or Socratic. The Reflective focuses on the other person—on making the other person feel good or comfortable. The Socratic focuses on the argument, the issue, the rhetoric of the moment. The Candidate uses rhetoric to focus liking on the self. Information combined with liking is then used to disarm the other person and get him or her to agree with the Candidate's position.

Lovable Chatterbox

The soft-spoken verbosity of this communicator is used to reduce hostility and encourage open communication. A Candidate dealing with a hostile individual will combine the warm, calm Reflective style with the Socratic question-and-answer technique to encourage conversation until the tension is reduced or eliminated. This should place the Candidate high on the list of nominees for a leadership position that requires dealing with difficult people. The Candidate, however, also uses this approach with people who aren't difficult, and this can definitely lead to despair and the desire to place a strip of tape over the lips of this gentle chatterbox.

Perhaps the most talkative of all styles, the Candidate is easier to tolerate than the Socratic or Magistrate because he or she does not speak with arrogance. The Socratic and Magistrate air of certainty tend to be missing in the speech of the Candidate. He or she will make use of the Socratic question-and-answer technique to lead you to a forgone conclusion, but there is no apparent impatience with your inability to reach or accept that conclusion. The Candidate will simply continue to talk, even if it seems to take forever. Like the Reflective, the Candidate will walk away from the situation if hostility begins to accelerate, but like the Socratic, he or she will come back for a second, third, fourth, ad infinitum attempt at the persuasive effort. Like the Magistrate, Candidates are committed to winning the argument, but they do it in a nicer way. As a result, the nonthreatening approach of this blended-style communicator makes it difficult for even the Noble to become angry with these repeated attempts at persuasion.

In John Houston's classic film, *The African Queen,* Katherine Hepburn (Rosie) provides an excellent example of the Candidate's pleasant powers of persuasion. Rosie is an intelligent woman who knows exactly what she wants, but she doesn't come right out and say it like a Noble and she doesn't use the question-and-answer technique as if she were a teacher. Rather, she presents her thoughts as questions to which she ostensibly does not know the answers. She speaks with a kind, slow, inquisitive tone, but she in fact does know the answers to her questions. In the following scene with Charlie, played by Humphrey Bogart, Rosie has decided they should launch their own private attack on the *Louisa,* a formidable German warship. Listen as she persuades Charlie:

ROSIE: Mr. Aurnot? What are these big, round torpedolike things?

CHARLIE: Oh, them? Them's oxygen hydrogen cylinders, Miss.

ROSIE: Mr. Aurnot?

CHARLIE: I'm still here, Miss. There ain't much any other place I could be on a 30-foot boat.

ROSIE: You're a machinist aren't you. I mean wasn't that your position at the mine?

CHARLIE: Yes. Jack of all trades, master or none, or so they say.

ROSIE: Could you make a torpedo?

CHARLIE: How's that, Miss?

ROSIE: Could you make a torpedo?

CHARLIE: A torpedo? Ask me to make a dreadnought, and do it right . . . A torpedo, Miss . . . you really don't know what you're asking. You see there ain't nothing so complicated as the insides of a torpedo. There are gyroscopes, compressed air chambers, compensating . . .

ROSIE: Yes, but aren't all those things, those gyroscopes and things, there only to make it go? Aren't they?

CHARLIE: Yeah. Yeah, go and hit what it's aimed at.

ROSIE: Well, we've got the *African Queen*.

CHARLIE: How's that, Miss?

ROSIE: If we were to fill those cylinders with that blasting gelatin, and then fix them so they would stick out over the end of the boat, and then run the boat against the side of a ship, they would go off just like a torpedo, wouldn't they?

CHARLIE: Yeah. Yeah, if they had detonators in the end.

ROSIE: We could—what do you call it—get up a good head of steam, and point the launch toward the ship, and just when she hits, we could dive off. Couldn't we?

Rosie persuades Charlie to begin their voyage and eventual attack on the *Louisa*. She doesn't raise her voice, and she doesn't order. She just quietly questions her way to the logical conclusion.

Talk, Talk, and Even More Talk

Like the Magistrate, the Candidate draws upon and uses a much larger set of characteristics than does a dominant-style communicator. Also like Magistrates, Candidates are more difficult to identify during the first few minutes of conversation. Unlike Magistrates, Candidates are not perceived as domineering communicators. They are perceived as *dominating* communicators because they dominate the conversation. Candidates, however, do not have the pushy or forceful tendencies of Socratics or Magistrates and as a result are not considered domineering, just talkative.

The Candidate is simultaneously warm, supportive, calm, and verbose. The Reflective is warm, supportive, and calm but not verbose. In addition, the Candidate lacks the listening skills of the dominant-style Reflective and as a result will dominate the conversation with incessant talk.

Chief Dan George in his role as Lone Watie in *The Outlaw Josey Wales* provides a humorous example of the Candidate's tendency to engage in talk, talk, and more talk. In one scene, Josey Wales (Clint Eastwood) sneaks up behind Lone Watie and puts a gun to his head. Lone Watie speaks in a slow, soft, warm, nonthreatening tone. He begins to explain why Josey was able to sneak up on him even though he is an Indian. He tells about the white man who has been sneaking up on Indians for years; he tells how his wife and two sons died on the Trail of Tears; he tells of his visit to Washington, what he wore, and the words that were uttered by the Secretary of the Interior. He even provides the names of the other Indians who went to Washington with him, and recites the newspaper headlines. He stops talking when he realizes Josey Wales has fallen asleep during his oration.

Later in the movie, Lone Watie unites with an Indian woman who talks even more than he, driving Josey to plead, "Can't you get her to shut up?" Josey, like most of the other Clint Eastwood characters, is a Noble.

Masters of the Parenthetical Aside

Because the Socratic talks in footnotes, the listener often gets lost in the conversation. The Candidate uses so many footnotes and so many parenthetical asides that the Candidate also gets lost. Candidates give so much additional, and often irrelevant, information about whatever or whomever they are talking about that they have to stop and say, "Why am I telling you this? I'm sorry, I got off the track. What were we talking about?"

Candidates often use so many parenthetical asides that I find myself giggling while they are speaking. I am amused by the fact that they can remember all of these details, and I am even more amused by the fact that they think I need to know all of this information.

Blending the Best of Two Worlds

Because so many of the Socratic and Reflective characteristics are compatible, the Candidate is not identified by the simultaneous use of differing characteristics as is the Magistrate. Rather, Candidates are identified by their ability to use Reflective techniques to modify or soften their Socratic tendencies. For example, Candidates view argumentation as desirable and constructive (Socratic), but they will make less than truthful statements to maintain the communication decorum (Reflective). They would prefer not to do this, and they will attempt to say what they really feel, but they will "give in" and tell you what you want to hear if you get too pushy. Similarly, Candidates openly engage in discussion, negotiation, debate, and arbitration, but they will withhold negative opinions to avoid open conflict. Again, they will begin by stating their negative opinion in a very tactful manner, but if the conflict accelerates, they will not restate their opinion. True to their Reflective nature, however, they will come back later to regenerate the discussion and advance the persuasive effort.

Listen to the Candidate sound in the following story, and witness the successful use of some of the Candidate characteristics.

In my last job, I was an account executive at the design division of an advertising agency. Part of my job was to present the client with various creative campaigns, and sell them on the best one. This was not always easy, especially if the concept was unusual or different. After I presented the concept to my client contacts, they presented it to their bosses if they felt it was acceptable. I was not included in those final presentations.

My creative team came up with a very different concept and style that the client had not used before. We felt they probably would reject it because it was unproved. The client was insecure about new ideas and refused to present anything that would not please the big bosses. Many of our concepts had died because they couldn't get past the client.

I knew this particular client quite well. I knew his likes, dislikes, fears, and professional background and the structure of his company. I knew the attitude of the big bosses, and I felt the concept would sell if it was pushed.

My client was reluctant to push, but I convinced him that it was in his best interest to do so. I think I knew just how far I could go, and I went right to the line. I said, "I know using scorn to sell a fragrance is a bit unusual, but let me share a personal story with you to illustrate how an irritating ad can actually motivate a person to buy a product. Do you remember those "ring around the collar" advertisements? Well, every time I saw one of those ads my blood would boil. To begin with, no one is so rude as to tell someone they have a ring around their collar, and even if they did, they wouldn't act like it was the end of the world. It's not like they discovered the person had leprosy or something. Secondly, they always made it seem like it was the woman's fault that the man had a ring around his color. I would just fume every time I saw one of those ads. Well, one day I went to a store to buy that product—not because I liked the ad but specifically because I was irritated by it. In my mind, I wanted to know that this product was so good that I could rationalize the irritation away, or I wanted to know that it couldn't live up to its claims, and I could file a false advertising charge. The same sort of principle is working here. The scorned woman concept will be irritating because it will hit a familiar cord in a lot of people. I know it will make me think about Jim. He broke my heart, but when I think of him, I think of why I was drawn to him. Men will have a similar reaction. Think of yourself. Haven't you had an experience where you wished you had been the one to create the scorned woman instead of the other way around? Or maybe you were the one who walked out. Didn't it make you feel just a wee-bit powerful?

I continued presenting the concept in a soft sell, round-about way, and I let the client warm up to it. Then I reinforced the decision and gave the client ammunition to sell the big bosses. I provided him with strategy, costs, art work, and so on. I even gave the client several pep talks to prepare for the big presentation. I did everything I could to support the concept, and to blunt negative reactions.

To make a long story short, I sold the idea to the client, who subsequently sold it to the big bosses.

Disarm the Opponent

The Candidate's persuasive effort differs significantly from that of the dominant-style Socratic. Candidates avoid the use of directive and controlling statements or the logical hypothesis (if-then-therefore) statements. Instead, they use personal self-disclosure statements to disarm the other person. The purpose of this technique is to encourage liking. Once liking has been established, the other person is more inclined to accept the Candidate's position or is more willing to break a rule for the Candidate or simply do what the Candidate requests. Recall the story of Sheila, Dave, and the theater tickets that I provided in Chapter 2.

Listen as Bill describes how Julie used this self-disclosure technique to establish a personal relationship and then how she got him to buy more than he really needed.

This conversation happened to me recently. I work for a beer distributing company. A secondary business we own is a carpet and linoleum company. One Friday night, I was trying to buy a carpet for my own personal use in a rental property. Julie is the salesperson I had to deal with to get this carpet.

I met her on Friday evening at 4:00 P.M. in her office. We spent an hour talking about what party she was going to, what she was going to do this weekend, and so on. We only briefly talked about the purpose of my visit, which was to purchase carpet. At first, this drove me a little crazy because I wanted to get the carpet and get out of there.

An hour later, we went down to the showroom to look at some carpet. I agreed to one of the first carpets I looked at, and then we proceeded to talk about everything but purchasing the carpet. She was really nice. It was like we had known each other all our lives.

We finally agreed on a very cheap price, and it was a done deal. Well almost. After we agreed on the price, she said, "Oh, by the way. You only need sixty square yards, but you have to buy the whole roll to get it at that price." There was about seventy-two square yards in the roll. I agreed to everything she said. When I got home and started thinking about it, I realized I had just been hustled by a Candidate.

I Know Someone Who . . .

Since the focus is on the self for the Candidate, arguments or evidence presented in the persuasive encounter typically center around the Candidate's personal experiences or the experiences of a personal friend. The experiences of strangers, as reported in newspapers or in research, are not offered as stand-alone evidence. For example, dominant-style Socratics will cite research findings as support for their contentions. They will say,

"The research suggests that . . ."

Candidates, however, will cite their own personal research–based conclusions as support for their contentions. They will say,

"I've read a lot of research on this and I believe that . . ."

Thus, the opinion of the self serves as the source of evidence to support a contention for the Candidate. The opinions of others count if—and only if—they are personal friends of the Candidate.

This personal verbosity is both an advantage and disadvantage of the Candidate's style. It is an advantage because it can be a very effective way of reducing hostility and controlling the outcome of interactions. When carried to the extreme, however, the Candidate presents a know-it-all image that is similar to that presented by the Magistrate during his or her less memorable moments.

The Candidate's focus on the self presents the other person with an advantage. The other person can use his or her knowledge of the Candidate's need to be liked as a means for controlling the outcome of the interaction. The other person simply takes the position advanced by the Candidate and paints a negative image of an individual who would support such a position. Since Candidates don't want to be viewed in negative terms, they will back away from their original position, and they can be persuaded to think about and accept alternative positions.

Simon is a Reflective who used this characteristic to win over a reluctant client whom he was able to identify as a Candidate. Notice how he analyzed the situation first and then planned a strategy that would meet the communication needs of a buyer who happens to be a Candidate. I've underlined his communication strategy.

I was trying to establish my clothes design business in the highly competitive London environment. My ultimate goal was to sell my designs in the King's Road. I had targeted a very up-market boutique with an excellent reputation for selling individual styles. My initial research revealed the buyer to be extremely critical of English designers. She preferred buying from trade shows, and she was extremely knowledgeable on all facets of the apparel industry.

An appointment with her was out of the question, since our profile fulfilled all her worst expectations of designers, so I just approached her in the store armed with clothing samples and quoting the names of prestigious buyers whom I had seen the previous week. I very cautiously suggested that the absence of an English designer decreases the stature of a boutique. I said,

"Some of the most recent research figures point to the importance of a design connection. When people are asked to identify the most prestigious boutiques, those with English designers consistently outrank those without. I know if I were a store owner, I would want to be on the top of the prestige list rather than the bottom. I have a very dear friend who even gets invited to social affairs he didn't used to get invited to. Now I don't know if carrying our line was totally responsible for his newly found social prominence, but it certainly didn't hurt him any."

I very concisely told her why she should stock our clothes, and I told her that I had chosen her store because of her ability to select with discrimination. I assured her that only the best stores would carry our line.

To further whet her appetite, I left twenty samples with her for a week. Three days later, she telephoned and placed a 200-piece order and thereby launched a long-term business relationship.

Simon controlled the outcome of the interaction by using the "I know someone who" technique and by taking advantage of the Candidate's need to be liked or thought of in positive terms. He created a scenario that suggested she would be one of the elite if she purchased his product.

Don't You Think . . .

Candidates use their Reflective techniques to soften their harsh Socratic tendencies when attempting to help someone solve a problem. Like the Reflective, Candidates offer help and ask questions. Like the Socratic and unlike the Reflective, they offer solutions. Their solution statements, however, are usually preceded by the words, "Don't you think . . ." Thus, the solution statements are offered as possibilities rather than directives. Furthermore, this approach allows the other person to take ownership of the solution. The other person says, "Yes, as a matter of fact, that is exactly what I thought we should do."

The soft-spoken verbosity and quiet, assertive style allow the Candidate to overcome some of the problems encountered by dominant style-Reflectives. For example, because they have the Socratic affinity for words, they are better able to establish their credibility and are not typically seen as conniving or deceitful. Because they can be assertive, they do not experience the same degree of personal frustration as does the Reflective. They do, however, experience this personal frustration when they are forced to back away from their position as conflict begins to escalate.

If You Can't Win, Then Change the Subject

The Candidate can be distinguished from the Socratic and the Magistrate by listening to the way he or she engages in discussion and debate. Recall that the Socratic presents a prima facie case and expects the other person to present a rebuttal. The Magistrate presents a prima facie case to which no rebuttal is expected. The Candidate does not present a prima facie case. Rather, he or she presents the position statement followed by a series of personal experiences meant to serve as evidence for the truthfulness of the position statement. The Candidate will listen to an opposing position from the other person if it is offered in a similar style but will change the topic if hostility arises. Even if there is no hostility, the Candidate will switch the topic on you if he or she thinks you are beginning to win the debate. Like the Magistrate, however, the Candidate is totally committed to winning the argument, and he or she will come back and visit the issue again.

When All Else Fails, Out-Vocabulary the Opponent

Candidates know a lot of words, and they love to win. When they find they are on the losing end of an argument and the other Candidate tricks haven't worked, they will simply out-vocabulary the other person. They will dig deep into their dictionary of terms and pull out some words that will totally baffle their verbal opponent. The other person will typically back off rather than admit he or she doesn't understand what the Candidate is saying.

HOW TO GET CANDIDATES TO DO WHAT YOU WANT

Interesting and charming communicators emerge when Candidates combine their affinity for words with their analytical abilities and their desire to create a warm, calm communication climate. Even at their worst, others tend to refer to Candidates as nice people who talk too much.

Like the others, this blended-style communicator has a communication premise that guides his or her behaviors:

The Candidate Communication Premise

Candidates are warm, analytical, and verbose communicators who believe that any problem can be solved with extended conversation. They are persuasive communicators who use rhetoric to disarm the other person and focus liking on the self.

In attempting to explain, predict, and control the Candidate or to be able to control your own style-associated behaviors if you are a Candidate, it is imperative that you understand the Reflective and the Socratic styles of communication. As with the Magistrate, you have to begin hearing the best and the worst of two different styles. If you skipped those chapters, go back and read them. The Candidate doesn't use Reflective in one situation and Socratic in another. Rather, he or she weaves the two styles together to create a unique blended style that sounds very different from the Socratic or the Reflective.

Candidates are identified by their ability to use Reflective techniques to modify or soften their harsh Socratic tendencies and their ability to use Socratic techniques to strengthen their softer Reflective tendencies. Thus, in being able to distinguish the Candidate from the Magistrate, the Reflective, or the Socratic, you must be able to recognize his or her ability to integrate compatible communication characteristics:

The Candidate's Integration of Compatible Characteristics

The Candidate:

Is warm, supportive, analytical and quite verbose

Combines pleasant Reflective style with Socratic question-and-answer techniques

Actively engages the persuasive efforts but will say nothing or say what the other person wants to hear if hostility escalates

Views argumentation as desirable and constructive but will make less-than-truthful statements to maintain the communication decorum

Openly engages in discussion, negotiation, and debate but will avoid conflict by changing the topic

Makes use of personal self-disclosure statements to disarm the other person and encourage liking

Uses rhetoric to focus liking on the self

Uses personal experiences and experiences of personal friends as
   supporting evidence

Uses personal verbosity to reduce hostility

Offers help, asks questions, and provides solutions

Uses the words "don't you think" to turn a solution statement into
   a possible alternative.

Changes the topic if he or she thinks you are going to win the
   argument

Unlike the Reflective, the Candidate:

Is concerned with the feelings of the self rather than the feelings
   of the other

Is not a patient listener

Can be assertive

Unlike the Socratic, the Candidate:

Is persuadable

Avoids directive and controlling statements

Does not present his or her position as a prima facie case

Candidate Strengths

It may take a bit longer to pinpoint this style, but if you listen and watch
carefully, you can hear the Candidate sound and work with it to guide and
control the outcome of the interaction. In gaining control, it is important
to recognize the strengths of the Candidate style of communication:

Rhetorical sophistication and openness.   Candidates use their well-
   developed vocabularies and their ability to create an open communication climate to arbitrate or negotiate interpersonal interactions.

Analysis and conciliation.   Candidates have the ability to see issues
   from many perspectives and are able to help others do the same. Thus,
   they have the potential to be successful problem solvers and peacekeepers.

Persuasiveness. Candidates have the ability to reduce hostility and guide behaviors with the use of words.

Patience and credibility. Candidates tend to think before they act, and they tend to speak from a base of knowledge. Thus, their remarks are usually given consideration, and they avoid unnecessary conflict.

Candidate Weaknesses

The problem areas of any given style prevent the other person from listening to or being persuaded by the message. In some instances, the problem actually causes the other person to do the opposite of what you are advocating. Candidates tend to have the following communication problems:

Verbosity. Candidates have a tendency to be redundant, to engage in nonstop conversation with the self, and to engage in information overload. The other person stops listening because the Candidate talks too much.

Vulnerability. Because of their concern for a pleasant communication decorum and their need to be liked, Candidates become easy prey for the strong-willed. Candidates are verbally attacked because the other person knows they will back down.

Indecisiveness. Also because of their concern for a pleasant communication decorum and their need to be liked, Candidates tend to be indecisive.

Egocentricity. Candidates focus attention on the self and the personal experiences of the self, causing others to perceive them as self-centered.

Rudeness. Candidates don't listen, and they have a tendency to interrupt or talk over the other person.

When attempting to persuade a Candidate, you must be patient and willing to listen. If you attempt to cut the conversation short or if you become overbearing, the Candidate will withdraw into his or her Reflective shell. He or she will say nothing or say what you want to hear, but you will not have persuaded the Candidate. Once you have accepted that you must listen to this chatty communicator, the key to persuasion rests on personal experience. Remember that the Candidate utilizes liking through personal experiences as a persuasive technique. You also must be willing to use this technique. You must allow yourself to be included in the Candidate's world of personal experiences, and you must bring the Candidate into your world of personal experiences. Let me show you what it sounds like when you are able to do this.

Suppose you have a volunteer who is working on raising funds for your organization. In fact, he is the chair of your fund-raising committee and takes a great deal of pride in developing personal contacts. Harry, your fund-raising chairperson, has been very successful, but you have a potential donor who is a very wealthy Noble and a staunch feminist. Her name is Ms. Jerome. You know that Ms. Jerome is intolerant of verbosity, and you suspect that she is more likely to donate if she is approached by another woman. At the same time, you know that Harry believes that he can talk anyone into making a donation. You don't want to usurp Harry's authority, and you don't want to alienate this very valuable volunteer. So how do you persuade Harry to want to send someone else to make the contact? Remember that Harry is a Candidate. On a sheet of paper, write out the words you would use to persuade Harry.

Here is what Lillian actually said to persuade Harry:

LILLIAN: Harry, have you seen Meryl Streep in her new movie *Cry in the Dark?*

HARRY: Yea, Joanie and I saw it last week at the Beverly Center. It was depressing to think about the injustice, but Streep's performance was wonderful.

LILLIAN: Do you remember the scene where she fights with her attorneys over her image, and she tells them that she can't or won't change her style to make the jurors happy?

HARRY: Ummm, yes . . . toward the end of the trial. Yes, I remember. I think she was silly because she could have saved herself if she would have shown some emotion.

LILLIAN: I agree, but that scene reminded me of our fiasco with Mr. Goldmeyer three years ago.

HARRY: (cringing with humorous remembrance) Goldmeyer! I've tried to wipe that incident from my memory bank.

LILLIAN: Yep, we really blew that one. You know, you and I are an awful lot alike. We do really well with people who like to talk and enjoy a good discussion. You are especially good at making friends with some of our hotsy-totsy clients. My weakness and, to some extent, your weak spot is that we have difficulty with the ones who just want to talk about the bottom line.

HARRY: (fondly remembering) Like Goldmeyer . . . that abrasive old coot!

LILLIAN: Well, I hate to tell you this, but we have another Goldmeyer to deal with, only this time it's a she, and she could be our biggest donor ever. She also happens to make Gloria Steinem look like the happy homemaker. Don't you think you should assign her to one of the women on your committee?

HARRY: Oh, I don't know if we have to do that. You know I've worked on some pretty tough cookies before. Do you remember Kathleen McConnell?

LILLIAN: I also remember that you had a few sleepless nights over the beach party incident, and Ms. Jerome would throw you out on your ear if she heard you call her a cookie. You have such a perfect record, and the board will be furious if we lose her. Do you really want to risk that?

HARRY: That is just what I was thinking. I think my best move is to send Sylvia. I'll coach her. If she doesn't reel her in, I'll give it a shot.

Lillian brought Harry into her world of personal experiences, and Lillian put herself into his world of personal experiences. In addition, she suggested that loss of liking might occur with a solution that differed from the one she presented. She allowed him to save face by giving him the chance to claim the solution as his own idea.

Is this manipulative? Of course, it is. But that is what persuasion is all about. Manipulation is negative only if you use it to accomplish evil or if you are deceitful. There was nothing evil about Lillian's goal, and she wasn't deceitful. She believed someone else should make the contact, and she used her knowledge about Harry's communication style to control the outcome of the interaction. She simply paid attention to how she said what she said. It took more time than her usual blunt Noble style would have taken, but her Noble style may have resulted in unnecessary conflict and the loss of a valuable volunteer.

Thus, in attempting to persuade the Candidate, keep the following four rules in mind:

1. Be prepared to have the interaction take some time.
2. Attempt to draw the Candidate into your world of experiences and place yourself in his or her world of experiences.
3. Use the Candidate's need for liking to your advantage. Show the person how doing what you want will make him or her look better.
4. Allow the Candidate to claim the solution as his or her own.

The tension that is present when two Magistrates attempt to persuade each other is missing in the Candidate's persuasive encounter. When two Candidates get together, there is indeed a lot of talking, but the talk is usually pleasant and quite entertaining. There will, of course, be an abundance of anecdotal stories exchanged. Who is most likely to be persuasive? The person with the best and most convincing set of personal experiences.

HOW CANDIDATES CAN GET OTHERS TO DO WHAT THEY WANT

Magistrates tend to be powerfully persuasive in the public arena and totally inept in the interpersonal encounter. The opposite is true of the Candidate. Candidates tend to achieve persuasive success in the interpersonal encounter, particularly if the other person is hostile. The patient, soft-spoken, verbose style of the Candidate creates a calming effect. He or she continues to chat with the other person and skillfully utilizes the Socratic method of teaching to get the other person to bring forth and explain his or her position. As the talk increases, the hostility decreases. Candidates do not do well, however, in the public arena. Their soft-spoken verbosity works against them because the audience gets lost in their quiet sea of words.

As you saw earlier, the Candidate is adept at using rhetoric to disarm the other person and focus liking on the self. This need for liking, however, can serve as a downfall for the Candidate. It is his or her weak spot, and the other person can take total control of the interaction with a personal attack. In addition, the heavy reliance on personal experiences as supporting evidence can weaken the persuasive effort, particularly if the other person is a well-read Socratic. Finally, the Candidate can sabotage his or her own persuasive effort with the same quiet sea of words that inundates the public audience. Thus, if you are a Candidate and you want to control the outcome of the interaction then you must add three rules to those already presented in the previous chapters:

1. You must listen and not just talk.
2. You must be willing to go beyond your own personal world of experiences when attempting to persuade a Noble, Socratic, or Magistrate.
3. You must not let your need to be liked overshadow your persuasive goal in the interpersonal interaction.

The Candidate is perhaps the most persuasive of all communicators. The quiet, rhetorical demeanor allows the Candidate to talk his or her way out of some very difficult situations, but this same demeanor can be responsible for creating interpersonal conflict because the Candidate simply talks too much for some people. The Candidate is the person who can talk his or her way into heaven or hell—depending upon whether he or she follows or ignores the rules I noted.

Chapter 8

The Senator:
Now You See Me,
Now You Don't

THE SENATOR SOUND

The Senator is a chameleon-like, strategic communicator who uses two distinctly different styles of communication to adapt to differing environments. The Senator switches back and forth between being a Noble and a Reflective. The Senator does not blend these two opposing styles together but instead attempts to blend into the environment by allowing the situation to determine which style is appropriate. In one situation the Senator may be totally Noble and in another totally Reflective.

Anyone who watched President George Bush on television during the Desert Storm conflict had an opportunity to view a Senator using both the Noble and Reflective styles in one setting. When President Bush spoke of Saddam Hussein or when he was offering a direct message to Hussein, the style was Noble—direct, curt, and crisp. He used absolute statements and spoke with certainty, using such phrases as "under no circumstances," "there will be no compromise," "this is intolerable," and "we will accept nothing less."

Then Mr. Bush would switch, with his Reflective style emerging as he talked about the people of Iraq and the allied forces. His tone softened, he dropped the absolute statements, and he focused on the personal aspects of the situation, using words like "pride," "concern," "feeling," "sadness," and "love." He talked of prayers and families and frequently said, "My heart goes out to . . ."

As I watched those speeches, I couldn't help but wonder if Mr. Bush mispronounced the name "Saddam" on purpose. Surely one of his advisers must have mentioned that he wasn't pronouncing it correctly. I also couldn't help but wonder if Mr. Bush's normally soft-spoken style caused Mr. Hussein to make his serious error in judgment. Did Hussein refuse to leave Kuwait because he thought Mr. Bush's Reflective style indicated that Bush was weak and indecisive? I believe Mr. Hussein did misjudge President Bush. George Bush does sound like a Reflective most of the time, and people do tend to perceive Reflectives as weak. Surely Hussein knew his military power was inferior to ours. So why did he risk what turned out to be an embarrassingly simple defeat? Perhaps it was because he viewed Mr. Bush as indecisive and too nice to carry through on his ultimatum.

Strategy in Motion

Perhaps the most clever of all communicators, the Senator views communication as a strategy for success or survival. This doesn't mean that Senators are more successful or more satisfied with their communication interactions, only that they make a conscious effort to control their environments with communication style. Listen for the strategic mind of the Senator in Tom's story.

This event occurred at work. I was speaking with a co-worker over the telephone. The other employee is a peer with much more seniority than I. We do not work together usually, but we are sometimes involved with the same project. A project she was working on was receiving very little attention, and our mutual boss asked if I would help out. At a meeting I made some drastic suggestions to address the problem. I said,

"This project needs to be placed first on our list of priorities. We can't treat it as a part-time activity. We need to set up a schedule and hold one person responsible for meeting that schedule."

These suggestions carried an unintentional implication that the job was not being done properly. [Here Tom realizes he was too direct — too Noble — in his approach.] A couple of days after the meeting, the other employee called me to discuss the situation. She did not know that the decision to go with my proposal had already been made. She started by making some suggestions as to what she thought should be done and how to do it. I let her have the floor until she was done — with no interruptions — and then, using as many of her thoughts [here Tom gains the information advantage] as possible, I slowly described what was happening with the project:

"I appreciate this information. It's very valuable. We will do the things you have suggested, and I'm sure that will help us meet our target date. I'm pleased with your selection of personnel, and I'm certainly going to use them. I'm adding some people simply because the scope of the project is bigger than you had originally planned."

I saw no reason to alienate her by saying my proposal had been accepted [here Tom is using his Reflective characteristics and the Hooded-Eye] instead of hers. I was straightforward with the information I gave her, I didn't try to flower the subject, and she seemed to appreciate the courtesy. There have been no repercussions.

Senators, more so than any of the other communicators, think before they speak. They think about the situation and whom they are speaking with, and then they choose the style they think will work best.

The Chameleon Approach

Senators are difficult communicators to identify for three primary reasons. First, there are fewer of them around; thus, it is harder to spot and analyze them. Less than 10 percent of the American population has developed the Senator style of communication. Second, Senators typically don't use both styles—Noble and Reflective—in the situation; thus you must observe them in more than one situation to know you are talking with a Senator. Finally, and perhaps more important, Senators may be strategic communicators, but they don't want you to know that. The next three characteristics illustrate how they accomplish this goal.

The Information Advantage

The Senator may be totally Reflective during one part of an interaction and totally Noble during another part of the same interaction. For example, in many communication interactions, the Senator listens as a Reflective but speaks as a Noble. This strategy helps the Senator achieve an information advantage. That is, the Senator does not speak as a Noble until he or she has gathered the information necessary to offer a "correct" opinion. The Senator gathers this information by being Reflective. Senators sit quietly and listen patiently while others talk, and because others initially think Senators are "harmless" Reflectives, they divulge tremendous amounts of information. Once the Senator has gained the information advantage, he or she will strike as a well-informed Noble. It is this information advantage characteristic that causes some people to view the Senator as a strong and certain leader while others view him or her as a serpent waiting in the grass to strike when least expected.

This negative reaction to the Senator occurs because the other person doesn't know what to expect. Senators are able to turn their Noble and Reflective styles off and on at will, so the other person becomes confused and isn't able to build a consistent set of expectations to guide his or her own behaviors. An observant person will come to appreciate the inherent strength of the Senator and think of him or her as a thoughtful Noble.

That is, in situations where the Senator is attempting to gain an information advantage, he or she will speak as a Noble but only after listening as a Reflective. Thus, instead of allowing the thought of the moment to come tumbling out of his or her mouth as would the dominant-style Noble, the Senator reflects on the situation and then speaks. The speech is that of a Noble, albeit a softer Noble than the dominant-style communicator. Counselors, therapists, and clergy have a need for the information advantage and therefore may develop the Senator style of communication.

Adapting to the Environment

The information advantage Senator is somewhat different from the Senator who switches styles to adapt to two distinctly different environments. The individual who has one style for the home and another for the workplace is an example of environmentally adaptive Senator. This is the person who, when complimented for being such a pleasant, patient individual, responds, "You ought to see me at work . . . I'm a real tiger!!" or it is the person who, when praised or criticized, for being such a tiger at work states, "You've never seen the other side of me . . . at home I'm a different person. I'm really very quiet and passive."

In the early days of my research, I found that women who have returned to work after being homemakers, some minorities, counselors, clergy, and therapists made up the sample of people who develop this environmentally adaptive Senator style of communication. These groups of people all have something in common: they must balance between two different worlds. If they are to be successful, they must be Reflective in some situations and Noble in others. Of course, not all women, minorities, clergy, counselors, and therapists score as Senator communicators. It isn't the gender, race, or occupation per se that determines the style; it is the environment in which an individual operates that creates the need for differing styles, and it is the individual's ability and desire to succeed in differing environments that causes the emergence of the Senator style of communication.

The Hooded-Eye Technique

Is it difficult to identify the Senator during the first five minutes of conversation? You bet! You will think that the Senator is either a Noble or a Reflective. Identifying Senators is made even more difficult by the fact that they are experts at using the Hooded-Eye technique. Sounds mysterious, doesn't it? Indeed, the Hooded-Eye does create a sense of mystery about the Senator. Essentially, the technique involves not letting the other person know how you really feel. When you speak with a Hooded-Eye, you show no emotion toward the issue at hand, and you don't reveal your position on it.

Think about the scene from *The Godfather* where Marlon Brando grabs James Caan and orders him not to tell anyone outside of the family what he is thinking. The Senator believes that you give the other person an advantage when you reveal your feelings and attitudes.

The dominant style-Noble does not utilize the Hooded-Eye technique; you always know where the Noble stands on an issue. The dominant-style Reflective attempts to use the Hooded-Eye by withholding negative opinions or saying what you want to hear, but nonverbal gestures usually reveal his or her true feelings. The Senator is the master of the Hooded-Eye technique, and this goes hand in hand with the information advantage strategy. It is the Senator who can speak with no emotion and with no hint of which side of the issue he or she favors.

The Senator also uses this technique to avoid open conflict. Listen as Maria explains a very strategic Hooded-Eye interaction.

My fiancé has a difficult time making a decision about things to do on the weekends. He also hates conflict as much as I. Instead of asking him what he would like to do this weekend, I simply gave him an either-or scenario, so he could make his decision easier. He could either sail to Catalina for the weekend in a regatta, or he could spend the weekend with me and my family for Father's Day. Naturally, I wanted him to come with me for Father's Day, and he wanted to go sailing. Instead of giving him a guilt trip, which I can do quite easily, I opted to stay neutral and let him make the decision on his own.

He chose to go sailing. Rather than participate in a very uncomfortable conversation that would have continued for days, I left it at that. This way the decision was easy and painless, and we both did what we wanted. He went sailing, and I visited with my father.

And Justice for All

As this strategic communicator and master of the Hooded-Eye gains the information advantage, he or she becomes more powerful. This combination of traits allows the Senator to sabotage a project he or she does not favor, and it allows the Senator to get even with you when you have violated his or her sense of justice. Senators do this by first gathering information that you willingly provide and then using this information to their advantage. Like the Reflective, the Senator is very patient, and like the Noble, the Senator is very determined. If it is important, the Senator will get even, but you will never be able to prove it. You may know in your heart that the Senator caused your downfall. You will never, however, get him or her to admit it, because the Senator's Hooded-Eye tendencies overshadow the Noble tendency to tell it like it is and the Reflective tendency to be concerned with your feelings.

I have tremendous admiration for a woman named Barbara who introduced me to the Hooded-Eye technique. We frequently discuss verbal strategies, and she laughs when she refers to me as a foot soldier. In her soft-spoken manner, she tells me that I'm right out there in front where everyone can take a shot at me, and she suggests that I learn to be a bush fighter. Bush fighters just sit in the bush where they can't be seen, and when the time is right, they strike, without warning. Sometimes the bush fighter strikes from behind, so the victim doesn't know who hit him or her. I love this metaphor, I am totally intrigued by the approach, and I have observed that it works. This approach is certainly not appropriate in all situations, but it is particularly effective when the people you work with resemble a pack of wild wolves.

HOW TO GET SENATORS TO DO WHAT YOU WANT

Like the other communicators, this dual-style communicator has a communication premise that guides his or her behaviors:

The Senator's Communication Premise

Senators are strategic communicators who use two distinctly different styles of communication to adapt to differing environments. They operate from an information advantage standpoint and utilize the Hooded-Eye technique to control the outcome of interactions.

In attempting to explain, predict, and control the Senator or to be able to control your own style-associated behaviors if you are a Senator, it is imperative that you understand the Noble and Reflective styles of communication. The Senator has all of the characteristics, behaviors, strengths, and problems of these communicators. The Senator is Noble in one situation and Reflective in another, or the Senator attempts to gain the information advantage by listening as a Reflective but responding as a Noble within the same communication interaction. In addition, the Senator can respond without emotion. Thus, in attempting to identify the Senator, there are four important points to remember:

1. Know all of the Noble and Reflective characteristics.
2. Observe the Senator in more than one setting.
3. Watch for the shift from Reflective to Noble, which indicates an attempt to gain the information advantage.
4. Watch for the Hooded-Eye. If you are observant but unable to detect an opinion or emotion in the other person, then you are probably talking with a Senator.

Senator Strengths

In addition to the Noble and Reflective communication strengths, the Senator has two unique strengths:

Adaptability. The Senator can switch back and forth between the two styles with little difficulty, providing for a wider range of possibilities in the communication encounter. The Senator, however, seldom—if ever—uses the Socratic style of communication.

Plausibility. Because the Senator gains the information advantage and speaks from a position of knowledge as well as with the certainty of a Noble, his or her ideas always appear plausible to the other person.

Senator Weaknesses

In addition to the Noble and Reflective communication problems, the Senator has one unique problem; *unpredictability*. The Senator may be perceived as fickle by those who observe him or her in more than one situation or by those who have fallen victim to the Hooded-Eye technique. As humans, we distrust and even fear people who are unpredictable, and this can create some serious problems for the Senator.

In attempting to identify the Senator, you must go beyond listening. You must be able to view the communicator from more than one perspective and observe the individual in more than one setting. The more you know about the communicator, the more you know about his or her communication needs, and the more likely you are to be able to control the outcome of the interaction.

The need to go beyond listening also applies to the other styles of communication. People don't just communicate in a vacuum. There are things going on around us all the time that may affect our ability to communicate effectively. In addition, it is important to keep in mind that personality does interact with communication style. It is possible to be a very nice or obnoxious Noble. A Socratic can be a charming or totally boring communicator, and a Reflective can be truly warm and caring or completely devious. Nice, obnoxious, charming, boring, warm, caring, and devious are personality characteristics. To use the information provided in this book, you must be able to separate personality characteristics from communication style characteristics. You can do something about communication style; you can't do anything about personality.

For example, if a sociopath is holding a gun to your head, it probably won't help if you are able to identify his dominant style of communication. In dealing with your average, semi–well adjusted human being, however, communication style—not personality—is the operative condition. You can take personality into consideration in attempting to predict behaviors, but it is your ability to control communication style that will increase your chances for controlling the outcome of the interaction.

If you are not a Senator but are attempting to persuade this dichotomous communicator, then you must be able to go beyond listening to observe the Senator in more than one setting and to work with the information advantage and Hooded-Eye techniques. It is a real challenge to be able to persuade a Senator. You have to be on your toes and thinking every minute. When you are good at doing this, you can draw the Senator into responding in a style that is most comfortable for you. You can get him or her to respond as a Noble or as Reflective. You can't, however, get the Senator to respond as a Socratic because the Senator hasn't developed the Socratic style.

Thus, it is the Socratic who will have the most difficulty persuading the Senator. The Noble and Reflective sides of the Senator will adamantly reject a Socratic persuasive effort; the Senator does not deal with or accept verbosity. Senators simply tune out the Socratic. As a result, Socratics must pay particular attention to controlling their verbose nature if they wish to persuade a Senator.

Think about two Senators attempting to persuade each other, with each in the information advantage mode and each attempting to utilize the Hooded-Eye technique. Talk about verbal agility and the game of words!

The strategy and cunning of a world champion chess match would pale by comparison. Who would win the persuasive tug of war between two Senators who can, indeed, be very strategic and very clever communicators? The one who gains the greatest information advantage.

HOW SENATORS CAN GET OTHERS TO DO WHAT THEY WANT

Senators have the ability to switch between the Noble and Reflective styles, providing for a wider range of possibilities in the communication encounter. Their underdeveloped Socratic style, however, renders them ineffective in a persuasive encounter with a Socratic. When they are in their information advantage mode, however, Senators can be very persuasive, as long as their unpredictable nature doesn't appear too obvious. If the switch from Reflective listener to Noble speaker is too dramatic, the other person will become overly cautious of accepting the Senator's point of view. Thus, if you are a Senator and you would like to control the outcome of the interaction, you must add the following rules to those presented in the Noble and Reflective chapters:

1. Focus your talent for adaptability on success rather than just survival. The Hooded-Eye may work at times, but in the long run, people want to know who you are, or they won't trust you.

2. Work on developing your Socratic style of communication.

3. Allow your two styles to blend. Work on letting your Reflective strengths modify your harsh Noble tendencies and your Noble strengths modify your weaker Reflective characteristics.

PART THREE

How to Use Style to Talk Your Way Out of Trouble and Into Success

Chapter 9

Gaining Power without Generating Resentment

THE LINK BETWEEN COMMUNICATION STYLE AND MANAGEMENT STYLE

Communication is the essence of leadership, and leadership almost always involves the management of other people. Thus, it is important to think about how communication style is linked to management style.

A number of characteristics associated with each communication style directly affect management style—for example, communication immediacy, which affects managerial decision making. Nobles give and expect immediate responses, and when faced with a problem or challenge, they immediately outline a plan of action and begin to implement it. Decision making for the Noble is rapid but not necessarily autocratic. That is, the Noble is as likely to ask for ideas from others as is the Reflective or Socratic but acts on that information in a more immediate manner.

The Socratic develops a plan for implementation only after a thorough analysis of all the variables. If that analysis means delaying implementation of the plan, then so be it. Socratics may be collaborative and ask for help from others, or they may be autocratic and announce the final decision that they have reached as a result of their own personal, thorough analysis. The point for consideration here is the time factor.

The communication time factor and its relationship to managerial behavior becomes even more apparent when we compare the Noble to the Reflective. Reflectives have no sense of communication immediacy; when faced with a problem, they see no reason to act immediately. They take a wait-and-see approach, which infuriates the Noble, who wants action immediately. (The Noble is probably the one to make the statement, "My boss couldn't make a decision if his life depended upon it.")

One of my former bosses is a Reflective, and I can recall cringing as he stated his philosophy of management: "Linda, it is always better to say and do nothing in most situations. When I don't follow this rule, it gets me in trouble." He and I worked well together as a team because our differing styles of communication were complementary in most situations. The communication immediacy factor, however, was a constant source of frustration. He would tell me that my fuse was too short, and I would tell him that his fuse was too long. We managed to achieve some form of compromise in many situations, but that is because we discussed our different styles and the results that were produced through use of these styles. Actually, my relationship with this Reflective boss did teach me that some problems do go away if you ignore them and that patience is an important management tool—and it may be that he learned that some problems don't go away and that dealing with them helps to avoid crises.

Reflectives, Socratics, Nobles, Magistrates, Candidates, and Senators are all capable of making decisions. They just make their decisions within a different time frame.

Style of communication also determines the way in which problem employees are handled. Directive and controlling statements are characteristics of the Socratic and the Magistrate, yet all managers, at various times, will be called upon to be directive or controlling. This is especially true with respect to handling the difficult employee because the manager's responsibility is to reduce or eliminate unacceptable behaviors. Each type of communicator may deal with a problem like absenteeism very differently as a result of their own unique communication needs.*

The Noble is likely to call the employee in and state, "We can't tolerate this amount of absenteeism. You need to improve your attendance." The Noble does not suggest how the employee should go about improving but simply expects the employee to gain control of the self. The Noble expects the problem to be solved by fiat. Furthermore, the Noble is likely to end the reprimand with an "or else" ultimatum.

The Socratic typically sits down with the employee and works out a detailed plan describing how the employee is going to go about improving. The Socratic will then keep a close watch over the employee. In doing this, the Socratic is engaging in directive communication and management behavior.

The Reflective, on the other hand, will simply look for improvement rather than elimination of the problem and may even ask the employee to suggest a possible solution to the problem: "How do you think we can solve this problem?" or "Is there anything I can do to help you solve this problem?"

These are three very different managerial approaches to the same problem and can be directly attributed to differences in communication style — and the reactions to these differing approaches will depend on the dominant style of the subordinate (a subject discussed in Chapter 11).† In order to be an effective manager or leader, it is essential that you gain control of your work environment. Paying attention to your personal style of communication and its impact on others can aid you in gaining this control. Remember that in order to meet your organizational goals

---

*For a full discussion on how the three dominant styles of communication result in differing approaches to the discipline interview, see Linda McCallister, "Rhetorical Sensitivity, Sex of Interactants, and Superior-Subordinate Communication" (Ph.D. diss., Purdue University, 1981).

†For a complete discussion on the subordinate's reaction to these different approaches, see Linda McCallister, "Predicted Employee Compliance to Downward Communication Styles," *Journal of Business Communication* (1983): 67–89.

and objectives, you must be able to explain, predict, and ultimately control behaviors.

CAN AN ORGANIZATION HAVE STYLE?

By now, you should be convinced that communication style can help you begin controlling your own destiny, but you probably have a number of questions. Thus far, we have assumed that the person you are communicating with is rational, fair, and committed to advancing the goals of the organization. But what if this isn't a valid assumption and the other person isn't fair or rational? Additionally, what if there is more than one person, say, in a group meeting? What if the other person is from another country? What if the other person is a member of the opposite sex? The rest of this book is devoted to answering some of these "what if" questions and seeing whether you can use style to control some of the more perplexing aspects of organizational life. We'll start by broadening our perspective and trying to answer the question, Can an entire organization have style? The answer to this question is a resounding yes. In fact, all organizations have style. You may not like the style, but nonetheless all organizations have style.

Organizational style refers to what you need to know and understand in order to behave or operate in a manner that is acceptable to the other members of the organization. Think about the words "climate," "atmosphere," and "feeling." All organizations have a certain climate—formal, relaxed, corrupt, friendly, and so on. Think about your current job and your former place of employment. Try to describe the climate or atmosphere that exists in both places. Are they different or similar? Now try to describe what helped create or shape the climate, atmosphere, or general feeling you have about each organization. If you can do this, you are describing organizational style, and your success is definitely linked to your ability to utilize this style.

"Culture" is a hot term being used to describe organizational style. I recently asked a group of managers and supervisors from a federal employees' credit union to describe their corporate culture. They described it as "becoming 'refined' professionally," "open and honest," "a small, friendly company that provides interesting challenges and has room to grow," "sometimes 'Mom and Pop,' Peyton Place, cliquish or sometimes a very 'home' environment which is pleasant," and "innovative and progressive, with individual teams working toward one goal." Together these descriptions create a verbal picture of the credit union's organizational culture—a small, warm, progressive company with the benefits and problems of a growing family. Call it style, culture, climate, atmosphere, feeling—or whatever else you like. The bottom line remains the same: organizations develop expectations regarding behaviors, and what will work in one organization may not work in another.

Organizations have style, and individual success is linked to your ability to understand and emulate that style. This isn't difficult. If you read and are observant, you can figure out the rules for acceptable behavior. When an organization's style standards are violated, however, negative results can be expected, as one embarrassing moment from my past illustrates.

Several years ago, I was visiting local corporations to develop and improve the ties between the business community and my university. IBM was one of the companies I was visiting, and the university was particularly interested in developing a private-public partnership with IBM. No one could or would tell me exactly why there was a problem between the two institutions, but I surmised that a couple of our professors or administrators had done or said something to alienate the IBM people, and as a result, there wasn't a lot of support for our College of Business. My assignment was to rebuild and develop relations between the two organizations.

It is extremely hot in Florida in June, and I selected a lightweight beige suit to wear to my meeting. I used a red bow tie, red shoes, and a matching red purse to create a professional yet stylish image for myself.

If you work for IBM, you may be laughing because you know what I am about to say. The minute I walked through the door and stood in the lobby of the big blue and gray building, I knew my attire violated the dress norms of IBM. My despair worsened as I was led down the sterile white corridors to the meeting room. My IBM escort was wearing a navy blue jacket and gray trousers, and when he opened the door and I saw five IBM managers in blue and gray suits staring at me, I prayed that a hurricane would suddenly strike so the meeting could be cancelled. I should have used communication style to try to overcome the image problem I had created, but I didn't. To the contrary, I knew I was inappropriately dressed, I knew my credibility was in question, and I knew I wanted to melt into the woodwork, so I let the negative aspects of my Noble style control me. I was overly direct, blunt, defensive, and curt in my responses, and the men did nothing to improve the situation. One man did most of the talking, and his comments were demeaning and sarcastic in tone—or at least I perceived them as such. The rest of the men sat around the table looking quite bored with the whole interaction. The meeting did not go well. On my way home, I kept reliving the meeting, shaking my head and saying, "I wish I hadn't said that!"

What should I have done? First, I shouldn't have focused on myself and my weaknesses. When I stepped into the lobby of the blue and gray building, I knew I had violated the cultural norms of the organization. At that point, I should have immediately begun thinking about power communication. I had a little legitimate power because I represented the university, but I already knew that was not a strong selling point. Obviously I hadn't done my research, and as a blond-haired woman dressed in beige and red, there wasn't much chance that the room full of men dressed in blue and gray were going to view me as a role model. Nevertheless, I should have been able to turn this potentially disastrous situation into a successful moment. Since I know how to use communication style to control the outcome of an interaction, I should have said,

"Gentlemen, it is no secret that relations between IBM and the university have not been good. There is a large rift between our organizations. We are the red and white, and you are the blue and gray. I am here today to listen to your comments, your ideas, and your perceptions about how we can begin to repair the rift. How can we make our differences work for us so that, together, we might better serve the people of southeast Florida? With your permission, I'd like to begin by having each of you share some of your thoughts about the university. Please don't feel that you need to be polite. We need to be honest with each other if we are going to heal the wounds."

With a few variations, this is what I said in my second meeting at IBM, and I listened intently to their comments. That meeting went smoothly, and I was able to accomplish my goals. To their credit, I should mention that there were two women present at the second meeting. Like the men, the women were dressed in blue and gray, but then, so was I.

HOW TO IDENTIFY THE POWER COMMUNICATORS

Let's take the concept of power communication further. It's not likely that everyone in an organization will have the same dominant style of communication, but probably one style is viewed as more acceptable than another. Look at those at the top of your organization and those who are being promoted. Chances are there is not an even distribution of people with different styles of communication but rather a predominance of one and a smattering of the others. This occurs because of the first rule of communication: *We expect the other person to sound as we sound.* Since we all tend to think that our style of communication is the best or correct style, we, when given the opportunity, tend to hire or promote people who sound as we do. Thus, the first step in identifying the power communicators is to listen to the people holding power positions. The majority of these people will have the same dominant style of communication, and these people are the power communicators. Power communicators, of course, differ from organization to organization, and sometimes they differ within organizations.

Power is an important part of organizational gamesmanship, but it isn't something you can count, touch, or package in a little box. It is an elusive term with different meanings for different people. Some view it as a goal to be achieved, some as a means to achieve goals.

Viewed simply as *the* goal, power can be abused, and it can become destructive. Organizational and individual needs are usually of little concern to the person who views power as the ultimate goal.

Viewed as a means to achieve goals, power helps bring about change in the organization. Without change, organizations become stagnant. Thus, power can be viewed as a positive force that allows the organization to be dynamic. Power communicators use their sources of power and their communication styles to bring about change. If, on the other hand, you are in a stagnant bureaucracy, you will use your power and communication style to stop any change that might occur. (Notice the university influence here.)

There are basically six different sources of power in all organizations:*

Legitimate power is inherent in position, title, or job description (you have power because you are the boss).

Expert power exists when you are better at doing something than anyone else (you have power because you are the expert).

Reward power exists when you are able to say, do, or give someone something that will motivate the person to continue performing some behavior. Recognition and salary are examples of reward power.

Coercive power, the flip side of reward power, allows you to force or compel someone to do something.

Informational power refers to your ability to make things happen because you have the information that makes change possible; your informational power increases as your knowledge about the organization increases.

Referent power refers to your ability to serve as a role model for others.

---

*These power sources were first identified and described in the research of John French and Bertram Raven. For a complete discussion of this groundbreaking research, see their "The Basis of Social Power," in D. Cartwright, ed., *Studies in Social Power* (Ann Arbor: University of Michigan, 1959), 150–67.

Power communicators are those people who use style of communication to activate or access the six sources of power that exist in all organizations. Let's see how you can use power communication to control those devious little organizational characters who are so fond of stabbing others in the back.

USING COMMUNICATION STYLE TO GAIN POWER AND CONTROL THOSE WHO WOULD STAB YOU IN THE BACK

I have to be honest: I don't have the answer for dealing with or eliminating those people who stab others in the back. If I had an answer that would work in all situations, I wouldn't be writing this book. I'd be basking in the sun on the French Riviera spending my fortune. What I do have are some strategies for minimizing the damage caused by these people.

There are a couple of things to keep in mind. First there are some people who have real emotional problems, and these problems dictate their behaviors. Thus, their behaviors don't really have anything to do with you. They act the way they do because of some psychological flaw, and unless you are a psychiatrist, there isn't anything you can do about another person's psychological problems. Second, someone who stabs you in the back has probably done or will do the same thing to others. If you are patient and remain in control of yourself, you will eventually get to watch the back stabber self-destruct. Finally, everyone knows who these people are, so there is never any reason for you to get into the proverbial contest with a skunk. When you engage in open warfare with the back stabber, you come out smelling equally bad. Consider the sad but true saga of Ralph and Charles.

Charles and Ralph are market researchers for an advertising and public relations firm. Because this is a small firm, Charles and Ralph are, in fact, the market research department. They gather and provide important information for the account executives. Most of their projects require a team effort, but Charles openly accepts all of the credit for their accomplishments, and he always uses the pronoun "I" when presenting their information in group meetings. Ralph is irritated by these behaviors and makes off-handed, sarcastic remarks to Charles, and he calls Charles the "glory grabber" when talking with the secretaries. Both Charles and Ralph want to become account executives, but Charles is angry over Ralph's tendency to take all of the credit for their work. Relations between Ralph and Charles are strained and becoming worse. Ralph and Charles are asked to make a presentation before a very important client. The president of the firm and the account executive will be present at the meeting, and Ralph "just knows that Charles is going to hog all of the credit for their work."

As expected, Charles spoke from the "I" perspective, and halfway through the presentation, Ralph interrupted and said, "Excuse me Charles, but I'd like to point out that this was a team effort. You didn't do this alone." Charles responded, "Well, they know that. They know I'm speaking for both of us. I didn't mean to hurt your feelings." Charles went on to emphasize the pronoun "we" throughout the rest of the presentation.

After the meeting, the president of the firm called Ralph into his office and said, "I've been seriously considering giving you a shot at being an account executive, but your comments today revealed a lack of maturity I hadn't noticed before. There was no reason for you to risk alienating our clients with your personal feud. I'm not blind, and I'm not dumb. I know what Charles is, and I don't need you to point it out in front of our clients. You have some growing up to do, young man."

Ralph talked his way into trouble and out of success; he should never have engaged in open warfare with Charles. Now I'm not suggesting that you cower in a corner and let people take advantage of you. I am suggesting that you need to be clever in your approach when dealing with less-than-honorable people. You need to think like the Senator and use communication style strategically because open warfare doesn't work. I am telling you this as a Noble who has engaged in open warfare and lived to suffer the consequences. I am also telling you this as a Noble who has learned to use the Hooded-Eye so that my true feelings are not revealed and has, indeed, lived to experience the joy of watching back stabbers self-destruct. By the way, don't let anyone tell you there is no joy in watching the wicked crumble or observing the mighty fall from an evil throne. There is joy. As a good Senator, you may not want to express this joy openly, but there is joy.

Let's do an instant replay. You are Ralph. Think about communication style and power. What can you do to control Charles and your own destiny? Think of a couple of strategies you can use to minimize any damage Charles might cause.

If you started by saying Ralph should just ignore Charles, then you have gotten ahead of yourself. You've provided a solution before analyzing the situation. Let's analyze first.

Ralph is a Noble. You know this from the information I gave you. Ralph engaged in hit-and-run communications with Charles rather than discussing his feelings about Charles's behaviors. Additionally, Ralph was under stress in the group meeting and as a result failed to filter his comments; he had a thought pop into his mind, and he let it fall right out of his mouth.

We know that Charles is not a Reflective (a Reflective says "we" and does not openly take credit for another person's work), and we know that Charles is not Noble (a Noble wouldn't call attention to the problem by focusing on the "we" during the rest of the presentation). Charles is either a Magistrate or a Socratic (he is verbose and detailed). I haven't given enough information to identify Charles's style specifically, but his style of communication isn't as important as the fact that he is a back stabber, a person who takes credit for another's work.

Ralph is Noble, Charles is a back stabber, and Ralph violated a basic business principle by airing dirty laundry in front of a client. Furthermore, Ralph shouldn't have let the problem get out of hand. It should have been handled before the meeting took place. This information combined with your knowledge of power should produce workable strategies.

Telling Ralph to forget about Charles is not an alternative because

Ralph is a Noble. He's not going to forget about Charles, and Charles isn't going to stop taking credit for Ralph's work.

Ralph can use his expert power and his Noble style of communication to minimize the damage. Since Ralph and Charles are of equal status in the organization, Ralph can simply inform Charles that they will be splitting the presentations from this point forward. When Ralph delivers his part of the presentation, he will present his comments from the team perspective without calling attention to the issue. Charles will probably continue to speak from the "I" perspective and in so doing begin the process of self-destruction. On the other hand, there is a slight possibility that Charles will begin to model his behaviors after Ralph. It's possible — but not likely.

Ralph can also use his expert power and his knowledge of legitimate and informational power to call attention to his own contribution. Ralph can ask for a "touch-base" meeting with the account executive before any group meeting. At the meeting, Ralph can go over the findings and ask the account executive for comments.

The "draft document approach" is a variation of the touch-base meeting. Ralph can send a draft copy of the information to the account executive and ask for his or her comments before producing the final document. Whether Ralph uses the touch-base meeting or the draft document approach, he should maintain the team perspective. His comments should sound something like this:

"Here is a draft of our report for the O'Connor presentation. We'd like you to take a look at it before we put on the finishing touches."

If Ralph doesn't like any of these suggestions, he can simply introduce Charles as the person who will present "our" findings. If he uses this approach, he may also want to have a cover sheet on the report with their names following the words "prepared by."

Let's take Ralph and Charles out of the picture and make this a little tougher. Suppose your boss is the one taking credit for your work. What do you do? If you're thinking there is nothing you can do, think again. If your boss is the CEO and there is no one over him or her, then you can continue to do the work and consider it an opportunity to gain experience while you are looking for another job. If your boss reports to someone higher and the work is submitted to this higher authority, then you can use the touch-base or draft document approaches, but use them with *considerable caution*. You need to understand your organization's culture and power structure before deciding on an approach.

The main point is that you need to be able to think like a Senator. Learn how to be a bush fighter, planning a strategy without letting everyone else know what you think or what you are going to do. Let's see if you are beginning to think like a bush fighter. Read the following story about Paula and Teri, and assume that you are the consultant. What do you advise Paula to do?

Paula is the director of subsidiary rights for a major publishing house in New York. Teri is the manager of foreign rights. Paula reports directly to the president, and Teri reports to Paula. In fact, Paula hired Teri.

Paula comments to Louis, a colleague and director from another department, that she is concerned about the increasing tension she feels in her department. Louis apologizes for not coming to her sooner and then proceeds to tell her that Teri has been undermining Paula within the department. He also tells her that he heard a rumor that Teri made some negative comments to the president about Paula's abilities.

Paula is shocked and angry. As she sifts through the information provided by Louis, she recalls a number of incidents and realizes that Louis is giving her accurate and valuable information. Teri has been undermining her within the department and with the president.

What's your advice? What should Paula do? Think about it for a minute, and then read on as I share with you what Paula actually did.

Paula used the Hooded-Eye to gather information with respect to specific comments made and actions taken by Teri. She remained neutral and didn't reveal her true feelings or emotions. She remained calm, warm, and supportive as she discreetly gathered information from employees.

She remained friendly with Teri and didn't reveal there was a problem. After she had gained the information advantage, she scheduled a meeting with the president to "discuss a problem." Paula is Noble, but she took the time to establish a warm interpersonal climate before she presented her problem to the president. They shared a laugh or two, and then Paula said,

> "I have a very sensitive problem, and I am desperately in need of your advice. I've watched the way you deal with people, and I'm hoping you will give me some guidance. There's been a lot of tension and conflict in my department recently. I did some investigating and found out that one of my employees has been seriously undermining my authority and credibility. I don't want to make the situation any worse than it already is, so I'm hoping you can lead me in the right direction. What should I do?"

The president asked Paula for an example of some of the things this employee was doing. Paula presented him with a well-organized list of specific, observed, and documented behaviors. She waited for him to ask her questions and responded calmly and concisely. She did not mention the employee's name, and she did not indicate that she knew the employee had engaged in these tactics with him. The president advised Paula to ignore Teri's behaviors for the time being. She wasn't exactly thrilled with that advice but nevertheless did as he requested.

Paula and the president had two more meetings to discuss this problem, and at their third meeting, he suggested that it would be in everyone's best interest to release Teri from her position with the publishing company. Without hesitation, Paula complied with this suggestion.

The president didn't tell Paula why he wanted Teri fired. Paula surmised that he also used the Hooded-Eye to observe and verify the behaviors she had strategically identified for him.

Paula chose the right strategy. It worked, so it was the right strategy. If it hadn't worked, it wouldn't have been the right strategy. Remember: Things that work in one situation or organization may not work in another. That's the beauty of the Senator style of communication: the Senator gathers information and knows what will work before striking.

Power is dormant until you activate it with your style of communication. Once activated, power helps you accomplish your goals, and your accomplishments earn you respect and recognition. Additionally, keep the following tips in mind as you begin experimenting with power communication:

- Power for the sake of power will not get you respect. At best, it will get you recognition as someone to be feared or avoided.

- Powermongers do exist. Your own efforts can be impaired if you ignore the fact that they exist.

- Powermongers are usually threatened by achievers. Use your own knowledge of organizational culture to deal with powermongers. In some cases you may not be able to do anything about them—and maybe you shouldn't even try—but you can avoid them.

- Power has limitations. Know the limits of your own sources of power. It can be very damaging to overextend the limits of your power.

- Power can be created. Analyze your organization, and activate your sources of power with communication style.

USING STYLE TO CREATE A CUSTOMER SERVICE MODEL INSIDE THE ORGANIZATION

Let's stop talking about less than honorable people and see how to establish a positive climate in the organization. Throughout history, people and organizations that pay attention to their customers have tended to survive. Those unconcerned with customer satisfaction may have short-term success but ultimately don't survive. Customer service won't override a bad or defective product, but a good product and excellent customer service will outperform an excellent product and bad customer service.

The customer service model for success can also be established within an organization. Internal customer service assumes that everyone is a customer to someone, and success is measured by the degree of customer satisfaction. Thus, managers service employees, employees service managers, sales services manufacturing, and so on. Leaders have customers too. Those who would be led are the customers, and in order to service these customers, leaders must listen.

A musical classic by Paul Simon and Art Garfunkel suggests that there is sound to silence—that silence does indeed communicate; that people talk but often fail to say anything; that people hear but often fail to listen to what's being said. We spend more time listening than we do speaking, writing, and reading, yet listening remains the most neglected of communication skills. In the educational process, little or no time is devoted to it.

Most of us cannot function as leaders without owning effective listening skills. Listening can mean the difference between being aware of or being oblivious to the impact of the unspoken problem.

Mary is a training coordinator for a large financial institution, and Susan is her manager. Mary is frustrated because she doesn't have the tools she needs to produce a professional-looking product. Her typewriter is old and in disrepair. Mary tells Susan about the problem, and Susan arranges to have the typewriter repaired. The service person ostensibly repairs the typewriter, but soon after Mary begins to type, the typewriter breaks down again.

Mary really wants to tell Susan that this is a hopelessly old typewriter that will never function properly and that she needs a new one—or better yet, a computer—if she is to be more effective in her job. Mary, however, is a Reflective, so instead of saying this, she merely reports that the typewriter has broken down, and Susan reissues a repair request.

Mary remains silent while the typewriter continues to malfunction, but she displays her frustration by referring to the machine as "my typewriter from the year one." With a definite edge of irritation in her voice, Mary hands the completed project to Susan and says, "The quality of the work is commensurate with the quality of the machine."

Susan is disappointed that the proposal does not live up to Mary's usual high standards. She calls Mary into the office and candidly relates her dissatisfaction. Mary becomes defensive and tells Susan that she is lucky to have gotten the proposal at all since most of her time was spent trying to get the typewriter to work.

Susan is surprised by Mary's reaction since she thought the typewriter had been repaired. Mary claims she told Susan that the machine was not working despite numerous repairs. Susan states that she recalls only being told that the machine was an "antique," not that it was still not working.

Both Mary and Susan displayed poor listening skills; neither listened to the nonverbal aspects of communication. Had Susan listened to the sounds of silence—Mary's offhanded remarks—conflict could have been avoided. Granted, Mary should have clearly communicated her problem to Susan, but it was Susan's responsibility as the leader to listen to the sounds of silence and deal with the problem before it became a conflict. Clearly Susan heard the offhanded remarks, but she did not listen to the implied meaning of these comments.

Susan, at least, thought she was listening. For many of us, there are times when we purposely don't listen because we don't like the other person or their style of communication.

Steve is a manager in a large electronics firm. Joe is a young, bright, somewhat abrasive engineer who reports to Steve. Joe tells Steve that he thinks it is possible to eliminate step two of the manufacturing process without endangering the quality of the product.

Steve hears what Joe is saying, but he doesn't listen to the suggestion because he doesn't like Joe very much. Joe is loud, he wears a lot of flashy gold jewelry, and he is a Magistrate. Surely anything Joe has to say is of little importance to Steve. Steve is pleased when Joe resigns to take a position with a competitor.

A year later, Steve finds out that Joe has been promoted to vice-president of his new company because he was able to save the company a considerable amount of money by eliminating step two of the manufacturing process. Joe's company is now producing the same product for less money, and Steve's company sales have decreased.

A farfetched example? Not at all. This sort of thing happens all the time and not just in manufacturing firms. A highly paid consultant might examine the situation and conclude that a technical problem existed, but this would be an inaccurate assessment. The technical problem was the result, not the cause, of the problem. The manager's ineffective listening skills caused a costly technical problem.

If you want to improve your listening skills, watch and listen to the Reflective. Teach yourself to use the Reflective's Rogerian response techniques and be patient. Let the other person say what he or she has to say without being evaluative and without jumping in to provide a solution before the sentence is completed.

It would be impossible to calculate the dollars lost because we don't listen to people we don't like, but the amount, I am sure, would be staggering. The dollars lost can be significantly reduced if we just listen to the other person as if he or she were a customer to be satisfied.

Chapter 10

Style, Gender, and the Organization

Let me take a very Noble approach to this topic and state my conclusion up front: gender has absolutely nothing at all to do with communication style. Men don't tend to be one style and women another. With all of the thousands of people I have tested, I find an equal distribution of males and females in each particular style. The styles, however, are not evenly distributed. There are more dominant-style communicators than blended-style communicators, and there are more Magistrates and Candidates than Senators, but there are no gender differences within each style.

Traditions and cultural mores may set up expectations regarding acceptable styles for women and acceptable styles for men, but biological gender does not cause women to be one style and men to be another. Nor does gender have anything at all to do with management or leadership abilities. There is no body of reputable, scientific research that suggests that men have some genetic trait that makes them better managers or leaders. Tradition and cultural mores may have placed men in these positions in the past, but these mores have been challenged, and the traditions are now being broken. Gender-based style differences are myths; these stereotypical beliefs can be shattered if we look beyond gender and examine communication style as a cause of behaviors.

I had several thousand workers describe the characteristics they liked and disliked about their bosses. I took the workers' most frequently used words and phrases and created a profile of an ideal leader. In general, workers are happy with a boss who is frank, direct, and to the point. At the same time, he or she listens, is willing to talk, is open to discussion and constructive suggestions, is receptive to new ideas, and is supportive. He or she is honest, kind, considerate, fair, friendly, patient, understanding, humane, open-minded, easy going, and has a sense of humor. The effective leader is intelligent, organized, professional, knowledgeable, and able to get results. This profile may sound like "Mom and apple pie," but it is, nevertheless, a profile of an ideal leader as described by real people. It's the sum total of the actual words used by workers who were describing the things they like about their bosses.

Take a good look at this description. This is not a "male" profile. It is also not a "female" profile. It is a profile that could describe either a man or a woman.

Now let's take a reverse look at what the modern worker will not accept from people occupying leadership positions. A bad boss is dishonest, disorganized, autocratic, sarcastic, critical, and arrogant He or she is prone to temper tantrums, self-pity, and self-promotion; doesn't listen, is unclear in communication and fails to keep others informed; procrastinates and is unable to deal with pressure. The bad boss can be a perfectionist who focuses on details and ignores the bigger picture. He or she is moody, closed-minded, opinionated, and indecisive. This person rarely accepts responsibility for his or her mistakes but gladly accepts credit for contributions made by others. Take a good look at this description. It is neither a male nor a female profile. It is, once again, gender neutral.

Now we know that ideal leaders can be either male or female, and we know that bad bosses can be male or female. What then do we know about the communication styles of these ideal leaders and bad bosses?

Look at the first two sentences describing the ideal leader. From a communication style perspective, we want a leader to be frank, direct, and to the point. At the same time, he or she listens, is willing to talk, is open to discussion and constructive suggestions, is receptive to new ideas, and is supportive. In a nutshell, this is a gender-neutral description of a person who can use all three dominant styles of communication, drawing upon the Noble, Socratic, and Reflective strengths.

Now look at the type of communication we don't want from people in leadership positions. We don't want our leaders to be sarcastic, critical, unclear, opinionated, or indecisive. We don't like it when they don't listen or fail to keep us informed. Each of these negative traits is associated with one of the styles in the Communication Kaleidoscope. Obviously people who communicate in this manner are not leaders.

Keep in mind that these descriptions of the ideal leaders and bad bosses were based on the reported observations of real workers who were talking about their real bosses, managers, and leaders. They were noting behaviors they observed, and when we group these behaviors together, we see that effective leadership has nothing at all to do with gender. Why, then, you may be asking yourself, is gender still an issue for so many people, and why is a chapter in this book devoted to gender?

The answer is simple. Our traditions and mores are in the process of change, but they have not been eliminated. Thus, while male and female leadership behaviors may not differ, our expectations regarding acceptable behaviors from males and females may still differ. That is, what we expect and accept from men may be different from what we expect and accept from women.

SHE'S A BITCH, HE'S A LEADER

I took the research one step further and examined the messages provided by the workers to see if they expected the same behaviors from their male and female bosses. I created three lists made up of terms used to describe both male and female bosses, only male bosses, and only female bosses.

From this analysis, something very interesting emerged. The terms "efficient," "aggressive," "demands respect," and "ambitious" appeared on the list describing positive aspects of male leaders, and the terms "totally efficient," "aggressive," "demanding," and "ambitious" appeared on the list describing negative aspects of female leaders. For example, one person said, "I like my boss because he's aggressive. He can really shake things up." But another person said, "I don't like my boss because she's too aggressive. She's all work. She should be more congenial."

Another person said, "I like my boss because he's ambitious. He's going to the top!" But another person said, "The thing I don't like about my boss is that she is ambitious. She should just do her job and not worry about getting promoted." The male and female leaders were displaying the same behaviors, but some people perceived these behaviors as unacceptable when displayed by a woman.

The complete analysis of the messages in this research led us to conclude that modern workers like their female leader if she is an effective communicator and if she actively assumes the role of mentor. The male leader is liked when he is an effective communicator and assumes the role of friend or buddy. That is, we want to get along with our male leaders, but we want our female leaders to nurture us and help us get promoted. My most recent observations with respect to communication style suggest that the Magistrate style of communication is not acceptable from a female who aspires to lead others.

HE'S A WIMP, SHE'S A LEADER

If there are behaviors acceptable for men but unacceptable for women, then there must be behaviors acceptable for women and not for men. Indeed, there are, but we don't tend to make as much of an issue of unacceptable male behaviors.

The words "too easy-going" were used to describe negative behaviors of male bosses, but there are a number of terms on the positive female list that indicate a female leader should be easy-going ("amiable," "flexible," "pleasant," "nice"). From a communication style perspective, it appears that the Reflective male is viewed as a weak leader (although that is in the process of change).

When I present my lists of terms to business students or seminar participants without telling them which list is which, the overwhelming majority select the female traits as the least negative, and the simple majority select the female traits as the most positive. This suggests that leadership is not just a male phenomenon. It suggests that we like the things female leaders do and that the presence of women in positions of leadership has helped shape our vision of what a leader should or should not be. Moreover, a close examination of the lists suggests that some significant changes have taken place with respect to our thinking about male leaders.

The terms "caring," "sensitive," "helpful," "complementary," "compassionate," and "thoughtful" appear on the list of positive male traits. Twenty years ago these words would not have been included on a list of positive traits describing male leaders. Today their presence suggests that male leaders display these behaviors and that we expect these behaviors from male and female leaders. You may argue that it is the women who tend to appreciate these behaviors the most. Even if this is true—and I'm not convinced it is—keep in mind that women make up nearly 50 percent of the labor force. This is an important statistic to remember because you cannot ignore the needs of half of your people if you truly aspire to lead others.

The bottom line of this discussion is that leadership skills are neither male nor female. The traits we like in male leaders are similar to those we like in female leaders, and both men and women have some areas in which improvement is needed. Of course, there are still some people who like certain behaviors in men and dislike those same behaviors in women and vice versa. Fortunately, those gender-based distinctions are rapidly disappearing.

When women first began making their presence known in the upper echelons of organizations in the 1970s, there was a lot of speculation that women would become "masculine" if they were allowed to do "men's work." That has not happened. We do not have a generation of women who look and think like Conan the Barbarian. We do have a generation of women who have learned to be assertive, and we do have a generation of women who are equal in stature and ability to their male colleagues.

We also have a steadily increasing group of male bosses who have adopted, or at least learned to display, positive, nurturing traits, which were, prior to the 1970s, considered "feminine." As our nation moves rapidly away from the manufacturing age and into the information age where the focus is on people and communications, this is a welcome and necessary change. Moreover, nurturing is a desirable and positive trait we should all work to develop. Nurturing does not mean "babying" another person. It means helping a person grow and develop by providing firm and consistent guidance to bring out the best in another and help that person be all that he or she is capable of being. Nurturing is a feminine strength, not a weakness, and it is something that men can and should learn to do.

Now let's see if we can use communication style to solve a problem and if it will work even when the person using it has no legitimate power. To make it even more difficult, this person is a woman. Thus, we have a woman who does not occupy a position of leadership, who is going to use communication style to solve a problem, and who wants to get others to do willingly what she wants them to do without generating resentment or anger.

Think back to the day when the first computer/word processor was introduced into your department and when word processing became part of the secretary's job duties. In the beginning, this new technology created more work and problems than it solved. Instead of improving the work environment, the word processor initially created a lot of busy work, irritation, and stress. Here is the problem:

Helen is a secretary in a large social service agency, and she produces work for several people, all of whom view her as their private secretary. Helen reports directly to David, the agency director. David managed to squeeze some funds out of his very lean budget to purchase a computer for Helen. He knows he needs to hire a second person because Helen's work load is so heavy, but there isn't enough money in the budget. The computer, David believes, will help Helen manage the work.

Two months after the computer arrives, Helen realizes that her work load has not become more manageable. To the contrary, her multiple bosses are giving her more work than ever, assuming that "the computer can handle it."

What do you think Helen should do? What would you do if you were Helen? This actually happened, so we know what Helen actually did.

Helen has worked for David for some time and knows him well. She knows he is a Noble and understands she must approach him as a Noble. She also knows that he clearly views himself as the boss and realizes the Noble approach must be softened with her natural Reflective style and that she must be the one to take care of the details (Socratic). After planning out her course of action, she begins by putting together a one-page document stating the problem, the cause of the problem, and possible solutions to the problem. Next she figures out the best time to talk with David because she doesn't want to approach him when he's in a bad mood or pressed for time. At the time she judges to be right, she knocks on the door, smiling and carrying a memo in her hand.

HELEN: David, I have something rather important I need to discuss with you. Is this a good time for you?

DAVID: (smiling) I don't know. This sound pretty serious. How much time do you need, and is it going to cost me anything?

HELEN: (walking toward the desk as she talks) It's not serious now, but it could be if we don't deal with it. I only need a few minutes, and it won't cost you a penny. In fact, it will save you money!

Helen hands the memo to David, which looked something like this:

To: David Smith, Manager
From: Helen Jones, Secretary
Re: Possible solutions to word processing difficulties

Problem: The new word processing equipment was supposed to help us meet our departmental goals in a more efficient manner. To date, the presence of the equipment has only served to decrease our abilities to meet departmental goals, and it has increased tension and hostility.

Cause: The equipment has not been properly integrated into our work environment. As a result, most of our colleagues do not understand the relationship between what they do or want done and what the machine is able to do.

Possible solution: I would like to conduct a 30-minute orientation session where I will:

1. Demonstrate the features of the machine.
2. Discuss cooperative procedures that will allow us to make optimal use of this new technology.

To make sure that everyone has an opportunity to attend these sessions, and to disrupt the flow of work as little as possible, I suggest that I present the orientation session several times with three or four people attending each session.

I have attached a schedule that seems workable.

As she begins to talk, she walks around to the back of his chair.

HELEN: We have a problem with the new equipment. Instead of helping us be more efficient, it is keeping us from being efficient.

DAVID: Why is that?

HELEN: (standing next to David and pointing at the memo) There appear to be some real misunderstandings about the word processor—what it can be used for, what it can do. It's a problem that I think we can easily correct with a series of short orientation sessions. I've prepared a time-table that should fit in with everyone's schedule. How does it look to you?

DAVID: It looks pretty good. You've covered all the bases.

HELEN: I can start the sessions tomorrow or I can begin them next week. Which do you prefer?

DAVID: Let's start tomorrow and get this problem solved.

HELEN: (walking in front of the desk) Consider the problem solved.

Helen begins walking out the door and then turns back to David:

HELEN: Oh, would you like to attend the first session?

DAVID: No, I don't think so. I know how computers work.

HELEN: Yes, I know you do, but I was hoping that you would observe me and give me some feedback on how well I do. Besides I'd feel a lot more confident with you present.

David could have agreed to be there to support Helen, but he didn't. He simply told her that he didn't need to be there since he had total confidence in her abilities. After the meeting, Helen sent a memo from David to everyone else informing them of the orientation sessions. After she completed the sessions, she sent a brief progress report to David summarizing the effectiveness of her problem-solution efforts. Helen got everyone to do willingly what she wanted them to do.

What does this scenario have to do with gender? Absolutely nothing— and that's exactly the point. Effective leadership, management, persuasion, or whatever else you want to call it isn't about gender; it's about communication style.

Take a few minutes to go back over this scenario and see if you can identify the Noble, Reflective, and Socratic strategies. If you think about it, it really is fun to see how you can use style to get others to do what you want without generating resentment or anger. Helen did it. You can do it, too.

DEALING WITH MALE EXPECTATIONS

Now let's get into the juicy part of this discussion. Whom do men and women like working for better? In my research, I ask workers if men or women make better managers, and then I ask them to justify their position.

I found that about 30 percent of those asked will create a new category and say that men and women are equal. Because that is the socially desirable response, I don't give them this category. I feel that the person who creates the category is more likely to be committed to that belief as opposed to a person who simply places a check mark in front of a socially acceptable answer.

We analyzed the justification statements provided by those who created this equality category and found that these are the people who have had experiences with both male and female bosses. People who create this category will say, "I've worked for both. Some are good, and some are bad. It's not whether the person is male or female that counts."

Each semester I do this exercise with graduate and undergraduate students, and each semester the percentage of people who create the equality category increases. More and more people are experiencing female managers, and a new experience is the only thing that can change an old belief or stereotype.

It should come as no surprise, however, that nearly half of the male workers in my research stated that men make better managers. What may come as a surprise is how they justified their belief. Men who state men are better managers tend not to provide specific, observed behaviors to support their assertion of male superiority. Instead, they use generalities and sexual stereotypes to suggest men do something better as managers. They suggest men are stronger, less emotional, and more aggressive. They also say such things as:

- Men handle authority with grace.
- Men have smarts.
- Men are able to put their foot [sic] down.
- Men make better managers because society has led us to believe this.
- Men make better managers because when our secretary is in charge, things don't run smoothly.
- Men make better managers because the women have not stepped up to the same level as men.

The primary communication strategy utilized by men who state men are better managers is the verbal attack. They support their assertion of male superiority by attacking or criticizing some personal female characteristic or activity. Their verbal attacks are general and stereotypical as opposed to specific or observational. They make such comments as these:

- Women are vulnerable.
- Women are not strong or aggressive.
- Women lose their niceness when they work too much.
- Women act impulsively and stupidly.
- Women are moody.

Remember that "aggressive" showed up on the list of positive male traits and on the list of negative female traits. Here, not being aggressive is considered a negative—a real double bind. Also, I must note that the term "moody" was used to describe negative aspects of both male and female bosses.

Some men believe women make better managers, but, alas, they are the minority. Only 20 percent of the men in my current research state women are better managers than men. Men who take this position support their assertion with multiple examples of positive behaviors—for example, "Women seem to be more organized and have the ability to handle pressure and multiple tasks at one time. They are also better communicators. This comes from working and raising kids."

How do you deal with male expectations if you are a woman and the man thinks women can't manage? Provide him with a new experience to replace his stereotypical belief. Demonstrate the profile of an ideal leader presented earlier in this chapter, pay particular attention to his dominant style of communication, and make an effort to use all three styles of communication to persuade him to do willingly the things you need done.

DEALING WITH FEMALE EXPECTATIONS

In the early 1980s, I appeared several times on the "AM Buffalo Show" in Buffalo, New York. My topics were communication, management, and women in management. One morning we were doing a session on how women apply management skills in the home. The host interviewed me, and then we took calls from home viewers. The first call I received was from a female viewer; I will never forget her words: "My boss is a woman, and she's a bitch. I would never choose to work for a woman." The show was live, there was no editing, and I hadn't been toughened by years of experience back then, so to say I was a bit shaken would be a tremendous understatement. That woman had either had a very negative experience with a female boss or was holding tight to a stereotypical belief about women—a stereotypical belief that is not shared by the majority of women.

Stereotypes are built on kernels of truth. You have probably heard people say, "Women don't like to work for other women" or "I work with a woman, and she says she would never work for a woman," or "women are the ones who don't want women in management positions." There are indeed women who openly expound that they don't want women in management or leadership positions. However, these women are the vocal minority. They represent the dissenting opinion, not the majority opinion.

The overwhelming majority of women in my research state women are equal to or better than men with respect to management abilities.

Only 20 percent of the women state men are better managers. Women support their assertions that women are better with specific, observed, positive behaviors—for example:

Women make better managers because where I work there is a man manager and a woman manager. The woman does a much better job of organizing.

Women make better managers because a manager's principal role is dealing with people. On the whole, women are more sensitive in this area and are able to motivate others without threats.

Women make better managers because the women I've worked under have been very organized, considerate, and productivity oriented. The men seem more distant and uninvolved.

Women make better managers because they are more sensitive in their interactions, and they are less likely to be crooks.

So the next time someone smugly states, "Women don't like to work for other women," simply smile warmly and say, "Yes, there are some women who feel that way. Fortunately, they are expressing a minority opinion. Most women recognize that gender has very little to do with management." Then provide a positive experience that will help alter their stereotypical beliefs.

MALE AND FEMALE MANAGERS OF THE TWENTY-FIRST CENTURY: WILL THERE BE A DIFFERENCE?*

Attitudes are changing as experiences change, but there are still a lot of places where the woman is the only manager or is one of a very small

---

*This is the title of the chapter written by me and my friend Don Gaymon, which appears in the book *Beyond Boundaries,* edited by Cheryl Friedly and Cynthia Lont (Fairfax, Va.: George Mason University Press, 1989, pp. 209–230). *Beyond Boundaries,* a fascinating book, focuses on cultural and gender diversity in communication and language.

group of female managers in the organization. In some organizations, a woman manager may still be trying to establish herself as an individual who is qualified to be counted among the ranks of successful managers. In some organizations, the woman is still being tested by her superiors. She is given more work and responsibility than is reasonable to expect, and she is still being asked to rise to the level of super boss — capable of jumping tall buildings in a single leap. But things are changing.

In the early days of civilization, male and female roles were very clearly defined. Men were the warriors, and women were the caretakers. But the world has changed, and the need for brute strength, force, and intimidation has given way to the need for human relations skills. As we move closer to the year 2000 and a service age society, men will be placed in a position of having to develop the nurturing, supportive, and interactive human relations skills that women have developed and displayed for centuries. More important, both men and women will need to develop their communication skills if they seek to lead others. This book is designed to help you gain the skills you will need for a successful future — a future that will see an equal number of men and women in leadership positions.

I end this chapter with the insightful words of a twenty-seven-year-old graduate student named Mark who said,

> "I think men and women are equal because an idiot is an idiot no matter what kind of underwear they may wear."

It should come as no surprise that Mark is a Noble.

Chapter 11

Talking with
Difficult People

THE ONE-ON-ONE INTERACTION:
IT CAN MAKE OR BREAK YOUR CAREER

A young doctoral candidate reported on time for her interview with a team of professors from a prestigious university. She looked forward to an exciting session. After all, representatives of this university had to be good. She was distressed, however, when only two of the interviewers appeared on time, and she was forced to remain in the waiting room until the others appeared. She became angry as her waiting time increased.

When everyone finally showed up, she was ushered into the room and found herself placed in a low-cushioned chair surrounded by seven interviewers in straight-backed chairs about a foot higher than her own. She forced herself to sit on the edge of the sofa chair to avoid sinking down into the cushion.

The chairman of the interview group then commented, "I don't believe anyone has seen your résumé. I'll pass it around so the others can see it."

"Incredible!" she thought. "How could anyone be so unprepared?" Once again, she waited, and her stress level rose as the men slowly passed her papers around the group.

As they spoke, the negative aspects of her Noble style began to dominate her conversation. She provided absolute and abrupt responses to questions presented and began to interpret the entire session as something akin to a Nazi inquisition. Finally, one of the interviewers said, "I'd like to return to a question I asked earlier that I don't think you answered fully." He barely had the words out of his mouth when she stood up, looked directly at him, and firmly stated,

> "I didn't answer the question because I haven't been allowed to fully answer any of the questions without being interrupted. Your attitude makes it apparent that you are not interested in hiring me, and quite frankly, I am no longer interested in working with you."

On that note, she left the room.

When the young doctoral candidate returned to her university campus, she ran into her adviser and began to relay her experience to him. As she spoke, her eyes began to fill with tears, and she slowly sank into the chair nearest to him. He listened intently to the details of the story and then suggested that they try to analyze what happened from a communication perspective.

He spoke calmly and explained that not only were her expectations shattered, but surely the expectations of the interviewers were also out of balance. He said,

> "Linda, these people expected you to communicate like a soft female, but in their eyes, you communicate like a tough man, and they weren't able to deal with that any better than you were able to deal with their communication behaviors."

Yes, I was the young doctoral candidate in this story, and no, I didn't get the job that I wanted so badly. Who was right and who was wrong in this interview is not important. What is important is that I should have been able to control my communication style to control the outcome of the interaction. If I wanted the job, it was my responsibility to make my communication style work for me instead of against me.

Whether you are applying for a job or trying to solidify your position within your current organization, it is the one-on-one interaction that will, ultimately, make or break your career. You must be able to combine your knowledge of organizational culture with your communication style capabilities to control the one-on-one interaction. If you aren't able to manage people problems, your ability to handle technical problems will probably be overlooked. And if you are able to manage the most difficult of people, then your technical shortcomings will probably be tolerated.

TALKING WITH YOUR BOSS, COLLEAGUES, SUBORDINATES, AND CLIENTS: IS THERE A DIFFERENCE?

Difficult people come in all sizes, shapes, colors, and ethnic origins. Men and women can be difficult, and your boss, colleagues, subordinates, and clients can be difficult. The one characteristic that all of these people have in common is that each has a dominant style of communication. How you talk to any of these people is dependent on that style. To whom you are talking, however, determines what you will or will not say.

During the course of your career, you may be called upon to deal with any number of work-related behavior problems, some more difficult than others. One of the most difficult problems you may encounter is sexual harassment. Current research reveals that the average company will pay out more than $1 million yearly to settle sexual harassment lawsuits, and if you cause your company, by your actions or inaction, to lose $1 million, your career will undoubtedly be broken.

Sexual harassment is not an exaggerated problem, and it is not an issue that affects only women. It isn't even an issue about sex. Like rape, sexual harassment is an issue of power, aggression, and cruelty that knows no gender. It is one person's attempt to use intimidation and threats to force another person to do something that he or she does not want to do; more important, it is against the law. We're going to look at sexual harassment from two different perspectives: to see how to use style to ward off unwanted advances and then to explore options in dealing with the accused sexual harasser.

First, one argument often offered in defense of a sexual harasser must be dismissed. Some people attempt to justify this repugnant behavior by saying that the victim dressed seductively and therefore she asked to be harassed. This defense, typically used in reference to a woman's appearance, is as much an insult to men as it is to women. It reduces the entire male population to an animalistic level, suggesting that men are unable to control their desires and that when confronted with an attractive woman respond like animals driven by the scent of the mating season. Only someone speaking from a position of ignorance would suggest that an attractive woman is "asking" to be harassed, and this assertion of ignorance is indeed an insult to men as well as women.

Research suggests that no one single approach to the problem of sexual harassment is more effective than another. Being direct, using humor, or ignoring the person are strategies that may or may not be effective. Two things, however, are clear: (1) it is your responsibility to let the harasser know that you want the behaviors to stop, and (2) you must be able to use your knowledge of communication style to accomplish this goal. Let's add another goal: to retain a professional, amicable relationship with the offender. That is, you want the offensive behaviors or remarks to stop, but you do not want to make this person your enemy. This isn't always possible, because some people really are scoundrels, but if you can do it, you are well on your way to becoming the master of your own destiny.

I'm going to provide three common scenarios, and I want you to think about a Noble, a Socratic, and a Reflective response to each scenario. (You might want to take out a piece of paper and write out your responses.) In the first scenario, you are the boss, and it is your subordinate who is engaging in sexually harassing behaviors.

Scenario One: Off-Color Jokes Meant to
Degrade the Opposite Sex

Each time your department has a meeting, John (or June if you are a male doing this exercise) takes delight in telling raucous jokes that degrade women (or men). You are the only female (or male), and the other men (or women) laugh at the jokes and then look at you. What do you say?

In the next scenario, it is your colleague who is engaging in sexually harassing behaviors.

Scenario Two: Unwanted Touching

Every time Donald (Donna) walks past you, he (she) pats your behind and says, "You're doing great work. You could really go far with this company." He (she) has just patted your behind again. What do you do or say?

In the third scenario, your boss is engaging in sexually harassing behaviors:

Scenario Three: The Request for Sexual Favors

You are having a business dinner with your boss in a hotel dining room. You are both attending an out-of-town conference. He (she) moves closer to you and says, "I can be very instrumental in moving your career forward. Why don't we go up to my room and discuss this?" What do you say?

Draw upon all three dominant styles of communication to create different responses to the same situation. (I didn't ask for responses for the Magistrate, the Candidate, or the Senator because the three dominant styles are the basis for these other styles. Once you can create the three dominant styles, you will be ready to move on to the others.)

Obviously you cannot rely only on style of communication to solve these sensitive problems because sexual harassment goes beyond style. If you were able to create a Noble, Socratic, and Reflective sound for each of the three scenarios, however, you are more than halfway there. You are beginning to see that communication is a matter of choice and that you can create different outcomes with style.

It isn't possible to predict which style would be most effective in getting each of the three harassers to discontinue the behaviors because you need to have more information about the people and situation. But we can create some stylized responses and see how they compare to the rebuttals you generated. As a rejoinder to John or June and the offensive jokes, imagine your mom placing her hand on your arm, raising her eyebrow and saying:

NOBLE RESPONSE: (calmly and without emotion) Save the sick jokes for the boy's locker room, John. This is a business meeting. They are inappropriate and offensive.

SOCRATIC RESPONSE: John, humor is a great thing in its place. This, however, is not the appropriate place for those types of remarks. A stag party, a locker room, or the little boy's room might be okay. This is a business meeting, so it's not okay. You know women tell some pretty nasty jokes about men, too. But I wouldn't tell them here, and I would certainly not tell them if you were the only man in the room. I am your colleague, and I am offended by those remarks. Please use some discretion from now on.

REFLECTIVE RESPONSE: (softly) Oh John. That was really sick. Would you say something like that in front of your mother or daughter?

Now let's try the octopus. Look the offender directly in the eyes, and calmly say:

NOBLE RESPONSE: And you, my dear friend, are going to have a broken arm if you don't keep your hands to yourself.

SOCRATIC RESPONSE: This is my right shoulder, and this is my left shoulder. If you feel the urge to pat me, please use one of these two parts of my anatomy. I'm not a football player, you know.

REFLECTIVE RESPONSE: I'm sure you mean no disrespect, but I don't think your wife or my husband would be pleased to see you pat me on the behind. A pat on my back or shoulder would be just fine.

Now for the tough one, your boss. Although your boss is wrong in making the remarks, it is probably a good idea to let him or her save face. You might say:

"I'm very flattered by your attention. You are a very attractive person, and if you weren't my boss, I'd consider the offer. But you are my boss, and these sorts of comments can place us both in jeopardy, so I'll simply say good night."

Let's try another response, but this time, we'll let your boss do some talking.

BOSS: I can be very instrumental in moving your career forward. Why don't we go up to my room and discuss this?

YOU: No, I don't think so.

BOSS: Aww, c'mon. We'll have a nice glass of wine. What can it hurt?

YOU: Your marriage . . . my life . . . our careers.

BOSS: Look, no one will know, and I will be most unhappy if I think you are unwilling to cooperate with your boss on such a simple matter.

YOU: You'd be even more unhappy if I gave you a disease and your wife divorced you and took you for everything you have.

Comments about disease usually stop these sorts of advances, but let's say this guy (or gal) is really a scoundrel. Let's say the advances keep coming, and your attempts at ignoring him, using humor, and making sarcastic replies simply aren't working. What do you do? You pick an appropriate time and place, and then you must specifically request that the behaviors be discontinued. Depending on the type of person you are dealing with, it is probably a good idea to let him or her have a second chance at saving face. You say,

"You may not be aware of the fact that your comments make me uncomfortable, but they do. Please stop suggesting that we have anything more than a business relationship."

If that doesn't work or your request is met with a threat, then you need to document everything that has happened and go to a leader who is in a position to handle the problem. Once informed of the problem, the leader has several options. If the next person on the hierarchical ladder chooses to do nothing, that person becomes liable in a sexual harassment lawsuit. Leaders, of course, do not ignore problems; they attempt to solve them. Let's briefly see how you do that.

How you deal with the sexual harasser is important because your behaviors will establish the ground rules for future behaviors. You will want to get his or her version of the story, and you may want to gather information from other sources. In doing this, you will need to draw upon your Reflective style of communication to get people to open up. You will need to ask questions in a careful and nonjudgmental manner to encourage honest responses.

Regardless of the outcome of your investigation, it is your responsibility to make it clear to the accused that sexual harassment is against the law. If your investigation leads you to believe that the person may have been wrongly accused, then you may want to get the two parties together to discuss perceptions and iron out any misunderstandings. If your investigation leads you to believe that there is a problem, then you must make it clear that any similar behaviors in the future will not be tolerated. This is not the time to be Reflective; this is the time to be a Magistrate. State that the behaviors are unacceptable, and clearly explain all of the conditions that constitute a legal definition of sexual harassment. Remember that your ability to control the outcome of these types of interactions can make or break your career.

TALKING WITH THE CHRONIC COMPLAINER

In most situations, personality shouldn't interfere with your ability to control outcomes. People are what they are, and each of us is in some way a little eccentric. We can't do anything about personalities, so we work with the elements we can control, like communication style. There are some personalities, however, that we cannot ignore. These are the people who go beyond annoying (where most of us fall) and yet still remain within the limits of what is considered normal human behavior.

Let's take a quick look at three of the most common personality problems you may have to encounter at work. We'll start with the chronic complainer.

A chronic complainer can be a Noble, a Socratic, a Reflective, a Magistrate, a Candidate, a Senator, or a Student. It isn't communication style that makes a person a chronic complainer; it's personality. A chronic complainer can be someone with a truly negative outlook on life or someone who, as the Yiddish expression goes, just likes to kvetch. They complain, but it really doesn't matter; they get over it.

The past is a favorite topic for the chronic complainer, so let's see if we can talk our way into and out of trouble with the person who always complains about what happened in the past. Our chronic complainer is a Magistrate who likes to kvetch.

You are the new principal of Chippewa High School. The former principal was unethical and used intimidation tactics to try to motivate his faculty. Connie is an excellent English teacher who used to coach drama. The school hasn't had a drama program in five years. You realize the arts are an integral part of a well-rounded education. You would like to motivate Connie to resurrect the the drama program.

PRINCIPAL: Connie, the school is badly in need of a drama program. There are a lot of artistic students who have no outlet for their talents. I'd like you to bring back the drama program.

CONNIE: Just like that (snaps her fingers) you want me to bring back the drama program? Do you have any idea what it takes to run a successful program? You know, I did this before, and it was one major headache after another. Every production was heart attack city. Karl [the former principal] would promise his total support and then provide nothing but complaints. He'd promise funds, and halfway into the production, he'd say there was no money, and the students and I would have to go out and beg for money and materials for our costumes and set. Then, God forbid, one of the students should get into a little trouble. Suddenly I'm the bad guy responsible for the actions of every student in the school. Do you know that the year we did *Arsenic and Old Lace,* he suspended my Teddy Roosevelt the day of our opening performance? Now you tell me how you do *Arsenic* without a Teddy!

PRINCIPAL: That was then, and this is now. You had a wonderful reputation as a coach, and the students need you. I'm asking you to do it. I know you'll be successful.

CONNIE: Yes, but you don't understand. I've tried this in the past and it comes out of my hide. I'm here until all hours of the night, and everyone else is at home with their families. The additional pay that I get works out to be about four cents an hour. And then there are the parents. If Johnny isn't home by eight, they . . .

PRINCIPAL: Connie! I'm tired of hearing about the past. I'm not Karl. I'll give you the support you need, within reason.

CONNIE: Within reason! Boy, I've heard those words before, and "within reason" usually turns into "the funds just aren't there."

PRINCIPAL: Enough with what used to be. Will you do the program or not?

CONNIE: No. I don't think it is in my best interest to do the program at this time.

What do you think? Can you do better? Before you start, here's an additional hint about the chronic complainer. If you want to get the chronic complainer to work with you, you must always acknowledge the legitimacy of the complaints. This requires drawing upon the grain-of-truth technique that is characteristic of the Reflective style. Once you have acknowledged that there is validity to the complaints, you can use communication style to control the outcome. For this scenario, use Connie's directive nature and attention to detail to get her to suggest ways to resurrect the program. With these suggestions in mind, think about how you could use communication style to motivate Connie to want to resurrect the drama program.

Now analyze what you just did. Will it work? Will you be able to control the outcome of the interaction? Give this scenario to a couple of your colleagues. Compare their responses, and talk about strategies for motivating the chronic complainer who actually has a lot of potential. Compare your strategies with mine:

PRINCIPAL: Connie, the school is badly in need of a drama program. There are a lot of artistic students who have no outlet for their talents. I'd like you to bring back the drama program.

CONNIE: Just like that (snaps her fingers) you want me to bring back the drama program? Do you have any idea what it takes to run a successful program? You know I did this before, and it was one major headache after another. Every production was heart attack city. Karl [the former principal] would promise his total support and then provide nothing but complaints. He'd promise funds, and halfway into the production, he'd say there was no money, and the students and I would have to go out and beg for money and materials for our costumes and set. Then, God forbid, one of the students should get into a little trouble. Suddenly, I'm the bad guy responsible for the actions of every student in the school. Do you know that the year we did *Arsenic and Old Lace,* he suspended my Teddy Roosevelt the day of our opening performance? Now you tell me how you do *Arsenic* without a Teddy!

PRINCIPAL: You are absolutely right. I've been going over the records, and your assessment of the situation appears to be correct. You were short-changed in the past. I'm hoping to change all that. I'm also hoping that everything I've heard and read about you is true. You have a wonderful reputation as a coach, and the students need you.

CONNIE: Thank you. I appreciate your comments, but you don't totally understand. I've tried this in the past, and it comes out of my hide. I'm here until all hours of the night, and everyone else is at home with their families. The additional pay that I get works out to be about four cents an hour. And then there are the parents. If Johnny isn't home by eight, they . . .

PRINCIPAL: There's absolutely no denying that this would place an additional burden on you that some of the other teachers don't share. But that's what separates the mediocre teachers from the truly outstanding teachers, and from what I've heard, you are not to be counted with the mediocre group.

CONNIE: No, I'm not. I take a lot of pride in my work, but I'm tired of this system's taking advantage of me.

PRINCIPAL: I can understand that, but I would like to take advantage of your talents. Will you do something for me? Will you put together a short proposal for me that illustrates how we can capitalize on your talents without taking unfair advantage? Tell me what it will take to create an ideal program.

CONNIE: You're not going to give me everything I want for an ideal program.

PRINCIPAL: You're probably right about that, but it does give us someplace to start. What I can guarantee you is that I am committed to helping you build your program, and I am willing to give you a written contract so you know what to expect. There will be no surprises or letdowns, and if it's all right with you, I'd like to use your proposal to try to generate some outside funding to help us eventually get that ideal program. What do you think? Will you give it a try? Will you put together a proposal for me?

CONNIE: All right. I think I can do that much, and if you're serious about the fund raising, I think I can give you some names of people who may be willing to help.

This really isn't so hard, is it? It takes patience, thought, and som planning, but it is possible to avoid unnecessary conflict when you pa attention to and effectively use communication style.

TALKING WITH EMOTIONAL PEOPLE

All normal human beings have emotions, and all of us have times when we are more emotional than usual. We may reveal our emotions differently, but we all have moments when emotions control our intellect.

Emotional moments are perfectly natural events, but it is unnatural for any of us to assume that emotions do not exist or that they should be kept out of the workplace. (Take note Nobles and Magistrates. This exercise is especially for you.) All of us should be able to turn emotional moments into productive moments.

When attempting to turn an emotional moment into a productive moment, it is crucial that you remain calm and listen. Let the other person talk because some of the emotion will be released through the talk. Keep in mind that you can't solve the problem as long as the person is emotional. Once the person begins to calm down, you can begin to deal with the problem at hand. To do this you must be able to utilize Reflective techniques to get the person to acknowledge the cause of the emotion and develop his or her own solution to the problem. In addition, you must be patient and tolerant and allow the person to respond in his or her own communication style. Remember, however, that an emotional moment is also a stressful moment, and in stressful moments, we gravitate to our dominant style, and the negative aspects of the dominant style become worse.

During stressful or emotional moments, each of the six communicators has a different communication focus. If you consider the central focus of the communicator, you will know what to expect and can act accordingly to control the outcome. For example, Nobles focus on the result rather than the process for attaining the result. In addition, during emotional moments, they are likely to be overly abrupt, intimidating, or rude and will probably see only two polarized solutions to the problem. As the leader, it is your responsibility to help Nobles visualize alternatives and the solution process. Utilizing Reflective techniques, you might say,

"The two alternatives you suggest are both possible. I'm very interested in knowing how you arrived at those decisions. Also, let me

229

play the devil's advocate for a minute and suggest that someone up the line is going to reject the solutions. If this happens, what else do you think will work and why?"

Socratics focus on the issue and the rhetoric of the moment rather than the result. When they are emotional or under stress, they are likely to talk incessantly and to suggest a thousand different probable solutions. As an effective problem solver, you will help Socratics visualize a result. You might say,

"You've done an excellent job of analyzing the situation. Of all the solutions you've suggested, I'd like you to select two that you feel have the best chance of success."

Reflectives focus on the other and making that person feel comfortable rather than dealing with the cause of the emotion. If they are experiencing an emotional moment, they are likely to be extremely apologetic and will agree with anything you suggest. Thus, it becomes your responsibility to help Reflectives focus on the self and the cause of the problem and to visualize a result that the self wants to achieve. You might say,

"John, I know you don't like to be directive, and I admire the fact that you don't cast blame on others. I like those qualities, but I desperately need your help and expertise with this problem. If this was a hypothetical situation and you were forced to identify the primary cause of the problem, and there was no one else around to make suggestions, what would you say, and how would you go about correcting the situation?"

Magistrates focus on the rhetoric of the moment as it relates to their internal knowledge and the need to win or be correct. They are likely to be verbose, inattentive, totally dogmatic, and arrogant despite the fact that they are the one experiencing the emotional moment. In order to deal with the Magistrate, you must use the Noble style to help him or her visualize alternative perspectives to the problem—for example,

"I like that. It makes a lot of sense. You're good at analyzing things. Create another scenario for me that might solve the problem. Can you do that?"

Candidates focus on the personal experience and the need to be liked by the other person. If their emotions are running high, they are likely to be extremely verbose and totally indecisive, and they will avoid dealing with the problem so you will not think of them in negative terms. As the person in charge, you can help Candidates visualize how a solution will enhance their positive image:

"You know, Gloria, you're going to have quite a feather in your cap if you can solve this problem. I remember when I first started here. I was always afraid I'd make the wrong decision, so I ended up being very indecisive—a lot like you. Once I learned how to make a decision and run with it, people began taking me seriously."

Finally, Senators focus on the situation and strategy. They may be more concerned with the fact that they have revealed an emotional moment than with finding a solution to the problem. As an expert communicator, it is your responsibility to help Senators visualize the problem and a strategy for solving it. A soft-spoken Noble approach is usually a fairly safe style to use with the Senator:

"Let's talk strategy for a minute. Given the information you have, what do you see as the main problem? Then given this, what is your plan of attack? How are you going to resolve this problem?"

Regardless of which type of difficult person you are dealing with, you will also want to utilize your Reflective techniques to get the person to discuss openly the problem and develop a solution to it. The Rogerian response techniques, I-messages, grain-of-truth messages, verbal qualifiers, and nonverbal support techniques are particularly helpful in dealing with emotional moments.

Think back to the last time you had to deal with an emotional moment and did not turn it into a productive moment. Recreate that moment. What did you do? What did you say? What was the result?

Think about the type of communicator you were dealing with, and try to recreate the scenario. Consider ways to utilize Reflective techniques. Anticipate what the communicator will say and how you will respond. Plan a communication strategy for turning an emotional moment into a productive moment.

There is a big difference between an emotional moment and a crier. Some people are criers, but that does not mean that they are having an emotional moment. If you are dealing with a crier, simply have tissues available and encourage the crier to continue talking. Don't focus on the tears. Just talk calmly, make the tissue available, and be tolerant of the crier's style of communication. Be mindful of the fact that men are just as likely to have emotional moments as are women, but they may reveal their emotions in different ways.

TALKING WITH THE EXPLOSIVE PERSON

We all dread dealing with the explosive person. We try to avoid this person because we don't want to deal with the explosion when it comes. Think back to the last time you dealt with an explosive person and you allowed your emotions, rather than your communication style, to control the outcome of the interaction. These moments are anything but pleasant, but they can be turned around.

You cannot use logic with an irrational person. Never argue with an angry person, because people tend not to rage if they have no one with whom to rage. Remain calm, and use silence as a verbal strategy. When the other person finally realizes that he or she is the only one exploding, the fireworks will end.

Second, keep in mind that you do not have to avoid the person; you only have to ignore the explosion. You can do this if you realize that the explosive person is not out of control. He or she is very much in control, and the explosive person knows that the explosion will control you. It will cause you to explode, it will intimidate you into acquiescence, it will cause you to leave the interaction, or it will allow the explosive person to avoid the issue at hand.

The third thing to keep in mind about some explosive people is that they enjoy the drama of the moment; they are bullies. They particularly like to bully someone when there is an audience. You can fall victim to the drama or you can create your own dramatic moment.

Suppose you call your department manager in and say,

> "Look, I know you're doing a great job, but you're over budget again, and to make matters worse, the word has come done that there will be an across-the-board 10 percent budget cut. You're going to have to get your figures in line."

Your department manager thinks he can intimidate you into exempting him from the budget restraints by flying into a rampage. He yells:

> "Are you crazy? Are they crazy? How the hell am I supposed to put out a product that's competitive? Do you think I can pull these results out of thin air? Cut someone else. Get rid of the nonproducers, or cut the fat in administration. My budget can't take any more cuts!"

If you wish to ignore the explosion or create your own dramatic moment, you need to be able to draw upon your Noble and Senator styles of communication. As a Noble, you may want to follow an explosive moment by calmly replying,

> "Are you done? If so, we can continue."

You might want to ward off the explosion before it occurs by saying,

> "You are not going to like what I'm going to say, but I want you to hold your temper anyway. If you feel the need to explode, you can take a walk or go get a cup of coffee and return when the urge subsides."

You may want to deal with the person whose voice begins to escalate in a meeting by placing your hand on his or her arm or shoulder and softly saying,

> "I know you're angry, but please speak softly and be objective."

Each time the person's voice begins to rise, raise your hand to indicate "stop," and softly say, "objective."

You may want to respond as a Reflective or a Senator by distancing yourself from the situation and changing the environment for the next interaction, as the following experience shows.

When I was teaching high school (a million years ago), I also coached debate. My debate teams were very active and quite successful, and I was constantly negotiating with my principal for resources to maintain the level of activity and success. Our negotiations typically turned into explosions, and I didn't get the resources I wanted.

I was frustrated by these experiences, so I went to see Karen, one of our counselors who appeared to have a fairly good relationship with our principal. She pointed out that Don, the principal, used the explosion to avoid giving me what I wanted. As I began to recall my numerous interactions with Don, I realized that the scenario was always the same. As soon as I made my request for the resource I needed, Don would shift the topic and explode about something one of my debaters or I had done that he didn't like. I would argue the issue with him and leave without my resource. Karen pointed out that I was not negotiating with Don; I was debating him. He always won, and I always lost.

I wasn't thrilled with this realization, but it did force me to think about my communication strategies. The next time I went in to talk with Don and the anticipated explosion came, I quietly stood up and stated,

"I see you are not feeling well. I'll come back later, and we can talk when you are in a better mood."

I came back at the end of the day, poked my head in his office, and said,

"If you are feeling better, I'd like to talk with you about hosting the regionals in March."

We hosted the regionals, we went on to the finals in two divisions, and I never lost another debate with Don.

USING STYLE TO CONDUCT AN EFFECTIVE DISCIPLINE INTERVIEW

Drug and alcohol abuse is pervasive, and it is a problem that we must learn to deal with and attempt to solve. We cannot solve a drug or alcohol problem for an employee, worker, or friend, but we can create an opportunity for the individual to solve his or her own problem. That sounds a bit Noble, but it is also reality.

Following are three dialogues in which the leader and the worker have the same style of communication. The leader observes the worker returning late from lunch—again. As the leader approaches the worker to discuss the problem, he notes the worker's speech is slurred and the smell of alcohol is obvious.

You might be asking yourself, "Is this a good or bad performer?" The answer to this question is, "It doesn't matter." The problem is alcohol, and from a legal standpoint, you must deal with this problem in a consistent manner. Your goal is to identify the drug or alcohol problem and make it clearly understood that the problem cannot continue. It isn't wise to use the alcohol problem as a excuse to get rid of an employee you don't like or one you look upon as a bad performer. The alcohol may be the reason for the bad performance, and a good performer will ultimately become a bad performer if the alcohol problem is not resolved.

NOBLE LEADER: You're late again.

NOBLE WORKER: No I'm not. I stopped in accounting to check some information.

NOBLE LEADER: No you didn't. You've been drinking again.

NOBLE WORKER: I haven't been drinking. I was in accounting. If you don't believe me, ask Allison. She's the one I talked to.

NOBLE LEADER: I can smell the alcohol.

NOBLE WORKER: Big deal. I had a beer at lunch. Is there a law against that?

NOBLE LEADER: Look, I see a pattern developing here. You come back late from lunch, and there's always alcohol on your breath. If this continues, I'll have to let you go.

NOBLE WORKER: Try it, and I'll haul your butt to court. I've got the best record in this department.

This isn't going too well. Maybe a Socratic can do better:

SOCRATIC LEADER: Mitchell, I'm beginning to notice a bit of a pattern here. This is the second time this week that you've returned from lunch late, and I believe it's happened on several other occasions this month.

SOCRATIC WORKER: Well, that's not quite accurate. It may appear that I am returning late, but actually I'm not. I like to run some errands right after lunch so that I don't have to interrupt my work in the afternoon. For example, I stopped in accounting after lunch today. I didn't realize that I needed to keep a log or ask your permission to perform my job.

SOCRATIC LEADER: That isn't the issue, Mitchell. The issue is that a pattern is developing. You return late from lunch, and each time there is the smell of alcohol on your breath. I'm sure you realize that drinking affects performance. Are you aware of the problems caused by alcohol?

SOCRATIC WORKER: Of course, I'm aware. With all of the media attention, who wouldn't be aware, and if I thought I had a problem, I'd be concerned. I did have a beer at lunch, but that does not mean that I have a problem. You are aware of the fact that alcohol is legal, aren't you? There is no law against having a beer with my lunch, is there?

SOCRATIC LEADER: Yes, I am aware of the fact that alcohol is legal, and no, there is no law against having a beer with your lunch. But when you continually return late from lunch and I can smell liquor on your breath, there is a problem. Are you willing to risk your job for a beer at lunch?

SOCRATIC WORKER: No, as a matter of fact, I'm not. If you are threatening to fire me, however, perhaps I should ask you if you are aware of the laws pertaining to wrongful discharge in this state. I just explained that I was not late.

Same result. Let's see if the Reflectives have better luck:

REFLECTIVE LEADER: Mitchell, I'm normally pretty pleased with your work, but I've noticed that you've been coming back late from lunch lately. Is there a problem we should talk about?

REFLECTIVE WORKER: No, not that I can think of. I wasn't actually late. I had to stop in accounting, and you know how Allison likes to chat.

REFLECTIVE LEADER: Oh yes, I know Allison, but that isn't what I am concerned about. I don't want to accuse you of anything, but I think you have been drinking again. Don't you think we should talk about this before Mr. Redding finds out and you lose your job?

REFLECTIVE WORKER: If you don't want to accuse me, then don't. If you want me to say that I had a beer at lunch, fine. I'll say I had a beer. That hardly constitutes a drinking problem, and why would you bring Mr. Redding into this? I have been a really good employee. You have no reason to threaten me like this.

What went wrong? The communication style expectations were met; each person had a style that matched the other person's style. Yet no solution was achieved, and in fact, conflict was generated and battle lines drawn.

In order to create a successful communication encounter, keep in mind that the timing and the situation are most important factors to consider in these instances; the communication style of the other person is of secondary importance. Although there is a point during the interaction where knowledge of the other person's style can help with the desired solution, your success depends on your ability to utilize all styles to conduct a proper discipline interview.

First, you begin by thinking like a Senator. The timing and situation are important. You need to speak with Mitchell when you observe the behavior, but not out in the open. Give Mitchell a chance to return to his desk or work area, and then arrange for a meeting in your office. It is your responsibility to control the outcome of this interview. In the discipline interview you have three goals:

1. To be sure that the worker is aware that a problem exists.
2. To agree on procedures for eliminating the problem.
3. To establish expectations for future behaviors.

You can accomplish these goals by moving in and out of your various styles of communication. (Remember, we all have the ability to use the three dominant styles; we just choose to use one more than the others.) You may find the following steps helpful as you attempt to resolve this problem:

1. Think like a Senator; develop your strategy before you speak.
2. Lead with your Reflective to establish an open, positive interpersonal climate.
3. Move to your Noble and clearly state the purpose of the interview.
4. Blend your Noble with your Socratic to create the Magistrate, and establish the agenda for the interview.

5. Move directly into your Socratic, and objectively describe the events you have observed and documented.

6. Give the worker an opportunity to comment on your observations. This is where you need to be aware of his or her style and use this information to maintain control of the interaction.

7. Agree upon a course of action for eliminating the problem.

8. Use your Noble to state clearly the expectations for future behaviors.

9. End with your Reflective by reestablishing the open communication climate.

Let's see what this sounds like in action:

VERSATILE YOU: Hi, Mitchell. Won't you have a seat. That's an attractive sports coat. Is it new?

MITCHELL: Fairly. I got it last month for my birthday.

VERSATILE YOU: It's very nice. I like it. Mitchell, I've enjoyed working with you, and you certainly have made some significant contributions to our department. Today, however, I need to speak with you about a problem I have observed. I am going to explain the problem, and then I am going to ask for your comments. When we are done speaking, I anticipate that we will have a solution worked out for this problem. Does that sound reasonable to you?

MITCHELL: Sure. This must be serious. You're so formal.

VERSATILE YOU: Yes Mitchell, it is serious, but it is something that can be solved. During the past month, I have observed you returning late from lunch on six different occasions. I have the specific dates listed here . . .

MITCHELL: Hey, I wasn't late. I was running errands. What is this anyway? I'm not . . .

VERSATILE YOU: Mitchell, I'm going to give you a chance to respond in just a minute. I need you to listen to what I have to say first. If we interrupt each other, we aren't going to get anything solved. I'd like to have this session end on a positive note, so can you hang in there for a minute while I continue?

MITCHELL: (reluctantly nods his head)

VERSATILE YOU: I first observed this change in behavior last month, but I ignored it, assuming that you were engaging in work-related activities. However, the end-of-the month reports came in, and they revealed a definite drop in your productivity and a significant increase in errors. I spoke with you on the third, the tenth, and the seventeenth. On each of these occasions, the smell of alcohol was obvious. Today the smell of alcohol is obvious. Drinking while on the job is strictly against company policy. This is a problem we must solve. Is there a reason for this change in your behavior?

MITCHELL: There is no change in behavior. I only had one beer at lunch. That's not a crime, is it?

VERSATILE YOU: I have documented the change in behavior. It's all here. I'd like this to be a problem-solving session — not a warning session, but that can occur only if you are willing to work with me. I'd like to help you, but you have to be willing to be truthful and talk about this problem. Would you like to talk about this with a professional counselor?

MITCHELL: If you think that would help.

VERSATILE YOU: I don't know if it will help. That part is up to you, but I'm willing to work with you. Here is the telephone number of Dr. LaBahn. I'd like you to call him and set up an appointment. After you've seen him, we will speak again. In the meantime, you must understand that alcohol during working hours is strictly forbidden. Failure to observe this rule will result in disciplinary action, and a continued decrease in your productivity could lead to dismissal. I don't want that, and I know you don't want that. May I count on you to observe this rule?

MITCHELL: I'll do my best.

VERSATILE YOU: Good. You're a valuable employee, and I'd like it to stay that way. If you feel you'd like to talk about this more, my door is always open.

There, that wasn't so bad. Was it? Of course, some people are more reluctant to acquiesce than Mitchell, but you can handle that if you continue to control the style component and if you focus on the company policy and your desire to work with the offender.

Over the years, I have noticed consistent behavior from substance abusers. When initially confronted, they deny that a problem exists. They are all embarrassed by the problem. Some try to hide their embarrassment with hostile or defensive behaviors, but nonetheless, they are not proud of their problem. No one wants to be an alcoholic or a drug addict. These people are typically ashamed of their problem, and in many cases they will seek help if they know you are willing to work with them instead of just threatening dismissal.

We can save organizations a lot of money and some valuable employees, and we may even be able to turn some nonproductive employees into performers by using communication style to handle problems properly. We can't reach everybody, but if we don't try, we won't reach anybody. Communication style can help us reach a few somebodies.

Chapter 12

Using Style to Climb the Corporate Ladder

NEGOTIATING SALARY IN A JOB INTERVIEW

Negotiating salary in a job interview is a bit different from asking for a raise. In the job interview, the company is trying to acquire a scarce resource, so you (the scarce resource) often have the advantage. If you are asking for a raise, the company already has you, so it has the advantage. In addition, employment contracts and unionized organizations often have strict guidelines or rules governing pay raises, and some organizations do not provide merit pay. Thus, your best opportunity for negotiating salary requirements is when you enter the organization.

The Reflective and the Candidate are the most uncomfortable with the task of negotiating salary. I want to show you a negotiation trick that will help these two communicators feel comfortable, and if it works for these two considerate communicators, it will work for the rest of us too.

The whole process begins with research, which, of course, is the basis for any good negotiation effort. Before going into the final interview where salary is going to be discussed, do your homework to determine the going rate for the position. Determine the salary range being offered by competitors and the salaries for comparable positions in the organization with which you are negotiating. Look at your current salary and determine the percentage of increase that would be appropriate given your new responsibilities. Put these figures down on small pieces of paper, and when your interviewer says, "What type of salary are you expecting?" You respond,

> "Well I've given this a considerable amount of thought. I did some research and found that the salary range for this type of position looks something like this [you show your first piece of paper with salary figures written on it]. Company Z, your closest competitor, has salaries at the high end of this range. This is my current salary [second piece of paper], and I think a 20 percent increase would be appropriate given the expanded responsibilities of this position. That would put me at the high end of the salary range for comparable positions within this company [show third piece of paper]. If we can get close to this figure [pointing at the high figure], we have a deal."

But suppose that instead of giving you a chance to take the lead, your prospective boss says, "I'm prepared to offer you a salary of $45,000." That is lower than you would like, so you respond,

> "I'm really excited about the possibility of joining your team, but we're not exactly in the same ballpark with respect to salary. I'm sure we can work this out. I've done some research and found . . ."

You continue with the previous scenario, and there is a good chance that you will get the figure you requested. I can testify that this trick works. I may be Noble, but I hate talking about salary. I devised this method of negotiating to get me past that uncomfortable segment of the interview, and it's never failed me yet. Moreover, I ask for the same amount of money the men ask for—and I get it. Yes, I know we have equal pay for equal work laws, but in reality, women still make less than men. Part of the reason that we make less is that we ask for less. Research shows that women tend to underestimate their monetary worth and tend to accept lower salaries than their male counterparts. If you ask for less, you will get less. Remember that salary is a negotiable item. It would be nice if the boss would say, "Your salary requirements are really too low. I'd like to start you at a higher salary," but there's not much chance of this happening. So do your research, and you probably will get what you ask for or close to it.

My negotiation strategies may be perceived as soft by Nobles, Magistrates, and maybe even some Socratics. As I said, these strategies are helpful for Reflectives and Candidates, who are uncomfortable with the salary aspects of an interview. These strategies will work for the other communicators too, but if you personally feel you want a stronger, more direct approach, certainly use one—as long as the person you are negotiating with isn't a Reflective or Candidate. If you are too strong with these communicators, he or she will smile and say, "That sounds reasonable, but I'll need to give it some thought [or I'll need to run this past my boss], and I'll get back to you." Unless there is no one else under consideration for the position, the message brought back will not be the one you want to hear. With that thought in mind, let's see what a successful negotiation with a Reflective might sound like:

REFLECTIVE: What sort of salary did you have in mind?

YOU: Well, I've given that some thought. It's my understanding that your company is competitive with respect to salaries. Would you say that's a fair assessment?

REFLECTIVE: Why, yes. I believe we are.

YOU: Good. I'm glad to hear you reinforce that piece of information because I'm truly excited about the possibility of working here. I think we can make that possible with a salary in the $60,000 to $65,000 range. Is that request in line with your salary structure?

REFLECTIVE: Not quite. That's a bit on the high side.

YOU: Is it really? I'm somewhat surprised by that. What is the top amount you are able to pay for this position?

REFLECTIVE: Actually $60,000 is our top end.

YOU: That's not really too bad, but it's the low end of what I expected. Do you have any room for flexibility?

REFLECTIVE: A little but not much. You know we're in the midst of a recession, and some of the people who've been around here for a while will be concerned about bringing someone in from the outside at that salary.

YOU: Ah yes, I know, but I'm not a new kid on the block. I bring a tremendous amount of experience with me, and I'm the type of worker your company needs during these tough times. How about if I accept the $60,000 with a clause in my contract for a salary review and a raise at six months?

REFLECTIVE: Hmmm, all right. That's sounds reasonable.

YOU: (shaking her hand) Great. I'm looking forward to being part of your team. When would you like me to start?

REFLECTIVE: As soon as you get your physical, and we process the paperwork.

That went pretty well. Now let's try it again. This time the person you are negotiating with is a Noble.

NOBLE: We can offer you $50,000 as a starting salary. Is that acceptable?

YOU: Well, not really. I was under the impression that you offered a competitive salary.

NOBLE: We do, but times are tough right now.

YOU: Yes, I understand that, and that's why you need to hire the best possible person for this job. You need someone who can carry you through the rough times. I'm that person, but $50,000 isn't appropriate for someone with my background and level of expertise.

NOBLE: What is appropriate?

YOU: $60,000.

NOBLE: No way. I can't do it. The budget's just too tight.

YOU: All right. How about if we meet halfway: $55,000?

NOBLE: That I can probably manage.

YOU: Great, then we've got a deal, but I'd like a salary review with the possibility for a raise in six months. Does that sound fair?

NOBLE: I can live with that. Welcome aboard.

Keep in mind that even Nobles and Magistrates may reject a salary request that sounds like a demand. Negotiations are give-and-take situations where style of communication is very important, but the other person's style isn't the only determining factor. It is the situation—the negotiating event—combined with your dominant style of communication that creates the communication moment. Successfully negotiating salary requirements is the process of blending negotiating skills with communication style skills to control the outcome of the interaction.

HOW TO NEGOTIATE A RAISE

It is easier to negotiate initial salary requirement because once you are inside, the organizational constraints influence wage increases. One thing, however, is certain: your chances of getting the raise you feel you deserve are less if you don't at least ask for it. Men tend to ask for more, and they get more, and this holds true with other resources not just pay increases. Consider Beth's story:

I did not get what I wanted when I did not ask for it. We had cubicle offices and window offices. I sat in the cubicles with several male colleagues. One by one they were moved into window offices, while I remained in the cubicles. Several males who were hired after me also went to offices. One i particular told me he was next in line for an office and that it had been part of his negotiations for the job. I presume they thought me content to stay in the cubicles since I did not voice my opinion either way.

Beth didn't get what she wanted because she didn't ask for it. It would be nice if we all received automatic pay increases commensurate with our merit, but "nice" isn't a quality attributed to most organizations. If you feel you deserve a significant raise in pay, you'll probably have to ask for it.

Performance is your best bargaining chip when you are seeking a raise. You must be able to demonstrate that you deserve a raise, and to determine how much of a raise you deserve, you need to quantify your performance. Look at your goals and objectives. Did you meet them, or did you exceed your performance expectations? If you were 20 percent over goal, then a 20 percent increase should be your starting point in your raise negotiations.

Timing is also a good bargaining chip. If you can give your boss something he or she want or needs (a new client or a sizable contract, for example) just before merit pay decisions are being made, you are more likely to get the raise you want.

Use information as a bargaining chip too. Find out what you are worth on the open market. What will someone else pay for your services?

Go into the negotiations prepared to place your chips on the table at the appropriate time and prepared to use communication style to guide the direction of the interaction. This means that you must know the dominant style of communication displayed by your boss, and you must use this information to control the outcome of the interaction.

HOW TO GAIN RECOGNITION AND GET PROMOTIONS

I start this section by showing how communication style can be used to get a promotion in two Socratic stories. In the first story, Brad, a Socratic who is a manager of financial analysis and reporting, explains how he approached his vice-president, also a Socratic, to discuss the possibility of a promotion.

Ray is the newly hired vice-president and corporate controller of our company. I didn't know it then, but he had (and still has) a Socratic communication style. He likes to sit and talk—kind of like a grandfather telling stories about the war or something. He is about fifty years old, born in Germany, came to the United States when he was a young teenager. He is what I call a regular guy. He prefers water skiing on the Colorado River to sunbathing in Acapulco.

My goal was to get out of the treasury department and into accounting. I had been in cash management for seven years—much too long.

I went up to the fourth floor where the executive offices are and went to see Ray. Surprisingly, he was not busy, and we began to talk. I began:

> "Ray, I understand you are looking to hire an accounting supervisor to be in charge of the general ledger system. I would like you to consider me for the position."

Ray asked me what my salary grade was. After answering, he replied that I was overqualified. We began to talk about my career to date at the company. We talked for over an hour. I didn't get the job, fortunately, because later he created a new position of financial analyst, which he hired me to do—a much more challenging job with better advancement opportunities.

Take heed, Nobles. Brad got recognition and a promotion because he took the time to sit and talk with the person who had the power to advance his career. He chatted with him for more than an hour, which is how he came to know that Ray liked water skiing on the Colorado River better than sunbathing in Acapulco.

Everyone take heed. Brad did not get the promotion he requested, but he didn't get angry. He stayed around to chat with his Socratic boss, and he eventually got a better promotion.

Now let's listen to a Socratic explain how she dealt with a Noble boss to get the promotion she wanted. Meiyi is a stockbroker, and she tells the following story:

Kent is the manager of our underwriting department. He talks firmly—straightforward, and to the point. He is results oriented without showing how to get the job done in detail. I consider him a Noble style communicator.

I needed to get his approval so that I could be transferred from the stock brokerage department to the underwriting department.

On the day of the interview, I dressed to look trustful and professional. I stated my strong wish to be transferred to the underwriting department and stated why. Later he asked whether I thought I would meet those requirements, which were strong accounting and auditing backgrounds and experiences. I told him frankly that I had quite strong accounting and auditing backgrounds, but I lacked experience. Furthermore, I emphasized that I was willing to work hard to get the job done above the average performance. One week later, I was informed of being admitted to work in the underwriting department.

I succeeded in getting what I wanted because a few days before the interview, I observed the manager and knew he was the kind of person who tended to expect the other people to express true feelings, he expects yes-no responses from the other person, he expects orderly, concise communication, and he dislikes listening to detailed expression. Therefore, even though I am a Socratic style communicator, I tried to make myself look more like a Noble style communicator during the interview.

Meiyi had the training necessary for the job, but she didn't have the experience required. She used style of communication to get the promotion anyway.

Now we'll look at how you can develop communication strategies to help you climb the ladder of success. I'll provide a scenario and some communication style information. Try to develop a strategy based on this information. You might find it interesting to compare your strategies with those of a colleague who is also reading this book. Think about your strategies, and then I'll provide a strategic analysis of some of the possible responses. Here is the scenario:

You are a marketing representative in the department of marketing, advertising, and public relations. You were named Marketing Representative of the Year twice during the three years you have been with the company, and your sales always surpass established goals. Your company paid tuition for your night school classes at the university, and you have just completed your degree in organizational communication. You have recently married, and the additional money will help you and your spouse purchase a home. You would like to be considered for the marketing manager's position that has just opened. Your only internal competition is a person who has been with the company for five years and was named Marketing Representative of the Year during your first year with the company. You have heard that your boss, the director of the department, is thinking about going to the outside to bring in some new blood. You want to be sure that your boss knows you would like to be considered for the promotion.

Your boss is a Noble. Keep in mind the following points for controlling Nobles:

- Be direct, and simply say what you have to say.
- Be concise and orderly.
- Start your conversation by stating your purpose or conclusion first.
- Identify your main points, and ask if the Noble would like additional information.
- Don't be offended or intimidated by the Noble.
- Tell the Noble if he or she has done or said something that bothers you.
- If you want the Noble to do something, try providing two alternatives from which to choose.

With this information in mind, create a communication strategy designed to increase your chances of being considered for the promotion.

Now try the same scenario but this time with a boss who is a Reflective. In addition to controlling the negative aspects of your own style, be reminded of the following points when attempting to persuade a Reflective:

- Take time to develop the interpersonal aspect of the conversation.

- Attempt to include or draw the Reflective into the conversation using Rogerian response techniques.

- Use a self-disclosure or I-message combined with a qualifier and a what-if statement to gather honest information.

- Avoid bullying the Reflective into doing what you want. He or she will get you in the end.

Let's do a brief analysis of possible strategies. With both the Noble and the Reflective boss, timing and environment are important. An effective strategy should include an appointment time and meeting location. If your office enhances your image, try to meet there. If your office is a mess, don't even think about meeting there. Also with both the Noble and Reflective boss, your internal competition is of no relevance. Your job is to present your attributes, not to criticize the competition. Both the Noble and the Reflective would find critical remarks about your colleague inappropriate. With these guidelines in mind, you might say to your Noble boss:

"Thank you for agreeing to see me. I know your schedule is tight, so I'll get right to the point. I'd like to throw my hat in the ring for the marketing manager's position. I've put together a one-page analysis of my productivity figures for the three years I've been with the company, and as you know, I've been Marketing Representative of the Year two of those three years."

With your Reflective boss, first engage in some polite conversation. Comment on something in the office, his or her clothing, something positive that he or she has recently accomplished, or something positive that is currently happening in the company. If you know the boss well enough, ask questions about the family, some other aspect of his or her personal life, and/or give information about some aspect of your personal life with which the boss may be familiar. Then proceed:

> "Well, listen. I know you're busy, and I don't want to take up your whole afternoon, so I guess I should tell you why I asked to meet with you. I know the marketing manager's position is open, and I am hoping you will consider me as one of the candidates. And if it's okay with you, I'd like to share a few pieces of information with you. I've prepared a brief analysis of my productivity figures for you to take a look at if you like, and you already know I've been Marketing Representative of the Year two of the three years I've been with you."

Calling attention to the outside candidates is an issue that can be raised with both the Noble and Reflective boss. For the Noble, focus on the bottom line: the company's investment in your tuition:

> "You may not know that I just completed my degree. That represents a \$10,000 investment that this company has made in my future, and I'd like to provide a return on that investment by staying and growing with the company. I heard a rumor about bringing someone in from outside, but that seems like a waste of your investment. I also want to give a little pitch here for continuity. I know our product and our company. You won't have to waste time training me. I can hit the ground running."

For the Reflective, focus on the interpersonal—the need to promote from within to establish trust and loyalty:

> "I am very pleased that the company's tuition reimbursement plan allowed me to complete my college education. It really makes me feel

good to know that my company was willing to invest that much money in my future. I'd like to show that the faith was not misplaced. I'd like to grow and develop with the company, and I think that's a major advantage I have over someone from the outside. The company has been loyal to me, and I am loyal to the company."

Your strategy with the Noble boss should *not* include reference to your recent marriage. Your strategy with the Reflective *may* include reference to your recent marriage, but be careful—it may work against you. The Reflective may feel that the promotion will place a burden on your new interpersonal relationship or that you need the promotion because of this new interpersonal situation. (I do not think the marriage should be an issue, but then I'm not Reflective.)

Finally, if you decided to use the either-or strategy with the Noble, make sure that you didn't actually issue an ultimatum. If you asked the Noble to choose between your quitting or your promotion, start looking for another job. In a communication such as this, the either-or strategy needs to include two positive alternatives.

I can't guarantee that your request for promotion will be granted on your first try. There may be organizational variables that will attenuate your communication efforts. But I can guarantee that you will gain recognition if you handle the moment correctly by controlling communication style.

The fastest way to get recognition in any organization is to be known as a problem solver. Three stories illustrate this point. The first story is provided by Keith, a Socratic who is a human resource administrator in the aerospace industry. Keith tells how his style of communication kept him from gaining recognition:

Pete is our unit manager and my boss. He has been with the company over twenty-five years and is well respected in his field. He is a Noble in his written and verbal communications. I am a Socratic and I tend to ramble on (as I have done here). I was trying to get a procedure that I am currently involved with deleted from existence.

I approached Pete to discuss my views and get his okay to proceed with my work. During our conversation, I had a great deal of trouble communicating my point and was confusing him because I was giving him a lot of detailed information. I explained at least a dozen things that were wrong with the procedure, and I went into great detail about the negative effects of the procedure. Because I was taking so long to get to the point, I was asked to come back at another time to continue our discussion. He was not mean about it, but he could not stand to listen to all that I evidently had to say.

Keith learned from this disappointing interaction. He provides the following story of a subsequent interaction with Pete:

My goal was to get a problem in our group reviewed and gain the approval to implement a solution. A task was being performed by a group that I thought should not have the responsibility. I wanted our group to take over the responsibility.

I told Pete that I felt this situation was a problem, and I asked that our group take over the responsibility of salaried promotions. I followed my statement with an example. Since I now know that he is a Noble, I tried to be very short and to the point. I have also learned that I need to make good recommendations, which I did. His response was favorable, and I was asked to put my thoughts down on paper so he could review them with his manager and the other affected group managers. In the end, my proposed solution to the problem was adopted.

One final example will show how style can be used to gain recognition as a problem solver. Laura is a Reflective but found that she needed to change that style to get the results she wanted. Laura explains:

I was talking with my boss, whom I would definitely classify as a Noble type of communicator. My goal was to get him to rethink his litigation strategy on a particular lawsuit being defended by our office. My boss wanted to be very hard-nosed in his interactions with the plaintiff, while I believed that the case would be settled at a lower cost to our client if we attempted to come to an amicable settlement.

I told my boss that he was acting too rashly and acting more out of ego than in the best interest of our client. He seemed shocked that I would actually tell him that he had a big ego, and actually, it was unlike me to do that, but I had just gotten fed up that particular day.

The approach worked. I think he was so shocked that I would actually speak to him that way that he listened to me and agreed that we would try my approach, which did, in fact, work to our client's advantage.

Laura went on to explain that she typically felt she didn't get what she wanted because she wasn't aggressive enough. She said, "I am not the type of employee who likes to complain about things, but I've learned that sometimes the squeaky wheel does get the grease."

Staying where you are can be comfortable. When you decide to move up or move on, you lose your comfort factor and introduce risk. When you say, "I'm going to try for a promotion," you place yourself in an uncertain environment, and you run the risk of rejection, which can be painful. I end this discussion on promotions with a story that might help reduce some of the pain you may encounter.

A few years back, I was at a writers' conference where I was fortunate enough to hear Terry Louise Fisher speak. Fisher is the co-creator, producer, and writer of the hit television series "L.A. Law" and a former producer of the very successful "Cagney and Lacey" series. She told us how she had gotten started in show business.

Fisher is a lawyer by profession and had been working as a district attorney. She had just returned from a trip exhausted and furious with the airline company for losing her luggage. The trip had not helped to instill her with a renewed sense of purpose as she had hoped; she dreaded the thought of facing another year as a district attorney. She was sitting slouched down in a sofa chair with her legs outstretched, her head resting on her hand, contemplating her less-than-exciting future when the telephone rang.

The friend on the other end of the line told her that one of the major entertainment studios was looking for an attorney. Her friend emphasized that it was imperative that she go over immediately and speak with the executive in charge if she wished to be considered. Fisher was exhausted, looked terrible, and didn't have a suit for the interview since her clothes were in transit somewhere in the Southern Hemisphere. But she ended up going for the interview, and despite the fact that she was totally unprepared and inappropriately dressed, she got the job.

She didn't quite understand what she had done to make such a positive impression. Shortly after she began in her new position, she visited her new boss and asked him what she had done in the interview that was impressive enough to make him want to hire her.

He responded that she hadn't impressed him. To the contrary, he had hired her because she was the least impressive of all those who interviewed for the position. He said he was tired of hiring dynamite, hot-shot attorneys who would be stolen away from him in six months by another studio or another division within the studio. He told Fisher he figured no one would want to steal her away, so he hired her; he figured he could count on her to stay around for awhile, and his turnover problem would be solved. Six months later, someone did steal her away, and her career as a writer and producer was launched.

This story illustrates the irrational way in which some hiring and promotional decisions are made. You can be eliminated from a promotion or a job opportunity for reasons that have little or nothing to do with you or your level of expertise. So while you are developing communication strategies to improve your chances of success, keep two simple rules in mind:

1. Don't take rejection personally.

2. Don't give up. If you don't get the promotion the first time you try, keep trying until you do.

MAKING THE LABOR-MANAGEMENT
PARTNERSHIP WORK

Motivation and employee morale are clearly a function of your ability to use communication style effectively. With style, you can increase employee morale and self-motivation, which, in turn, will result in increased productivity. Ineffective communication can have the opposite effect. As you read the memo on the following page, see if you can hear the sound of a Magistrate manager talking his way into trouble. As you read this, keep in mind that *this memo is real*. Also note that the spelling and punctuation are presented exactly as they were in the original memo.

You may be thinking that this memo doesn't have anything to do with communication style—that this is simply a memo written by an idiot. You are partially correct. This memo was written by an idiot; the spelling and grammar provide testimony for this assertion. But this "idiot" is a manager, and this manager is clearly a Magistrate. If this manager's comments about low productivity were presented in a Reflective style, they would not be so offensive, and we might be willing to overlook the spelling and grammar errors. It is the arrogant Magistrate style, however, that evokes an intense reaction from the reader and causes us to label him an idiot.

The manager thought that this memo—hand printed on yellow lined paper, duplicated, and then distributed, via the departmental mailboxes, to the entire sales force—would motivate his staff to do a better job. But within six months from the time that it was distributed, a 100 percent turnover in the sales force occurred. Obviously this memo wasn't the only factor involved in the turnover, but it was indicative of the manager's overall communication and management style, which ultimately cost his company a tremendous amount of money. I have a file full of similar memos from people who occupy positions of leadership in organizations. This is not an isolated example.

We rely on communication to manage and motivate. We use it to resolve conflict and facilitate innovation and to negotiate, conciliate, arbitrate, evaluate, and coordinate. Keep in mind that communication and

Actual Managerial Memo Sent to Members of a Sale Team

To all sales reps.

The following will be implemented while I am on vacation.

1. Radio's are to [sic] loud!! Either low volume or not at all, it's your choice!

2. All special price cards & folders are in my desk. Muriel will ok [sic] all prices.

3. Very few people are making 50 outgoing calls todate [sic]. This is being checked everyday [sic] so if you don't make them you will have to tell Mr. Smith why you aren't.

4. Some salespersons are doing nothing more than sitting and waiting for the calls to come in. If this does not stop, I'm sure I can find some additional work for you to do since you have nothing to do!!

5. Order errors are at their peak! If these are not reduced, your commissions will be minimal because we will start a policy of dollar amount penalty for each credit that is written on your behalf. We are not paying you for numerous mistakes.

6. If anyone disaggrees [sic] with me on any of the previous policys [sic] just let me know and we can discuss it on your exit interview before you leave the company.

When each of you joined this company you wanted an opportunity to accell [sic] in supply sales and make money. We have given you the means, the tools, and the training and now it's up to you to show us you can do the job. It's my decision as to whether you make it or not.

With the supply division having a quota of $20 million + [sic] I need salespersons that can produce!! With errors, personal conflicts, and wasted time being the main cause of low productivity this is the problem I want eliminated <u>NOW</u> not later.

motivation are not one-way processes. The impact of this statement can best be shown by the following story, which appeared in a Detroit newspaper a number of years ago.

A large manufacturing firm felt it needed to improve employee relations and sent the management team to an expensive management training seminar for a week where the managers learned, among other things, that they should express love and kindness to their employees. Upon returning to the work environment, one of the managers encountered an employee, put his arm on his shoulder, and said, "I love you!" The employee, who had not attended the seminar, promptly punched his manager in the nose. A costly and lengthy grievance procedure followed the incident.

The point is that communication and motivation are two-way processes. When I conduct training seminars for employees, they all comment that their bosses need to attend. When I conduct seminars for managers, they all comment that their employees need to attend. Both are right. Labor-management is a partnership; both parties need to be actively involved if the partnership is to work. Some stories will show you how easy it is to make this partnership work.

John is an auditor, and he communicates as a Magistrate. He provides the following story of an unsuccessful communication encounter:

I was speaking with our regional sales manager, and my goal was to get him to agree to my audit findings and recommendations.

I went into his office and brought two large folders with me. We shook hands, and I sat down on the other side of his desk. I stared off by telling him all the positive things I found during my audit. Then I launched into a diatribe on my negative findings. I provided detailed recommendations for all of my negative findings that I thought were very helpful, but as I look back on it, I probably sounded like I was lecturing or scolding him. I tried to convince him that all of my recommendations were correct.

He got very defensive and started to take personal shots at me—I think because I backed him into a corner, and he knew it would not make him look good when my audit report was sent to his boss. I was too aggressive at this meeting. He rejected my recommendations, he went to my boss and complained about me, and now I think I have a permanent enemy.

John learned from this experience and decided to try and use his knowledge of communication style to get his own manager to do what he wanted without resentment. John explains his communication strategy:

I was in charge of a group of employees who were supposed to be gathering signatures to get Proposition 103 placed on the ballot for voting in the upcoming election. Collecting signatures is not part of our work requirements because Proposition 103 [an attempt to limit fees charged by insurance companies] is a political issue, and employees are under no obligation to support political issues endorsed by their employees. Nevertheless, there was subtle pressure put on us to collect the signatures because the company would benefit if the proposition was passed by the voters.

The employees asked me if I would try to get them time off work if they gathered a certain amount of signatures. My manager is not the type of person to let employees off early as a reward. My first thought was to go in and tell her that the company really didn't have any right to ask us to do this, but we would if we could have some time off.

I thought about it and realized that would be too aggressive. So I simply approached her and asked if she had any ideas on how I could motivate my group to gather signatures. She then asked me what I thought. I said I thought maybe time off would motivate the workers. I think by not pushing my ideas on her immediately (as I normally would), I was able to be successful in my goals. She agreed to the time off.

I'm not saying the employer was right in pressuring the employees to collect signatures. I'm just saying John used communication style to get what he needed to motivate his employees. The employees were willing to collect the signatures as long as a reward was attached. John got them the reward.

For another look at how a Magistrate can develop communication strategies designed to motivate, read the story of an unsuccessful encounter supplied by Jan, who is a branch manager for a credit union:

My goal was to get Allen, one of my tellers, to use the car sale screen to cross-sell auto loans to members at his window. I told him that he had the fewest number of car sale inquiries on our team and that I needed everyone on the team to do as many inquiries as possible to win the contest. He said he didn't have time when the line was long. Then I explained to him why we were doing this: because we need to cross-sell to bring in new business. He still didn't buy into it.

Allen is a Reflective, and Jan's bottom-line approach has no impact on his behaviors. As a Reflective, Allen's primary concern is for the people who have to wait in line. Jan has to address those needs first if she is to motivate Allen to cross-sell.

Jan decided to introduce some flexibility into her Magistrate style of communication. She provides a more successful communication encounter with a membership counselor whom Jan described as very Socratic:

My goal was to get her to be more cooperative and be part of the branch sales team.

I took her to lunch and listened to what she was saying, not only about the branch but about problems in her personal life. I asked open-ended questions, such as, How do you think our branch can attain its sales goal for the campaign? I heard her ideas and told her I thought they were valuable and ones we could use in the campaign. I tried to be empowering and supportive, giving her a sense of ownership. She has been very cooperative since that meeting.

John and Jan are Magistrates who found they were totally ineffective in motivating their employees to want to do the work they needed done. When they attempted to use some of their Reflective characteristics, they created moments of success by motivating their employees to do what was needed without generating resentment or anger.

You can bring about positive change even if you aren't the person in charge, as Sharon, a loan quality manager, reveals in her story. Sharon is Reflective, and she explains:

I was discussing a personnel issue with my Noble boss, who was in the process of writing a very direct memo without much forethought. The subject of the memo was based on hearsay and not documented. My goal was to get my boss to listen and to let the entire issue be brought out in order to prevent an explosion.

I suggested that she not send the memo without evidence and an opportunity to discuss facts with the person involved. I explained how a related incident had occurred with me and how I responded to what I perceived as an attack. As a result, she decided not to send the memo, but scheduled a meeting with those involved to obtain the facts and resolve the issue.

Sharon is a problem solver. She used her Reflective style of communication to motivate her boss to pursue a course of action that reduced conflict.

Good management and effective leadership are not difficult to achieve. It does take time to plan communication strategies designed to motivate others, but the rewards are tremendous.

Chapter **13**

Surviving the
Group Meeting

When a hundred clever heads join a group,
one big nincompoop is the result.

C. G. Jung, 1957

GROUPS, HORSES, CAMELS, AND
TWO SHIPS PASSING IN THE NIGHT

Jung's Noble description of the group is something most of us can visualize. If you've lived any time at all on this earth, you've been subject to the sometimes-dreaded group experience. There are almost as many definitions of the term "group" as there are different types of groups. For our purposes, "group" is a collection of people who interact with each other over time to accomplish a common goal. This type of group may be called a task force, a council, a committee, or a board. The label isn't important, but understanding the group process is of utmost importance.

Groups, like communication style, have a degree of predictability about them, and you can learn to manage predictable behaviors. The most predictable thing about groups is that they have a life cycle.* If you understand the life cycle, then you know what to expect. This doesn't change the fact that certain things will happen; it just means you can plan for these things to happen. The five stages of the life cycle are: Forming, Storming, Norming, Performing, and Adjourning.

Forming stage. Members come together to find out about each other and define their group goals. They talk about themselves to try to establish some interpersonal relationship between and among members, and also talk about the task to be performed.

Members often engage in "flashing" behaviors, similar to the chest-beating ritual apes go through when they gather to discuss whatever it is that apes discuss. Group members flash information about themselves to other members, and this flashing helps to establish norms, guidelines, and rules regarding acceptable and unacceptable behaviors for group members. Reflectives might not engage in these behaviors, sitting quietly listening as the Socratics, Magistrates, and Candidates dominate the conversation, or they might chat quietly with whomever they are seated near. Nobles engage in flashing behaviors if they deem the project important. Otherwise they sit quietly and think about things they would rather be doing, or they will bring other work with them to the meeting and complete it while the meeting is in session.

Members learn how to be comfortable with each other, and the climate for future interactions is established. This can be a particularly troublesome stage for Nobles and Magistrates, who would like to skip it entirely. These two results-oriented communicators make comments like,

---

*For a more complete discussion of this life cycle, see B. W. Tuckman, "Development Sequence in Small Groups, *Psychological Bulletin* (1965):384–99, and B. W. Tuckman and M. A. C. Jensen, "Stages of Small Group Development, Revisited," *Group and Organization Studies* (1977):419–27.

"Let's skip the chitchat and get right to the task at hand" or "We all basically know each other, so let's get right down to business." These sorts of remarks violate the sense of group decorum of the Socratics, Reflectives, and Candidates, and interpersonal conflict is generated.

The forming stage is a natural and necessary part of the group development process. When you allow the natural formation to take place, you can expect to hear polite and casual exchanges of personal information between and among members, and you can expect a series of questions and answers aimed at clarifying perceptions regarding the precise nature of the task at hand.

Storming stage. The group now begins to discuss in earnest who is going to be responsible for what. Differences are aired, polite conversation is abandoned, and individual personalities and communication styles emerge. The storm really begins to brew when group goals conflict with individual needs. Group members stop their flashing behaviors and begin jockeying for position. Each member attempts to define his or her status within the group and to set limits regarding individual contributions to the group effort. Conflict between members and emotional responses to the task at hand are to be expected. Informal subgroups may form as individual members begin to link up with other members who share a similar persuasion.

Effective groups resolve individual differences that emerge during this second stage or can capitalize on the differences to bring about the group goal. Some groups get stuck in the storming stage because they are unable to resolve individual differences. When this happens, we end up with the proverbial camel: a horse put together by committee. Like two ships passing in the night, each member does his or her own thing, and group synergy is never achieved. Some groups avoid conflict at all cost and end up producing an acceptable but mediocre product.

Norming stage. Members now begin to make constructive use of conflict. Conflict aimed at sorting out the best parts of differing ideas and viewpoints is a healthy, normal, and necessary part of the group process.

During this middle stage, members express their opinions and begin to develop common or shared opinions of what needs to be done. Group cohesion begins to emerge, and members begin working together as a unit.

At this time, members begin to realize individual contributions to the overall goal and begin accepting responsibility for the final product. You can expect to hear supportive statements and can expect task discussion to focus on the division of labor—who will be doing what to produce the final product.

Performing stage. If the group makes it to this stage, they will be functioning like a well-oiled machine. Everything comes together; loyalty, trust, and supportiveness are evident among members, and a blending of individual and group goals is achieved. Suggestions, comments, ideas, and criticisms are provided with a supportive tone, motivation is high, and members are comfortable with the roles they have assumed. Conversation focuses on perfecting the final product, and compromise with respect to remaining details is easily achieved.

Adjourning stage. As the life cycle of a group draws to an end, members begin to engage in parting rituals. They pat each other on the back and make reassuring statements about the fine decisions they have reached. They may even make reference to an earlier disagreement and how the discussion cleared the air and allowed them to come up with a better decision. The group adjourns, and members await their assignment to another group.

All effective groups pass through this life cycle. If you understand that each phase of the cycle is a natural and necessary part of the development process, you can use your knowledge of communication style to guide a group through the process to achieve the stated goals. Additionally, you can bring about a group synergism that is greater than the sum of its parts; you produce an end product that is superior to anything one individual member could have produced.

That sounds simple enough, so why doesn't it work? Mainly because the group is made up of human beings.

DEALING WITH FRUSTRATING PEOPLE IN GROUP MEETINGS

We find people frustrating when they don't sound as we sound, when they don't do what we want them to do, and when they don't do it the way we want it done or in the time we think it should be done. Handling these frustrations is difficult enough in the one-on-one interaction, but put six people in a group, and the frustration increases at an exponential rate.

Imagine a group with each of the six different types of communicators. Everyone sounds different, everyone has a unique set of communication needs, and everyone has a set of behaviors linked to their dominant style of communication.

Socratics and Candidates are concerned with establishing agendas, defining problems, and discussing possible solutions. They say things like,

> "One of our problems is that we need to sell this product to the over-forty group if we are going to make a profit. Why don't we begin with some brainstorming activities and try to identify some of the reasons why a forty-five-year-old would want to buy this book."

The Candidate will elaborate on this comment:

> "Yes, it is important to keep track of our comments, and it is also important that we try to develop a total understanding of our range of possibilities. I've been in groups where one person kept the list and when the discussion began, we never got around to reviewing all the ideas."

Senators and Nobles are concerned with the agenda because they know it is a tool for controlling the flow of information, but they aren't terribly interested in discussing all possible alternatives. Senators will listen, make objective/nonjudgmental statements, and seek participation by others so they can begin to gain the information advantage. They will say,

> "Over 30 percent of the nation is now above the age of forty. Do you think their needs are different than those under forty?"

Nobles jump right to the solution and avoid long discussions. They say,

"Age doesn't make a difference. The book topic is the only thing that counts. This is a topic everyone can relate to. Let's just concentrate on marketing the topic."

Magistrates respond by placing some value on what has just been said. They have a need to evaluate and criticize, positively or negatively, all of the ideas or opinions. They say,

"I think you overgeneralize; however, your general idea does have some merit. There may be some similarity of needs that we could tap into. I have a plan I believe will work. Let me explain."

The Magistrate will then present a lengthy, detailed plan. It will be presented as a finished product, and, in the mind of the Magistrate, there should be no objection to it.

The Magistrate is the group member who may attack any idea that he or she did not originate and heave personal insults at anyone who dares to suggest that these ideas are less than perfect. A Magistrate who takes on the aggressive role will speak in a thunderous voice and attempt to stop discussion. He or she will say,

"Look, we're wasting time here! This is a good solution. Let's just run with it and move on to the next item."

The Noble is the one who is likely to engage in open confrontation with the Magistrate—not over the issue but over the style. The Noble says,

"Hey, knock it off. You aren't the only one with an idea."

If the issue escalates into a full-blown argument, the Noble will say,

"Yeah, whatever. This isn't worth the effort to argue about it. If it blows up, it's your problem."

At this point the Noble will cease to be an active member of the group, and if at all possible, he or she will seek a way to resign from the group.

The Candidate and Socratics will discuss, at length, the Magistrate's proposal, but the Reflective and Senator will sit back and just observe. If the Magistrate's proposal is passed and they don't like it, they will quietly sabotage it.

To prevent this type of disastrous group ending, appoint someone with some knowledge of communication style as the group chairperson or leader. In addition to being tolerant of differing styles and paying attention to the communication needs of each communicator the chairperson should serve as a gatekeeper, an encourager, and a summarizer.

As a gatekeeper, the chair makes sure everyone has an opportunity to speak:

"Tom, you've been kind of quiet. Would you like to add anything to the list we've generated?"

As an encourager, the chair should sense if Tom is reluctant to speak and, with a warm Reflective style, encourage him to make a contribution:

"Tom, you always take a creative approach to things. I'll bet you have an idea floating around in your head that you'd love to share with us. Remember, this is a brainstorming session, and that means that every idea is a potentially good idea."

Finally, an effective chair summarizes the feelings of the group to ensure that everyone is in agreement on what has been said and where the group is going.

If you begin to look at these behaviors or roles as being valuable and necessary to the group process, then these people will no longer be so frustrating to you. These are all predictable behaviors. If you can predict the behaviors, you can control or manage them.

BUT I THOUGHT YOU SAID . . .

When you don't listen to the other person's style, miscommunication takes place. There's a saying that sums up the process of miscommunication: "I know you think you heard what you thought I said, but what I said was not what you heard."

A story provided by Carri, a Noble human resources administrator with a manufacturing firm, illustrates this point:

My goal was to get a lower-paid worker to relieve the receptionist on breaks.

Most of our clerks are women, and most of our low-level salary people are young males working in shipping and receiving. I was looking for someone to relieve the receptionist when she went on breaks and thought it would be a good idea to use someone who makes a lower salary since this function is basically unproductive time. I suggested to Steve, "Why do we have to use all women on the telephone? Why can't we use a guy from the shop?" He took this to mean, "Why are we discriminating against women and making them answer the phones?" That put him on the defensive, and it took some talking on my part to explain that was not my intention.

Multiply the one-on-one misunderstanding by six or eight, and you have the group misunderstanding quotient. Everything we have talked about in this book so far will help you avoid these misunderstandings.

WE'RE SAYING THE SAME THING . . .

One of the most aggravating things that happens in the group experience is that you make a suggestion that is totally ignored, but ten minutes later, when someone else makes the same suggestion, it is hailed as the idea that will save the world. Another variation of this irritating experience is that you take a position and another person takes the same position but it sounds as if the two of you are in conflict. You scratch your head and say, "But I think we're saying the same thing."

These two phenomena are easy to explain: both are the result of communication style differences. If you say something that is ignored but is accepted when stated by someone else, you probably are not using the preferred power style of communication. For example, you may be Reflective, and the person who gets recognition for saying what you said may be Noble. The reverse could also be true: you may be Noble, and the acceptable (power) style may be Reflective. If you are the Noble being ignored and you feel you need to make a comment, you might say

"I am in total agreement with Margaret, and I want to thank her for saying it in a much nicer tone than I did earlier."

If you find yourself debating someone who is, in actuality, on the same side of the issue, then you are probably talking with a Socratic or Magistrate. This is when you might use a Reflective technique to dispel the illusion of a conflict:

"I think we are saying the same thing. Are you saying . . ."

If you pay attention to what you are saying and how you are saying it, most communication misunderstanding can be resolved.

HOW TO AVOID DESTRUCTIVE ARGUMENTATION

Some people tend to be very aggressive when attempting to get their proposal accepted. It is possible for you to refocus this aggression. You might say,

"Anthony, I'd like you to serve as the devil's advocate for our group. For every solution we develop, I'd like you to write down a list of possible problems. We can then discuss each of the problem areas and select a solution that appears to be most workable."

By taking this approach, you have redirected Anthony's dysfunctional energies and encouraged his involvement in a functional task development role.

Effective delegation of duties can also help reduce destructive argumentation, and delegation can serve as a motivational tool. Some managers have difficulty delegating because they assume the task won't be done correctly unless they do it themselves. Others assume they won't be given credit if they delegate. These are faulty assumptions, to say nothing of the fact that the lack of delegation will increase conflict within a group. People need to feel that they are an important part of the group, and effective management involves getting work done through other people. The following guidelines should help you effectively delegate:

1. Select people who are most likely to succeed. When someone who lacks expertise volunteers to perform a task, create a mini-team by pairing that person with someone who has the expertise.
2. Clearly identify the expected results in an assignment statement.
3. Use active listening techniques to foster accurate transmission of information.
4. Agree upon ways to be kept informed on a timely basis.
5. Agree upon measures that will be used to evaluate progress and the formal evaluation of results.
6. Establish an action plan with expected deadlines.

It is always a good idea to put these items in writing. The written document serves as a reference for the leader and the group members, and it can help reduce misunderstandings.

Brainstorming is another communication technique that can be helpful in reducing destructive argumentation. Brainstorming is designed to help group members generate an extensive number of ideas or solutions to a problem by temporarily suspending criticism and evaluation. During brainstorming, everyone is asked to suggest as many solutions as possible, and the group chair lists all of the possible solutions on a chalkboard. There are four basic rules that guide successful brainstorming sessions:

- No criticism is allowed until all possible solutions are listed.
- Farfetched ideas are encouraged because they may trigger more practical ideas.
- All ideas are acceptable.
- Many ideas are desirable.

Once all of the ideas are generated, the group begins evaluating the possible solutions. They discuss the advantages and disadvantages of each solution and select the best solution.

Keep in mind that conflict is a necessary and valuable part of the group process. If you eliminate all conflict, the group members will lose their critical evaluative capabilities. You goal is to control unnecessary and destructive conflict by controlling communication style.

DEVELOPING STRATEGIES FOR SUCCESS IN THE GROUP MEETING

Groups are complex and difficult communication encounters, but they are a way of life in most organizations. An understanding of the group's life cycle and a knowledge of communication style can help you manage the group process—certainly no easy task. All of the problems you encounter in one-on-one interactions are intensified in the group setting. Instead of being concerned just with the communication expectations of one other individual, you must be concerned with many different expectations, many different roles, and some hidden agenda roles. There are some procedural ways to help bring about a positive group experience:

1. Always prepare an agenda for any group meeting.
2. Prior to the meeting, distribute lengthy documents to be discussed at the meeting to encourage people to participate from a position of knowledge.
3. Take notes or use a secretary. This is especially important if procedures, policies, or action plans are being developed.
4. Summarize the points covered and agreed upon during the course of the meeting.
5. Delegate individual and subgroup tasks in writing, with established deadlines for completion.
6. Verbally recognize behaviors that contribute to the completion of group goals.
7. Act as a positive role model.

Diane, a senior loan officer for a savings and loan association, illustrates how rules combined with communication help when simple communication fails:

My goal was to get my staff to keep me informed on the status of their work.

At our staff meeting, I specifically stated that each person was to send an E-mail [electronic mail] to me by Monday morning. I explained that each person was to give a listing of the work accomplished for the past week and a plan for the upcoming week. I suggested that each person take the last half-hour every Friday to do an inventory of accomplishments and a status of all loan files.

The first Monday when I looked for the reports and saw that all but one person had turned them in, I sent an E-mail to everyone—naming and thanking the ones who did the reports and giving the one who didn't until the end of the day to send the E-mail. I had tried to do this in the past, but I never provided a specific time frame for completion, and as a result, I failed. Once I provided a specific deadline, it made all of the difference in the world. They took notice of the direction and turned the reports in on time.

The group is simply an extension of the one-on-one interaction. You need to be tolerant of and skilled in using all of the styles to manage conflict and control the outcome of the interaction.

Chapter **14**

Talking about
Sensitive Issues

PERSONAL HYGIENE:
COMMON PROBLEM, UNCOMMON SOLUTIONS

Poor personal hygiene is a tough and common problem in organizations. When we conducted our research on aspiring leaders, personal hygiene emerged as a category of things people don't like about their bosses. A significant number of people indicated the thing they liked least about their boss was:

He or she doesn't use mouthwash.

He spills food on himself.

He doesn't use a hanky to clean his nose.

He doesn't excuse himself when he passes gas.

He scratches himself in front of everyone.

He or she has body odor.

We'll save the issue of what to do with a boss with a personal hygiene problem for later; right now, let's assume the person with the problem is your employee.

Everyone has worked with someone who has a problem with body odor, but no one wants to be the one to talk to the offender about the problem. You may be working with someone right now who offends your olfactory senses, and this person may be a very good employee or volunteer worker in all other aspects. Let's call this worker Mike, and let's assume that Mike reports directly to you. Mike deals directly with clients, so you must call Mike in and talk with him about this odor problem. Think about it for a minute, and then grab a piece of paper and write out a communication strategy. How will you approach Mike, and exactly what will you say to him?

If you wrote anything out without first assigning Mike a dominant style of communication, then the odds are six to one in favor of your talking your way into trouble. Remember: communication strategy is based on knowing the other person's style. Once you know that, you know his or her expectations, and then you can adjust your own style to meet those expectations and control the outcome of the interaction.

If you didn't assign Mike a dominant style of communication, don't feel badly. We all gravitate to our dominant style of communication in a stressful situation, and the negative aspects of our dominant style become worse in a stressful situation. Talking with someone about body odor is a stressful situation, so it is natural that you would have responded in your own style.

Writing the communication strategy out on a sheet of paper is certainly less stressful than actually saying the words in a face-to-face interaction. Yet there is a fairly good chance that the words you wrote are classic stereotypes of your dominant style — as the following stereotypical responses of communicators under stress show:

NOBLE: You need to take a shower. You smell.

SOCRATIC: (after first talking with a number of other employees and/or clients to see if others have detected the same odor and to determine if a real problem does indeed exist) Mike, I've spoken with a number of your co-workers who have observed a problem that I, also, am

277

concerned about. I've also spoken with a couple of your clients—Bob Smith and Margaret Murphy—who have confirmed that there is something we should discuss. As you know, interacting with people, particularly clients, requires a certain amount of finesse, attention to grooming, and an awareness of how we affect others. A number of us have observed that you are having a bit of a problem with personal hygiene. I think you should address this problem because smell can be very offensive to some people.

REFLECTIVE: (after opening with some pleasant chitchat) You know Mike, we are really pleased with your work, and I certainly like you as a person. I'm sorry I have to talk to you about this, but there have been some comments about your . . . well . . . about . . . (softly) personal hygiene. Is there a problem we can help you with?

SENATOR: (after first determining where the conversation should take place to ensure that Mike will be most receptive and least defensive about what is going to be said, and after beginning with some pleasant chitchat) Mike, it appears that you are having a problem with body odor. You'll need to do something to take care of this as soon as possible.

MAGISTRATE: (after verifying that others are bothered by the problem) Mike, it's very important that we always make the best impression possible when dealing with our clients, and it's important that we be able to work together as a team. I've noticed that you are having a problem with body odor, and it's something that you should take care of immediately.

CANDIDATE: (after some pleasant chitchat) We are really pleased that you are part of our team. It is always good in any situation to try and make sure that everyone is able to work together in a pleasant environment. Sometimes we have to talk about things that seem to be a problem, but that is only to clear up the problem . . . not to criticize you or anyone else. No one likes to be criticized. Helpful suggestions are more useful. Are you aware of any problems that we should be concerned with?

Let's analyze these responses. If you are Noble, you simply identified Mike's problem and stated he should take care of it. It is not your problem, and Mike should not be offended by your comments. It is simply something that needs to be addressed, and if you had a similar problem, you would want someone to tell you. There is no need for discussion.

If you are Socratic, you first check with co-workers and clients to verify your impressions. Then you use these impressions as evidence to support your assertion and provide a statement that establishes the need for good personal hygiene. You then state the problem that has been observed by the multitudes and end with a directive for Mike to improve and an additional reason as to why improvement is necessary, which may include a statement of consequences. You may even have suggested a plan for action, and you probably used the pronoun "I" in you directive statement.

If you are Reflective, you say something positive first; then you apologize for the remarks you are going to make; then you state that others—not you—have observed or reported a problem. This problem is very softly verbalized, and then you ask if something can be done or if you can help Mike with the problem. You probably use the pronoun "we" in suggesting that you and Mike could work together to solve the problem.

If you are a Senator, you think strategy first. You identify where the meeting should take place so that Mike will be comfortable and least likely to be offended by your remarks. Then you state that there appears to be a problem, but you do not indicate that others are concerned with it. After identifying the problem, you suggest that Mike is responsible for solving it promptly. There is an inherent assumption that Mike wants to and will solve the problem. No discussion is necessary, but you allow some face-saving by using a tone that implies, "It's no big deal; it just needs to be taken care of."

As a Magistrate, you will verify that others have observed the same problem, but you won't necessarily tell Mike that you have done some investigative reporting. You will, however, provide justification for elimination of the problem. Like a Socratic, you will probably use the pronoun

"I" to make your directive, but like the Noble, you assume Mike should take ownership of the problem and the solution.

Finally, if you are a Candidate, you really didn't want to do this exercise, but if you did, your message contains a series of qualifying statements. These statements are either apologetic, or they are potential excuses or explanations for Mike's "alleged" problem. You may have checked with other people to see if they have noticed the odor, but you probably didn't actually state the problem in your message. You may have tried to get Mike to talk about the problem without actually saying there is a problem.

The stereotypical messages I provided are actually taken from these group exercises I conduct in my seminars. People really do say these things! I say these things; you say these things; we all say these things.

Why do we say these things when we know we need to consider the other person's dominant style if we want to control the outcome of the interaction? Because we don't want to talk about body odor. No one wants to talk to someone about odor. We are under stress, and when we are under stress, we cling to what we know, relying on the familiar. We know our own personal style of communication, but we don't know the other styles well enough to use them without planning or practice. That is why this section of the book exists.

Mike was the hypothetical person in this exercise. Would you have responded differently if Mike was Sarah? Your answer is probably no, unless you are a male Reflective. Reflectives who happen to be men tend to suggest that women should talk to women about these issues. I don't agree with this, but then I'm _____. Ah yes, I've already told you that. I must be getting Socratic!

Finally, there is at least one chance in six that you actually did talk your way out of trouble. If you assumed Mike's style of communication was the same as yours, then your message could be very effective. Candidates have to get around to stating the problem, but once they do, the problem can be solved. Even the Noble can be effective. Let's listen in as Noble Natalie talks to Noble Mike.

NOBLE NATALIE: (pulls Mike off into a corner, places her hand on his shoulder, raises her eyebrows, and looks him directly in the eyes) Mike, listen, I need to tell you this. You really need to take a shower. You have body odor.

NOBLE MIKE: (surprised and attempting to smell his armpits) Me? Get out of here. Really? I took a shower.

NOBLE NATALIE: Can't you smell yourself now?

NOBLE MIKE: Nah, I haven't been able to smell anything since the operation. An elephant could be standing here and I couldn't . . . hey, has anyone else noticed this?

NOBLE NATALIE: Don't worry about it. Use some deodorant after you shower from now on, and everything will be okay.

NOBLE MIKE: Geez, I feel like an _____ !

NOBLE NATALIE: Hey, it's no big deal. It can happen to anyone. Listen, as long as I have you here, can we take a few minutes and go over the Clark account?

NOBLE MIKE: Sure . . . Natalie . . . thanks.

NOBLE NATALIE: No problem. Let's get to work.

Now let's add a little more stress and tension into this topic. Suppose the one with the odor problem is your boss. Several of your clients have made comments to you, and you are really bothered by the problem because the two of you are making joint calls this week and must drive together in the same car. Your boss is a Socratic, and her name is Gloria. What do you say?

You guessed it! This is where I remind you that style isn't the *only* thing to consider when planning your communication strategy. Style may be the only thing you can actively manipulate in an interaction, but it is not the only thing that you can readily identify. Status and hierarchy are pieces of information that you might want to consider as you are constructing your strategy. Gloria is your boss, and depending on the type of relationship you have with her and the type of person she is, it may be inappropriate, or even detrimental to your career, for you to talk with her about this problem.

If you did decide you wanted to talk with her, your comments might sound something like this:

YOU ATTEMPTING TO BE SOCRATIC: Gloria, do you remember the annual meeting last year that was held in Chicago?

SOCRATIC GLORIA: Remember? How could I forget it! It was my first time in Chicago, and I took advantage of every minute. Rush Street, State Street, Michigan Avenue, Water Place Tower, the museums, the stores, the ambience of a city alive. All of the district managers got together for a special dinner at the top of the Sears building. It was breathtaking. I think that is the tallest building in the city, isn't it?

YOU ATTEMPTING TO BE SOCRATIC: Uh, yes, I believe it is. I've been to Chicago a number of times, but I always find it thrilling . . . but I was thinking specifically of the training sessions we attended. Do you recall the dress-for-success speaker?

SOCRATIC GLORIA: Yes, as a matter of fact, I do. I thought he was a bit flashy for someone who was supposed to be an expert on business attire. I think it is fairly safe to say that most businessmen do not have manicures or wear silk shirts to the office.

YOU ATTEMPTING TO BE SOCRATIC: Yes, I see your point. I was thinking more of his discussion on colognes and fragrances. Do you feel that body chemistry and personal hygiene are important to success?

SOCRATIC GLORIA: In some instances, no. In others, yes. If someone is offensive, then it could be harmful to his or her career, and the person should be concerned.

YOU ATTEMPTING TO BE SOCRATIC: Yes, I agree with you. I know I would want to know if I were offensive, and I'm sure you would want to know too. Since we have to work with the public, this is an important issue . . . and that is why I thought I might ask you if you are aware of the fact that your perfume has a strong and somewhat negative odor?

SOCRATIC GLORIA: Oh, my goodness no. I hope I haven't offended you. What kind of negative odor? You know, I've always been very conscious of my . . .

Gloria is indeed Socratic, and you made a valiant attempt at being Socratic. You used the Socratic question-and-answer technique to lead her to conclude that body odor is important.

If you decide it is not in your best professional interest to approach your boss about odor, be advised that you don't have to ignore the problem. If you don't think you can approach your boss, then consider talking with his or her boss (this assumes you have an open door policy). If you don't have an open door policy, consider sending an anonymous note to his or her superior. (Reflectives and Candidates love this approach, but don't use it with your subordinates.) If you do decide to go one level up, be sure to write or speak in that person's dominant style.

GOOD EMPLOYEE, BAD HABIT: WHAT DO YOU SAY?

Personal hygiene is a good employee, bad habit type of problem. The problem isn't keeping the employee from being productive, but the habit may be creating a problem for the rest of the work force; you need to try and change the employee's behavior without generating resentment or anger. Remember, this is a good employee, so we are not talking about a discipline interview. We are talking about a work habit interview where your goals are to allow the employee to save face and allow him or her to suggest ways to solve the problem.

Start by identifying the employee's dominant style of communication. Then, in the order presented, use the following steps to guide the outcome of the interaction:

1. Establish a positive interpersonal climate.
2. Describe in objective, nonevaluative terms the habit you have observed. Don't say, "It has come to my attention" or "Others have reported."

3. Indicate why it concerns you.

4. Ask the employee for reasons.

5. Listen, don't talk, while the employee explains his or her reasons.

6. State that the situation must be changed, and ask the employee for ideas on how the problem can be solved.

7. Discuss each idea offered.

8. Agree upon a specific action to be taken.

9. Set a specific follow-up date.

If you use this format and your knowledge of communication style, you should be able to talk to just about any employee about any topic.

Sometimes you have a good employee who isn't quite as productive as he or she could be. You don't want to have a discipline interview, and the problem doesn't really qualify for a work habit interview. You just want to talk with the employee to see if you can help him or her improve. John, a chemist with a major oil company, reveals how he used his Reflective style of communication to motivate Eric:

My goal was to get Eric to listen to instructions better and to organize his priorities to accomplish more assigned tasks.

I sat down with him and said,

"Eric you're really getting a lot done on the residue project you're working on. You know, there are still a few details that need to be improved. I've talked about these before, but I think you may need to listen better or write these things down as we talk. I know that there are a lot of details that need to be followed through on, and I, myself, need to really concentrate on listening for these detailed projects, and then write the information down so I remember it."

This approach worked, and Eric did improve in both areas.

HOW TO MOTIVATE SOMEONE AFTER DENYING HIS OR HER REQUEST FOR A PROMOTION OR A RAISE

What happens when you have an excellent employee who has requested a promotion, but organizational constraints prevent you from granting it? Here is a scenario:

You are the director of a large government agency. The person who heads up your word processing center has requested a promotion from AOA2 to AOA3 because the AOA2 job description does not include supervision of others. You have given this person the unofficial title of director, and the job does require the supervision of six lower-ranking employees, but there are no AOA3 "lines" available. Thus, you cannot honor the request for promotion. You do not want to lose this valuable employee. You do have control of your budget.

The director of the word processing center is a Magistrate. Be reminded of the following:

• Be assertive and use the Noble style to control the flow of conversation and information.

• Be prepared to listen to a lengthy but certain Socratic response.

• Be aware that the Magistrate is concerned with the bottom line and the details.

• Because this is a bad-news message, be prepared to utilize Reflective techniques to reduce hostility.

Now write out a strategy.

If you think you did fairly well with this strategy, let's change the scenario a bit and see how you adapt. Suppose you don't like this person who heads up your word processing center. This person's style of communication annoys the devil out of you, and you would be happy with a resignation. This person is competent but interpersonally irritating. What is your strategy?

Let's go back and analyze your first strategic message. If there is anything in your message that justifies this promotion denial, you are in trouble. This person is going to be angry, and rightly so. To add to the anger, this person is a Magistrate and will express this anger in great detail. If you didn't start off your message with your own expression of anger over the injustice of the bureaucratic system, the rest of your words will have no impact.

Your strategic communication plan should also include time to listen to the lengthy diatribe that the Magistrate will deliver, and it should include some method for you to remain calm and pleasant while the Magistrate insults the system, the structure, and the universe in general.

Finally, your plan should include a statement that indicates you will work within the system to bring about a reclassification that will match the job responsibilities, and you may want to offer some other resource as consolation for the disappointment. You have control of the budget, so it may be possible to send the Magistrate to a personal development seminar or purchase some equipment that would make the job easier.

You may want to offer to relieve the Magistrate of the supervisory duties, but you need to be careful with that offer. Magistrates like to be in control, so there is a good chance that your offer will be turned down, but there is always the possibility that the offer will be accepted, and then you are left without a supervisor.

Now let's take a look at your second message. You may have chosen to be very Noble and perhaps even cavalier about delivering the bad-news message to this Magistrate whom you dislike. If you did that, you talked your way into a whole heap of trouble. Keep in mind that this is a government agency; this person isn't about to quit. Furthermore, developing tolerance for differing styles of communication is what this book is all about. Leaders develop the tolerance. Your message to the Magistrate whom you dislike should be no different from your message to the Magistrate whom you value.

Deserving people often get passed over for promotion, they don't get the raise they would like, and they often don't get the job they would like. This is a fact of life that most people can live with if the situation is handled correctly. You don't want to create enemies over these issues, even when you are turning someone down for a job. I received a rejection letter some years ago that actually made me feel good about myself, and I encourage you to use it as a model for your bad-news messages:

The position of _____ at (name of organization) has been filled. Your interest in the position is appreciated. We were pleased with the high quality of the applicants. While this was good, it meant that we did not have the opportunity to invite extremely well-qualified people, such as you, to be our colleague.

Having completed this process we are interested in evaluating our efforts. We are particularly interested in the perception that you have of the way we interacted with you. If you have any suggestions to share with us, we would appreciate your sending them to us.

Please keep (name of organization) in mind, and we hope that you will explore any of our future opportunities that may arise in your field of interest. We wish you every success in the future.

HOW TO FIRE AN EMPLOYEE WITHOUT CREATING HOSTILITY

Most of us work to support our families, and many of us define ourselves in terms of the work we do, so denying a person the opportunity to work is a serious matter. It is not something that should be taken lightly, so we will not approach it lightly here.

Communication style and factual information are the two most important factors to consider when denying or granting a promotion. These same two variables are crucial to the termination process, but the individual's self-esteem is of equal importance. This is true regardless of whether you are firing a good employee or a bad one. You may wonder why you would want to fire a good employee. The answer is simple: you don't want to fire a good employee, but you may be asked to deliver this bad-news message because of financial cutbacks. In addition, in this age of mergers and takeovers, many good and loyal employees are being terminated. It isn't easy to fire anyone, and it is particularly difficult when it involves a loyal employee, so we'll start with the bad employee first.

Keep in mind that *termination of employment should never come as a surprise.* Otherwise you leave yourself wide open for a lawsuit or set yourself up as a target for revenge. Having said that, let's see if you can fire someone for nonperformance. This is the scenario:

Fred has been with your company for about a year. He is a very pleasant young man but terribly irresponsible. He is habitually late, and he has the highest absentee record in the department. He is so personable that his co-workers often cover for him. He makes everyone laugh and is good at making people feel good about themselves. He is a computer programmer, but his lack of attention to detail causes him to make an unacceptable amount of errors. You have conducted several discipline interviews with Fred and have documentation on his performance, as well as the interviews. You informed Fred that termination would result if there was no improvement in his performance and attendance. He has shown no improvement, and you must fire him.

Fred is a Candidate. Be reminded of the following guidelines:

- Be prepared to have the interaction take some time.
- Draw the Candidate into your world of experiences.
- Attempt to place yourself in his or her world of experience.
- Use the Candidate's need for liking to your advantage.
- Allow the Candidate to claim the solution as his or her own.

In addition, follow the guidelines for the discipline interview presented earlier in the book (pp. 238–239), and, of utmost importance, draw upon Reflective techniques to allow Fred to maintain his self-esteem.

What is your strategy?

Let's try one more. The person you are going to fire is Big Bertha Blowhard. She is the epitome of a Socratic, and while some people hate her, others love her and look upon her as a leader. She has a problem with absenteeism and errors, just as Fred does. You have documented the discipline interviews and her performance.

Be reminded of the following Socratic guidelines:

- Do not expect the interaction to be brief.
- Be prepared to present a thorough analysis of the problem.
- Don't become defensive when the Socratic begins to lecture.
- Be prepared for and appreciate the Socratic recall ability.
- Look for the humor in the parenthetical aside.
- Use the Socratic thoroughness, attention to detail, and anecdotal stories to your own benefit.

In addition, follow the guidelines for the discipline interview and allow Bertha to maintain her self-esteem.

What is your strategy?

What you say to both Fred and Bertha should be the same, but how you say it should differ because their communication styles differ. If you want the interaction to go smoothly and you don't want anyone to come back and shoot you, then you need to address their communication needs. As stressful as you may find these interactions, they are more stressful for the person who is about to lose his or her means of support. Your strategies may include information about employment that would be more suitable for Fred or Bertha, but there should be no attempt to lecture these two individuals on the merits of good work habits. Do not attempt to evaluate their personal attributes; simply focus your remarks on the problems with performance and attendance. Remember that the behaviors—not the people—are unacceptable.

It is difficult to fire an employee when there is justification, but it is painfully difficult to terminate an employee without cause. If you must deliver this bad-news message to a valued employee, keep in mind that this is not a discipline interview. If anything, it is a counseling or problem-solving interview. It wouldn't take a lot of effort to turn this unpleasant task into a session where you help the person examine alternatives. I'm not going to give a scenario for this distasteful personnel decision. Instead, I want you to think of one of your valued employees—the one most likely to be terminated if financial cutbacks had to be made. Consider his or her style of communication, review the Reflective techniques, and then try to create an entire scenario. Write out exactly what you would say and exactly what you think your employee would say. Unless both you and your employee are Noble, you will need a few sheets of paper to complete this exercise. When you are done, set it aside for a couple of days; then go back and read it. If you are pleased with the way it sounds, take it to your employee, explain why you wrote it, ask him or her to read it, and then ask for an honest evaluation. If the employee is a Reflective, Candidate, or Senator, use your communication skills to get an honest response. If your employee says you accurately predicted his or her responses and that he or she would feel comfortable with your remarks, then you have mastered the Communication Kaleidoscope, and you are well on your way to being able to talk almost anyone into almost anything.

I offer this exercise as a challenge. Try it and see how much you know about communication style. Try it and see how far you have come in learning how to control the outcome of an interaction. Try it and see how good you feel about being able to turn a bad-news message into a positive communication moment.

The dreadful topic of termination also applies to volunteer workers. There are times when you have a volunteer who isn't working out. You can't fire volunteer workers because you don't pay them, and you don't want to create negative feelings if your organization depends on volunteers for survival. What do you do? You transfer them to activities where their "expertise and talents can be better utilized." You see, I can be Reflective too.

HOW TO RESIGN WITHOUT BURNING BRIDGES

Now it's time to take a look at what you might want to say when you fire yourself. You may decide to terminate your own employment for any number of reasons: to retire, relocate, change careers, get a better position, or because you hate your job, your boss, or both. In any event, you will need to offer a letter of resignation. This letter is an important document because it may be the last communication moment you will have with the organization. In some instances, you will simply resign in person without offering a letter. Whether in person or in writing, some thought needs to go into your parting remarks. You will indeed leave a lasting impression if you say, "I quit!" and walk out the door, and that lasting impression may come back to haunt you. So let's try creating communication strategies for two different resignation scenarios. For this exercise, write out a letter of resignation.

In the first scenario, you resign for a better position:

You have been with your company for ten years. You have accepted a position with a competitor that has offered you a significant increase in salary and a higher-level position. You began looking for a new position when you found out that your current company was hiring new people at a salary that nearly matched yours. You have enjoyed working for this company and have made some very significant contributions during the decade of your employment.

Your boss is a Senator. You like her and have worked very well with her over the years, but you feel she could have done more to get you the salary increase you felt you deserved.

What is your strategy?

In the second scenario, you resign a job you hate:

You are making a lateral move because you hate your job. You boss is an unethical tyrant and bigot who has made your life miserable. Nevertheless, you have managed to make some significant contributions to the company.

You are sure that your boss would not have his job if he were not related to the president of the company.

Your boss is a Noble. He is also obnoxious.

What is your strategy?

I'm sure you have figured this game out by now and realize that both letters should look the same. A letter of resignation is a formal business document, not a critical commentary. When you leave an organization, it should be on a positive note because the last thing you say may be the only thing remembered. In addition, critical remarks offered in anger from a person leaving a corrupt organization will typically have little impact. Once I received a copy of a resignation letter from a young professor that included the following words, which describe the treatment she received from the other members of her department:

> "These messages have been intended to diminish my integrity; embarrass me in front of my students; disregard the recognition which my work has received; reinforce my "junior" status; coerce me to act with warmth and deference toward senior professors; deny me the opportunity to make mistakes and learn and develop from them; attribute my teaching success to my skill at "mothering" as opposed to my competence; hold me to a unique set of standards; and belittle my expertise. I do not choose to continue working in an environment which operates out of these types of performance expectations."

Everything this outstanding young professor wrote was true, but it had absolutely no impact on the organization because the person to whom it was addressed was part of the problem. Her words fell on deaf ears and served only to create a negative parting image. A simple, dignified letter of resignation would have served her better.

A letter of resignation should be written with the style and flare of the Senator. The first paragraph offers the resignation and states the date when it will be effective. The second paragraph offers a brief summary of your contributions to the organization, and the final paragraph offers a word o thanks for the "experience" you have gained during your time with the organization. If you truly enjoyed working for this organization, you may want to add a paragraph highlighting some fond memories or recognizing some memorable people. Regardless of whether you loved or hated your job, the letter of resignation should be Noble, with the light touch of the Reflective. It is the Senator at his or her best.

ALLOCATING OFFICE SPACE: A DIRTY JOB, BUT SOMEONE HAS TO DO IT

Allocating office space and cutting the budget are two of the more distasteful things leaders must do. No matter what you do or say, someone is dissatisfied, particularly in the case of office space. People are actually territorial creatures, and office space is a territory with special meaning. For many, it is a resource that establishes status. There are those who stalk this resource, and when it becomes vacant, they pounce on it like a lion waiting for its prey to fall.

When I was the assistant dean of the College of Business at Florida Atlantic University, I had the horrible, miserable, and unwanted task of assigning office space. Murder, torture, and life-long hatred were thoughts that passed through the mind of the professor who didn't like his office assignment!

The layout of the college was quite interesting. A series of offices with small windows formed the rectangular base of the building, and there was another series of offices without windows that formed an internal rectangle. The dean and the department chairs occupied the four corner offices of the outside rectangle, and the full professors occupied the offices with the small windows. Occasionally an associate professor would get an outer office with a window, but usually the associate and assistant professors were assigned to inner offices without windows. The assistant professors often had to share their office with another low-ranking creature. There was no formal policy to mandate this arrangement, but nonetheless, it was the law of the land.

During my first year as czarina of office space, a full professor was shot and critically wounded by his lover. As he lay dying in his hospital room barren of any flowers sent by the members of our faculty, the line of professors laying claim to his office space began to form. This experience showed me that there are some situations where reason, logic, and communication style will have little impact on persuasion. No matter what I said or how I said it, the professor who wanted that office was not to be persuaded otherwise.

Confronted with this challenging dilemma, I did the most reasonable thing I could think of: I gave the problem to the dean and told him to make the decision. He gave the office to the full professor who would cause the most grief if denied the office space. That professor moved into his new office the day before his fallen comrade's life support machine was turned off.

Perhaps a better method of allocating scarce resources is to have the people who must share the resources contribute to the development of a policy or guidelines for distribution of the resources. Decisions are then made in accordance with the guidelines or policy, and communication style is used primarily as a way of presenting or explaining the guidelines or policy.

Epilogue

I'm Glad I Said That!

Publius Syrus defined speech as "the mirror of the soul." To Democritus, speech was envisioned as "the image of life," and Talleyrand spoke of this inalienable right as a "faculty given to man to conceal his thoughts." Communication style embraces all of these perspectives and more. Communication is the most important and most complex thing we do. It can shape our careers, our lives, and our world.

I've shared some of my most dismal communication moments in this book because I believe we can learn as much from failure as we do from success. I still have communication fiascos but not nearly as frequently as I used to, and when I do control my communication style, I control the outcome of the interaction.

You too can control the outcome of your important interactions if you control your communication style. One final story will illustrate this point. Carolyn, a design department secretary, explains:

I have a faculty member who is an aggressive Magistrate. He loves to come in making sudden demands and wanting immediate attention. My goal was to have him respect my personhood — my own demands and responsibilities — and to indicate that respect in his behaviors toward me.

When he comes in without greeting me and wants me to look at his task to be done right this minute, *I say,*

> "Herb, I don't mind helping you out, but right now I have several projects with deadlines I need to meet. Also, I like to be treated with consideration and appreciation. It makes me more eager to get the work done for people who treat me nicely."

He usually immediately apologizes, and we discuss a workable time frame. He does try to improve, but I have to remind him.

Carolyn is a Reflective, and if she can train a Magistrate professor to treat her the way she wants to be treated, she can train anyone. You can do it too. You can use your style of communication to talk your way out of trouble and into success, and you can increase the number of times you hear yourself saying, "I'm glad I said that!"

Appendix

Communication Style Profile

As you read each statement that follows, think of the way you actually communicate, not about what you should do or wish you would do. If the statement describes the way you communicate most of the time, mark an "A." If the statement does not describe the way you communicate most of the time, mark a "B." You must mark either an A or a B for each statement.

_____ 1. I am direct, straightforward, frank, and spontaneous when I talk.

_____ 2. I tend to give my opinions on issues openly.

_____ 3. I do not tell others about my personal feelings.

_____ 4. I tend to say what I think, and I expect the other person to do the same.

_____ 5. I tend to be a "tell it like it is" person.

_____ 6. I tend to avoid long discussions that involve a lot of details.

_____ 7. I tend to say what I have to say in as few words as possible.

_____ 8. I tend to make a lot of "you should" statements.

_____ 9. There is a right and a wrong way to do most things.

_____ 10. I tend to be impatient when listening to others.

_____ 11. If I think my friend is making a mistake, I will tell him or her what I think.

_____ 12. I don't like to argue a position, but if I'm sure I'm right, it is important that the other person know he or she is wrong.

_____ 13. I will interrupt a person who is talking too much.

_____ 14. If I receive a lengthy memo, I usually read only the first and last paragraphs and skim over the rest.

_____ 15. The first thing I think of is usually what I say.

_____ 16. If I observe an irritating habit, I tend to tell the other person about it.

_____ 17. I like to deal with the "big picture" and let others deal with the details.

_____ 18. I will tell my friend if he or she has bad breath.

_____ 19. I admire people who say exactly what they think.

_____ 20. I get irritated with people who are not decisive.

_____ 21. I think words are very important, and I enjoy using them.

_____ 22. I really like to sit and talk with other people.

_____ 23. I view argumentation as a constructive activity.

_____ 24. I enjoy debating and discussing different issues.

_____ 25. Instead of just telling someone my opinion, I tend to lead the person through a series of questions and answers to help him or her reach or understand my conclusion.

_____ 26. I am very exact and detailed when I tell someone how to go about doing something.

_____ 27. Sometimes it appears that people tune me out when I am talking.

_____ 28. I tend to give other people advice on what they should do.

_____ 29. In any given situation, there are usually many alternatives from which to choose.

_____ 30. I have an excellent ability to recall details.

_____ 31. I enjoy analyzing all of the various aspects and details in a given situation.

_____ 32. I tend to explain things by using anecdotal stories and hypothetical examples.

_____ 33. I often provide lengthy historical reviews of events and am able to provide names, dates, and the details involved.

_____ 34. I tend to make if-then-therefore statements (if this happens, then this will happen, therefore we should . . .).

_____ 35. I seldom make absolute or final statements (e.g., "This will never happen").

_____ 36. I enjoy discussing abstract or philosophical concepts.

_____ 37. I get irritated with people who make quick decisions without analyzing all of the details.

_____ 38. I enjoy trying to persuade another person to accept a position that I support.

_____ 39. I tend to use a lot of descriptive adjectives and clauses in my written and oral communication.

_____ 40. Sometimes I am accused of being redundant.

_____ 41. I am willing to listen to another person, but I really don't like to give advice on what to do.

_____ 42. I share my personal feelings with others.

_____ 43. Other people tend to tell me their problems.

_____ 44. I often feel frustrated because I don't actually say what I really feel.

_____ 45. I am polite, supportive, and warm when I talk.

_____ 46. I will withhold my opinion if I feel expressing it will generate conflict.

_____ 47. I like to reflect on things for a while before making a final decision.

_____ 48. Other people tend to interrupt me when I am speaking.

_____ 49. I will laugh at an unfunny joke to make the joke teller feel better.

_____ 50. I will simply keep quiet rather than say something that will hurt the other person's feelings.

_____ 51. I have very good ideas, but my suggestions are often ignored.

_____ 52. I do not respond to another person who is angry.

_____ 53. I would not tell my friend that he or she has bad breath.

_____ 54. I try to show the other person that I am listening by nodding my head and saying, "yes, I see," "uh-huh," and so on.

_____ 55. I tend to be a very patient person.

_____ 56. Sometimes I indicate that I agree with the other person even though I really don't.

_____ 57. I am usually soft-spoken.

_____ 58. I will tell the other person what he or she wants to hear instead of what I really believe to avoid conflict.

_____ 59. I don't feel obligated to state my opinion when I am talking with someone with whom I disagree.

_____ 60. I tend to "give in" more than other people, and sometimes this bothers me.

SCORING

Give yourself 1 point for each A on items 1 through 20.
This is your Noble score.
Total number of Noble points _____

Give yourself 1 point for each A on items 21 through 40.
This is your Socratic Score.
Total number of Socratic points _____

Give yourself 1 point for each A on items 41 through 60.
This is your Reflective score.
Total number of Reflective points _____

```
20
19
18
17
16
15
14
13
12
11
10
 9
 8
 7
 6
 5
 4
 3
 2
 1
    NOBLE          SOCRATIC          REFLECTIVE
```

Your scores indicate the degree to which you tend to use each of the three styles of communication at this particular time. Everyone has some of the Noble style, some of the Socratic style, and some of the Reflective style, but it is the combination of scores that creates your unique communication profile. If you wish, you can plot your scores on the graph on the preceding page for an easily interpreted picture.

Noble, Socratic, and Reflective: The Three Dominant Styles

Everyone has the potential to use all three styles, but people in general tend to use one style predominantly. This tendency is revealed by the scoring patterns that emerge on the test. More than half the people who take this test will have one high score and two lower scores. If you had one high score and two lower scores then you are a dominant-style communicator. You can be a dominant Noble, a dominant Socratic, or a dominant Reflective. The high score is your dominant style of communication—the style that you use most of the time. The higher the score is, the higher is the degree of use for that particular style. For example, you might have the following scores:

Noble	17
Socratic	10
Reflective	2

These scores indicate that the Noble style of communication is your dominant style; the Socratic is your backup style (you use it if you have to, and you really think about it); and you seldom use your Reflective style.

Let's try another. Suppose your scores look like this:

Noble	8
Socratic	15
Reflective	8

If you scored like this, then you are a dominant Socratic. You are most comfortable with the Socratic style, and you use it most of the time. You occasionally use your Noble and Reflective styles, but it doesn't take too long for someone to figure out that you are going to give a very lengthy response to any question you are asked.

If you scored high on the Reflective style and lower on the Noble and Socratic styles, you fall into the dominant Reflective facet, and your scores might look like this:

> Noble   7
>
> Socratic   10
>
> Reflective   14

If you are a dominant-style communicator, you tend to use one style most of the time, and when you are in a stressful situation, you rely almost entirely on that one style. Dominant-style communicators are the easiest to identify. They are classic archetypes; they so clearly are what they are.

The Magistrate and the Candidate; Blending Two Styles

The blended-style communicator is a bit more difficult to identify at first because he or she has taken two styles, has blended them and uses them simultaneously. There are only two types of blended-style communicators. If you scored high on both the Noble and Socratic styles, you are considered a Magistrate, which is a Noble-Socratic blended-style communicator. If you scored high on both the Reflective and Socratic styles, you are considered a Candidate. The blended-style communicator does not switch back and forth between the two styles. Rather, he or she creates a unique style profile by combining the traits of two dominant styles. Examples of Magistrate and Candidate scores are:

Magistrate		*Candidate*	
Noble	12	Noble	7
Socratic	14	Socratic	12
Reflective	5	Reflective	11

The Senator: A Dual-Style Communicator

If you have a high Noble score and a high Reflective score, you are considered a Senator, which is a dual-style communicator. You have developed the ability to switch back and forth between these two styles of communication. You do not use these two styles at the same time, as do the blended-style communicators. Rather, you use one or the other style, depending on the situation. If you are a dual-style communicator, your scores might look something like this:

Noble	12
Socratic	7
Reflective	13

How to Interpret a Flat Scoring Pattern

If your scores were equally distributed and the line you drew on your scoring graph was almost flat, then you have a homogeneous score, but that does not mean you are a homogeneous-style communicator. It does mean that you are a student of style.

Flat scores tend to be low, which may indicate you are unsure of yourself in a communication encounter and therefore hesitate to engage in the communication process actively. Low scores may also indicate you are unaware of how you communicate. A flat score might look something like this:

Noble	9
Socratic	8
Reflective	8

In the early days of the research, people who had flat scoring patterns were considered errors in the research. I've learned at lot since those early days, and I don't think of flat scorers as error anymore, but the true homogeneous communicator is actually very rare. It is possible for you to be using all three styles mixed up together, but it is not very probable.

I find that less than 5 percent of the people have equally distributed— homogeneous—communication style scores. A very small percentage of this already small group indicate that they actually use all three styles to create successful moments. Those people, by and large, tend to be in jobs where their success is measured by how well they deal with different types of people, especially difficult people. A human resources manager might emerge with a homogeneous score. This is particularly true when the corporation views the human resources manager as the person who is supposed to keep everyone calm and happy. These are the people who are using style to create success.

Most of the people who have evenly distributed scores, however, are actually searching for a style. They tend to be going through a period of transition. They are in the process of adapting to a new environment or environments, and as a result, their communication style is in a period of transition and change. Students are learning about style and how to use style to adapt to change. Someone who is going through a traumatic divorce or someone who has made a dramatic shift in job responsibilities might have a flat score.

The more probable explanation for scores that are equally distributed is that you responded to the statements according to how you think you should communicate or how you wish you would communicate instead of how you actually do communicate.

If you had equally distributed scores, take the test again, and try to be as honest as you can with yourself about what you actually do. You might also have a very good friend take the test for you: Have your friend score the test according to his or her perceptions of how you actually communicate. If you don't want to do either of these two things, simply read the book. By the time you finish, you will be able to identify your dominant style of communication.

Index